HOW TO READ LIKE AN ANTI-FASCIST

How to Read Like an Anti-Fascist

STORYTELLING AND NARRATIVE LITERACY FOR YOUNG PEOPLE

Annette Wannamaker

FORDHAM UNIVERSITY PRESS   NEW YORK 2025

Copyright © 2025 Fordham University Press

All rights reserved. No part of this publication may be reproduced, stored in a retrieval system, or transmitted in any form or by any means—electronic, mechanical, photocopy, recording, or any other—except for brief quotations in printed reviews, without the prior permission of the publisher.

Fordham University Press has no responsibility for the persistence or accuracy of URLs for external or third-party Internet websites referred to in this publication and does not guarantee that any content on such websites is, or will remain, accurate or appropriate.

Fordham University Press also publishes its books in a variety of electronic formats. Some content that appears in print may not be available in electronic books.

Visit us online at www.fordhampress.com.

For EU safety / GPSR concerns: Mare Nostrum Group B.V., Mauritskade 21D, 1091 GC Amsterdam, The Netherlands, gpsr@mare-nostrum.co.uk

Library of Congress Cataloging-in-Publication Data available online at https://catalog.loc.gov.

Printed in the United States of America
27 26 25   5 4 3 2 1
First edition

To Mom, Dad, and Oma, my fellow travelers

Contents

PREFACE: FASCISM, RESISTANCE, AND THE CONFOUNDING CASE OF *HARRY POTTER* ix

Introduction: American Neofascism, the Child, and Children's Literature 1

1 Stories about Stories: Reading Fascistic Rhetoric 31

2 The Order of Story 65

3 Fascism Is the Patriarchy 86

4 From Margin to Center: An(Other) Point of View 111

Conclusion: The Ends of Story 135

ACKNOWLEDGMENTS 153

NOTES 155

INDEX 183

Preface
Fascism, Resistance, and the Confounding Case of *Harry Potter*

> Americans today are no wiser than the Europeans who saw democracy yield to fascism, Nazism, or communism in the twentieth century. Our one advantage is that we might learn from their experience. Now is a good time to do so.
>
> —TIMOTHY SNYDER,
> *On Tyranny: Twenty Lessons from the Twentieth Century*[1]

In 2017, Timothy Snyder published a pocket-size how-to guide, *On Tyranny: Twenty Lessons from the Twentieth Century*, that offers twenty pieces of advice for surviving and subverting the growing neofascistic movement that is threatening democracy in the United States. The premise of the book is that we'll be better able to resist fascism if we come to understand it. Chapter titles are framed as individual actions—"Believe in truth," "Defend institutions," and "Do not obey in advance." Chapter 9 instructs readers to "Make an effort to separate yourself from the internet. Read books." He recommends both fiction and non-fiction titles, and discusses Ray Bradbury's *Fahrenheit 451* and George Orwell's *1984*, explaining that these "classic novels of totalitarianism warned of the domination of screens, the suppression of books, the narrowing of vocabularies, and the associated difficulties of thought."[2] The 24/7 news cycle, with its continuous "breaking news," and the speed and ubiquity of the internet prevent us from slowing down to think deeply and carefully, he argues, making a case that "any good novel enlivens our ability to think about ambiguous situations and judge the intentions of others."[3] The books he recommends are all ones written for an audience of adult readers, with one exception,

J.K. Rowling's *Harry Potter and the Deathly Hallows*, which he argues "offers an account of tyranny and resistance."[4]

The *Harry Potter* novels seem an obvious choice of books to inspire young people, and adults as well, to understand and resist fascism. Voldemort and his followers are obsessed with purity of blood and they persecute Muggles (non-magical humans) and Mudbloods (magical humans from non-wizarding families). The Death Eaters are fascistic in their obsession with race, their veneration of an authoritarian leader who promises to rid the wizarding world of impurities, and their oppression of those considered Other. Our heroes, steadfast in their resolve, are depicted as champions of oppressed minorities as they lead an underground revolt and defeat Voldemort and his followers in a final battle on the grounds of Hogwarts.

Interestingly, the *Harry Potter* books have been vilified by members of white[5] supremacist groups, who condemn them for their overt messages about racism. For example, the night before the 2017 "Unite the Right" rally in Charlottesville, Virginia, which brought together multiple neofascist groups from around the nation and ended with the deaths of three people, torch-carrying white supremacists chanted "Harry Potter isn't real!" alongside neo-Nazi slogans like "Blood and soil!" and "Jews will not replace us!" As David Neiwert of the Southern Poverty Law Center explains, "Harry Potter Isn't Real!" is a "seemingly odd chant, which in many ways reflects the alt-right's fluency in popular culture, [which] is directed at White nationalists' enmity towards multiculturalism, since the underlying thesis of J.K. Rowling's massively popular youth-fantasy series is about combating prejudice, racial and otherwise."[6] Clearly, both the Right and the Left recognize the power of popular culture and children's literature to both affect and reflect opinions, identities, and worldviews.

Some on the Left have argued that the *Harry Potter* novels encourage youth activism. In a *Teen Vogue* essay titled "Why 'Harry Potter' Means So Much to the Parkland Activists," Ella Cerón draws parallels between the teenagers depicted in the novels and a group of Florida teenagers turned gun control activists after a 2018 mass shooter at Marjory Stoneman Douglas High School killed 17 people, most of them teenagers. In both cases, Cerón writes, "a small group of teenagers [had to] do the crucial work that an ineffective government refused to take on."[7] She notes that David Hogg, one of the group's leaders, compared Florida's Governor to Voldemort and that another leader, X Gonzáles, wrote a viral Twitter post that read: "You know, when I said I wanted the real world to be more like Harry Potter I just meant the teleportation and the magic stuff not the entire plot of book 5 where the government refuses to do anything about a deadly threat so the teenagers have to rise up and fight back."

Fascism, Resistance, and the Confounding Case of *Harry Potter*

These examples are anecdotal evidence, but one academic study demonstrates that the books increase readers' empathy toward out-groups and their understanding of others' perspectives. A group of sociologists concluded, after conducting interviews with readers, that, "When a fictional character comes alive in the mind of the reader, it can create empathy and reduce prejudice. Reading the novels promoted 'positive attitudes toward stigmatized groups.'"[8] Reading fiction, the authors of the study speculate, creates "extended contact" with characters as we get to know their internal lives, backgrounds, psychology, and motives over time in ways that can gradually lead to empathy and "theory of mind," an understanding that other people experience the world in ways that are different from our own. It's not clear though whether this "extended contact" can happen with any works of fiction, and not just *Harry Potter*.

Significantly, they also note that just watching the *Harry Potter* films did not have the same effect on respondents' attitudes, and that those surveyed who had only seen the films were more likely to identify with Voldemort than those who had also read the books. Film, a sequence of moving images and sounds, changes how we make meaning, shifting our attention to the visual, especially when a large screen provides a space for spectacle. Movie villains are often more interesting than heroes. In the films, the platinum-haired Malfoys have striking Aryan features and the Death Eaters share a goth aesthetic and matching tattoos: They are dark and alluring. Furthermore, identification with a fictional character on the page or screen is complicated, even in a pop culture narrative based on the Western hero myth where we're supposed to root for the easily identifiable "good guys" and boo the "bad guys." In this case, a kid who identifies with or roots for a villainous character on the page or screen is not necessarily a villain—they might just be a rebel.

The question of whether the *Harry Potter* narrative inspires anti-racist, anti-fascist thinking is further complicated by contradictions in the narrative itself. While the books use racial identity in the wizarding world as a metaphor for white supremacy, the racial makeup of the human characters undermines this narrative. All of the main characters, the heroes and the villains, are white. The few people of color take on secondary roles, and none are fully developed characters. As children's literature scholars Sarah Park Dahlen and Kallie Schell note, "The inclusion of one-dimensional racialized characters fills a superficial diversity quota."[9] Additionally, Park Dahlen and Ebony Elizabeth Thomas argue that this almost all-white wizarding world presented through the perspective of white characters can "uphold white supremacist views that people of color are not essential, even in a fantasy world built in the imagination."[10] People of color reading the books are not given an opportunity to identify with a character like themselves and white readers are not asked to stretch their imaginations beyond identifying with the white, Western, male, heterosexual, cisgendered protagonist whose perspective is centered throughout the seven-volume series.

Harry Potter is a unique case because the narrative is an international phenomenon that stretches over decades and includes far more than just the books. There are films, sequels, prequels, websites, toys, games, costumes, active fan communities, theme parks, and whole college courses devoted to the series (I designed and taught such a class at my university). Their author is an international celebrity who comments upon and continues to reshape the meaning of the books. For instance, shortly after the release of the seventh novel, J.K. Rowling announced that Hogwarts's Headmaster Albus Dumbledore is a gay character, even though there's no direct mention of his sexuality anywhere in the books, which are relentlessly heterosexual in all of their pairings. Most significantly, over the past few years, Rowling has made a number of anti-trans comments on social media, even mocking women who have transitioned for calling themselves women.

Should the author's celebrity status influence our understanding of the novels she created? Can we still promote *Harry Potter* as an anti-fascist text when its highly-visible author is promoting transphobia? Context matters. Neofascists in the United States are scapegoating and oppressing members of the trans community, most especially trans children. Books featuring LGBTQ+ characters are being banned in state after state, some of which have passed "don't say gay" laws that prohibit school discussions about sexual and gender identities. If homophobia and transphobia are characteristics of the new fascism, does the fact that the books have no LGBTQ+ characters undermine their anti-fascist message? Finally, we have to ask as well if British books with no main characters of color maintain or subvert, reveal or smooth over the ideology of white supremacy, which is central to American fascism.

I propose here that there are many other options, books for younger readers that more directly characterize and confront aspects of neofascism in the United States. In the chapters that follow, I make the case for a handful of carefully selected books for young readers that highlight and challenge various facets of American fascism: white supremacy, settler colonialism, scapegoating of Others, dualistic thinking, "us" versus "them" narratives, sexism, homophobia, transphobia, xenophobia, antisemitism, Islamophobia and a reassertion of patriarchal power often disguised as "family values." Fascism is a dangerous ideology, one that can lead to an authoritarian government and the oppression of human rights. Neofascism is an existential threat to our struggling multi-racial democracy,[11] it is not going away anytime soon, and we have a responsibility to prepare ourselves and our nation's young people to combat it. Books, of course, are not a panacea, but I argue here that they can be one part of a pro-democracy, anti-fascist education for both children and adults. I also focus attention on all-ages popular culture texts because children's literature and pop culture are connected: Both are dismissed as being "low art," formulaic, simple, and mass produced, but both, I would argue, have a far greater influence on our collective worldview than "high art," lofty texts aimed solidly at an audience of educated adults.[12]

Academic writing is supposed to "stake a claim" and "carve out territory," apt metaphors for an institution steeped in colonialist discourse. I don't "stake a claim" here to any knowledge that doesn't already exist. Instead, I see myself making connections among disparate-seeming texts and ideas, weaving a web of threads that brings patterns into relief. If fascism, as an ideology, is created through a web of story, then learning about the nature of story, the way stories construct meaning through connections to other stories, and how stories both reflect and shape our view of ourselves and the world we inhabit, might be a way to understand and counter the totalizing narratives central to fascism.

I am not a specialist in education and this is not a book about teaching methods. Education departments research pedagogy, the science of teaching, but I study what educators call "content," the subject matter that is the focus of the lesson; in my case, literature for children, teenagers, and young adults. My field is the humanities,[13] which means I'm most interested in understanding how stories work, how they affect us, and what we do with them. While books are taught in classrooms, I focus here on the way that books, all by themselves, being the transformative inanimate objects that they are, teach readers.

I started this project by asking what seemed like a simple research question: What sorts of stories are out there that inform young readers about American neofascism and its foundations in our long history of authoritarianism? I've lectured on Holocaust literature for young people in my courses and at the Zekelman Holocaust Center in Farmington Hills, Michigan, so my first thought was to revisit those texts.[14] Holocaust literature is, by nature, didactic: It teaches us about the horrible ends of fascism, it preserves memory by passing it to the next generation, and its stated goal is "never again," the idea that learning about atrocity will help to prevent it from happening again in the future. After I re-read a few novels, though, I realized that they wouldn't work for this project. While twenty-first-century fascism in the United States resembles European fascism in the twentieth century, it is different in significant ways. American neofascism is solidly based in US history and culture, drawing upon our existing prejudices and mythologies. It is rhizomic, weaving its way into our lives in small, everyday ways that feel normal, or "just the way things are," which may explain why many people don't seem to recognize neofascism for what it is. American neofascism is wired, fueled by a complex media ecosystem that allows users to create ideological bubbles for themselves. How could one book possibly depict such a complex system? As is the case with Holocaust literature, the answer is that there is no one book, which is why we need to consider multiple books, each of which highlights a different aspect of fascist ideology, one part of the elephant we're working together in the dark to understand. As Philip Nel noted in his book *Was the Cat in the Hat Black? The Hidden Racism of Children's Literature and the Need for Diverse Books*, racism is "a many-headed hydra. We need to battle it on as many fronts as possible."[15]

I'm an English professor who has spent the past twenty-five years researching and teaching children's and young adult literature at Eastern Michigan University. Before I was an academic, I worked as a newspaper journalist. My last two years working as a reporter at the Charlottesville *Daily Progress* in the late 1980s involved covering the higher education beat, which included the University of Virginia. That's why I was inspired to switch careers from journalist to English professor—I wanted to be part of a university, not just an observer. Transitioning to graduate school meant learning entirely new ways of thinking, reading, and writing focused on sharing ideas with small groups of other specialists working within the same discourse community. The more time you spend in academia, the smaller and smaller these communities become: you end up participating in insular conversations that mostly involve invoking names, using arcane terminology, and quibbling over minutia. Academic jargon, or any other kind of jargon, exists for a reason: It's shorthand for bigger ideas. There's nothing wrong with shorthand, slang, or jargon—as long as you're not leaving people out of the conversation. I believe it is vital to include more people of all ages in conversations about our civic well-being, which is why I've worked to make this a book that can be read by students, not just specialists. Cultural theorist bell hooks argues that, "any theory that cannot be shared in everyday conversation cannot be used to educate the public" and that theory that is "highly abstract, jargonistic, difficult to read, and containing obscure references" is a means of maintaining the "intellectual class hierarchy" that dominates institutions of higher education.[16] For these reasons, I'm doing my journalistic best to avoid jargon and to distill complex concepts into accessible English, and I'm doing my academic best to lend credibility to my arguments using sources and theories that are helpful for explaining bigger ideas. I am also focused on what children's literature scholar Kenneth Kidd calls "books for beginners," texts for readers of various ages that introduce complex concepts and theory.

I define an anti-fascist literature for beginners by building upon the work of scholars who study literature and media aimed at children, teens, and young

Fascism, Resistance, and the Confounding Case of *Harry Potter*   xv

adults; historians and philosophers who have analyzed fascist systems from the past; and journalists and political scientists who are working to understand American neofascism and its origins in the long history of authoritarianism in the United States. I focus on contemporary, mass-produced, easily-accessible books written in English that address various aspects of American authoritarianism and neofascism. Because neofascist ideology is spread out and intricately woven into the fabric of our everyday lives, it is difficult to pin down. My strategy for managing it has been to stick pins into some of its many tendrils and to focus on tangible, specific examples in hopes that the parts will assemble themselves into a comprehensible whole, or at least a mappable web. I've organized chapters around different aspects of neofascism: fascistic rhetoric, contested histories, a reassertion of patriarchal values, the scapegoating of Others, and fascist storytelling and mythmaking.

    Before I move on, I think it's important to tell readers a little bit about myself, to identify a few of the identities, affinities, and intersections that shape my point of view. I grew up a military brat, living in enlisted neighborhoods on and around Air Force bases on three different continents in the 1960s and 70s. My home was multigenerational, bicultural, and bilingual: dad came from small-town South Carolina and mom from small-town East Germany. Her mother, my Oma, lived with us too, but never learned English. She told me stories in German about life during two world wars, under fascism, under communism, and then as a refugee. The four of us, and our black and white cat named Boots, packed up our home into boxes and put it all back together again someplace new, on average, about once a year. Family was a constant, but the culture around us changed with each new place. I went to ten different public schools, moving each time in the middle of the school year, which means that, like many other Third Culture Kids,[17] I learned how to be a new kid, make new friends quickly, and deal with bullies. My immersions in multiple cultures gave me an invaluable informal education, but my nomadic K-12 formal education was continuously disrupted, inconsistent, and incomplete. To compensate, mom took me to the library. The books I read outside of school—ones for children and for adults, both fiction and nonfiction—helped to supplement my formal education, albeit, in a haphazard kind of way. And genre fiction—fantasy, horror, and science fiction—offered stability through fictional places and story structures that grounded me in the ever-shifting landscape of my childhood.

    Life now is far less interesting: I'm a cisgendered, white, older, middle-class woman living in a suburb of a Midwestern college town with lots of bookstores, coffee shops, and places to put in a kayak. I'm currently in the privileged position of being a tenured full professor at a regional university with a strong faculty union that protects academic freedom and supports scholarship. I'm able to write this book, not because I'll perish if I don't publish, but solely because I feel compelled to write it. My motivation is a simple and earnest one: A functioning democracy requires an informed and thinking electorate, and books are one way readers of all ages can educate and empower themselves. This is a hopeful and patriotic project because, as I'll discuss later, mass cynicism and skepticism create a perfect breeding ground for fascist propaganda. If we are going to work to preserve democracy, we must counter these with hopefulness, something many books written for young readers provide.

HOW TO READ LIKE AN ANTI-FASCIST

Introduction
American Neofascism, the Child, and Children's Literature

> It would be so much easier, for us, if there appeared on the world scene somebody saying, 'I want to reopen Auschwitz, I want the Black Shirts to parade again in the Italian squares.' Life is not that simple. Ur-Fascism can come back under the most innocent of disguises. Our duty is to uncover it and to point our finger at any of its new instances—every day, in every part of the world.
> —UMBERTO ECO, "Ur-Fascism."[1]

Aesop's fable "The Boy Who Cried Wolf" is a story that we share with children to teach the value of words. It's about a shepherd boy who cries "Wolf!" because he thinks it's entertaining to see all the townspeople come running to his aid. He laughs at them, then does it again, taking power away from the word with each repetition, with each breach of trust. Finally, of course, a real wolf appears, but this time, the boy's cry of "Wolf!" goes unheeded because he is no longer believed. In some versions of the story the sheep get eaten, and in the one I heard as a child, the boy gets eaten as well. The stated moral is that if you lie too many times, people won't believe you anymore. But it's also a story about how some words should never be misused because their meaning is vital to a community's survival. Once such a word, a communally agreed-upon distress signal, loses its meaning, the entire community suffers.

"Fascism" is such a word. After decades of overuse and misuse, it has become unmoored from its original meanings and is often, today, used simply as an insult to hurl at political opponents. It's not a word used in polite conversation, and the person using it is not usually taken seriously. That is perhaps why people have been so reluctant to use it to describe what is happening in twenty-first century America. I was reluctant to use it too, at first, when I started this project in early 2018. But with each passing year, as I learned from experts in fields like political science and history, it gradually became clear to me that what is happening right now in the United States is indeed the rise of fascism. Experts have been trying to warn us for years, but those warnings haven't reached the general public, maybe because fascism is a complicated concept that can't be boiled down into a sound bite or maybe because calling someone or something "fascist" is the equivalent of crying "Wolf!" long after the word has lost its ability to warn.

Fascism, at first, seems simple and easy to recognize: the image of goose-stepping, black-booted men stiff-arm saluting the strongman leader, everyone dressed in red and black. Our collective, mass media-influenced image of what fascism looks like is tied to a specific time and place when fascism was fully formed into a brutal dictatorship, but it doesn't acknowledge the slow, years-long process by which a fascist ideology develops or the way that American neofascism is distinct to the character of the United States. "The language and symbols of an authentic American fascism would, of course, have little to do with the original European models," writes Robert O. Paxton, author of *The Anatomy of Fascism*. "They would have to be as familiar and reassuring to loyal Americans as the language and symbols of the original fascisms were familiar and reassuring to many Italians and Germans, as Orwell suggested. Hitler and Mussolini, after all, had not tried to seem exotic to their fellow citizens. No swastikas in an American fascism, but Stars and Stripes (or Stars and Bars) and Christian crosses."[2] America's neofascists cloak themselves in red, white, and blue; Christianity; and jingoistic slogans like "America First." Paxton and a number of other experts have been raising the alarm for quite some time that the MAGA movement is indeed fascistic and an existential threat to democracy in the United States.

Paxton explains that fascism is "something that is better understood as a process," which means it cannot be easily summed up in a "neat general definition."[3] He reluctantly boils his book-length definition down to one sentence near the book's end:

> Fascism may be defined as a form of political behavior marked by obsessive preoccupation with community decline, humiliation, or victimhood and by compensatory cults of unity, energy, and purity, in which a mass-based party of committed nationalist militants, working in uneasy but effective collaboration with traditional elites, abandons democratic liberties, and pursues with redemptive violence and without ethical or legal restraints goals of internal cleansing and external expansion.[4]

His definition highlights the ways in which fascist ideology is linked to emotions, specific states of mind, and to storytelling. Contemporary fascist leaders and their surrogates tell their followers stories that provoke strong emotions like fear or humiliation: immigrants are "swarming" across our nation's borders, drag queens are "grooming" our children to question their gender identity, Black Lives Matter protestors are a threat to our safety, liberal elites and communists at schools and universities are brainwashing our young people, feminists are threatening the structure of the traditional family, and "Democrat-run cities" are sites of decay and corruption. This collection of stories forms a dark vision of life in the United States, reinforced through constant repetition to form a cohesive mythology of a once-great nation in decline. Fascist ideology can lead to authoritarianism when people who have been convinced that their nation has fallen into disorder elect a leader who promises a new order. In his influential essay, "The Five Stages of Fascism," Paxton encourages researchers to "study fascism in motion" and to study it within a cultural context, "spending at least as much time on the surrounding society and on fascism's allies and accomplices as on the fascist movements themselves."[5] This is the approach I have taken for this project.

In the decades after World War II, researchers, with the benefit of hindsight, analyzed the conditions, threads of thought, propaganda, and the existing prejudices that worked together to spread fascist ideology in Europe. This research is useful for recognizing patterns, the ways that neofascism in the United States resembles twentieth-century European fascism. But since fascism is a system embedded in a nation's distinct history and character, it is also necessary to consider the factors that make twenty-first-century American fascism unique. In his book about digital demagoguery, Christian Fuchs writes that, "If one argues in a historiographical manner that fascism includes only the societies associated with Hitler in Germany and Mussolini in Italy, then one risks not being able to argue for the potential historical return of fascism."[6] History does not repeat itself but it is instructive, and historians and political scientists have been among the first to sound the alarm that the United States is on a path toward authoritarianism.

While the descriptor "authoritarianism" feels foreign and far removed from a nation so "exceptional" as the United States, we already have a long history of supporting authoritarian ideals, movements, and individuals, as well as a long history of resistance and civil disobedience[7]. For instance, Hitler was a great admirer of our Jim Crow laws, Henry Ford, and our Aryan character, writing in *Mein Kampf*, "The Germanic inhabitant of the American continent, who has remained racially pure and unmixed, rose to be master of the continent; he will remain the master as long as he does not fall a victim to defilement of the blood."[8] From the KKK to the alt-right, authoritarianism in the United States has been consistently characterized by racism, settler colonialism, sexism, homophobia, transphobia, xenophobia, and antisemitism.[9] This is why, in his book *Teaching Anti-Fascism: A Critical Multicultural Pedagogy for Civic Engagement*, Michael Vavrus argues that in the United States, anti-fascist thinking and activism must "support anti-racism, decolonization, migrant protection, feminism, and anti-patriarchal policing of sexual and gender boundaries, all of which are bedrocks of critical multicultural education."[10] Critical multicultural education, which I also advocate for here, has long been a target of the American Right, which characterizes anti-racist teaching and books as "woke," a term used to pejoratively characterize education that encourages young people to question and to think critically about our institutions, histories, ideologies, and the stories we tell and are told.

On Behalf of the Children

We tend to associate fascism with one person, the charismatic fascistic leader, a Hitler or a Mussolini, but US neofascism runs much deeper than Donald Trump, as an individual, or even the MAGA movement. As I'll discuss in upcoming chapters, fascism has woven its way into institutions at the national, state, and local levels where the Right is working to enact policies and laws that are anti-democratic. Significantly, a number of these policies are being created "on behalf of the children." For example, in its sprawling 885-page 2023 report, *Mandate for Leadership: The Conservative Promise* (known widely as Project 2025), the highly influential Heritage Foundation laid out its recommendations for governance of the United States once a Republican was sworn in again as US President. Dozens of conservative activists representing a variety of political action groups contributed to the report, which includes an introduction by Kevin D. Roberts, the foundation's president. From its very first page, children in need of protection from liberal forces and cultural decay are invoked as justification for myriad regressive policy proposals. "Look at America under the ruling and cultural elite today," Roberts writes. "Inflation is ravaging family budgets, drug overdose deaths continue to escalate, and children suffer the toxic normalization of transgenderism with drag queens and pornography invading their school libraries."[11] A renewed conservative agenda, he promises in the report's introduction, will focus on "4 fronts," the first of which is to "restore the family as the centerpiece of American life and protect our children."[12] Some of the proposed policy changes designed to protect children include eliminating the Department of Education and the Head Start Program, which provides free pre-school education to low-income families. Instead, the authors propose funding for "promoting father involvement" to "keep a consistent male figure in the minor's life,"[13] "school choice," ways for conservative families to opt out of public education, and "parental rights," which supersede the rights of children.

Much vitriol in the report is aimed at "radical gender ideology,"[14] a queer trans feminist bogeyman that threatens the father-headed family as a foundational patriarchal institution and, thereby, the well-being of America's children. In the name of protecting the Child,[15] Roberts urges a new conservative administration to delete the terms "sexual orientation and gender identity ... diversity, equity, and inclusion ..., gender, gender equality, gender equity, gender awareness, gender-sensitive, abortion, reproductive health, reproductive rights, and any other term used to deprive Americans of their First Amendment rights out of every federal rule, agency, contract, grant, regulation, and piece of legislation that exists."[16] This list of prohibitions against a flood of words that threaten the patriarchy seeks to cement normative gender and sexual identities. Through its thoroughness about what it seeks to exclude, the report ensures that women and girls are only officially acknowledged as cisgendered, heterosexual, baby-making subjects of the patriarchy. Furthermore, Roberts argues that "Pornography, manifested today in the omnipresent propagation of transgender ideology and sexualization of children" should be outlawed and that, "the people who produce and distribute it should be imprisoned. Educators and public librarians who purvey it should be classed as registered sex offenders. And telecommunications and technology firms that facilitate its spread should be shuttered."[17] In the report, the Child in danger of corruption from nefarious cultural forces is used as a powerful symbol to justify regressive and oppressive policies meant to move the nation toward a fascistic future in which gender boundaries will be firmly redrawn.

Meanwhile, at the state and local level throughout the United States, book bans are surging and most of the books being banned are works written specifically for children and young adults. Books written by and featuring BIPOC (Black, Indigenous, and people of color) are among the most banned, as are books by and about people in the LGBTQ+ community. Worried parents, whipped into a frenzy by right-wing television personalities who warn about the looming threat of "critical race theory"[18] and of young people being "groomed" by teachers to adopt LGBTQ+ identities, have been crowding into school board meetings around the nation to demand more control over the formal education of young people. "Don't say gay" laws have been passed in several states to shield children from learning about sexual and gender identity, with many school systems even prohibiting sex education of any kind, teaching abstinence instead. Multiple US states have passed laws prohibiting transgender children from receiving gender-affirming medical treatment, using bathrooms aligning with their gender, or playing sports. School and public librarians around the nation have been forced to purge their shelves of offensive titles that might end up in children's hands, with librarians in some states even being threatened with jail time if they refuse to cull their collections. School and university curriculums are being impacted as well in states that are banning the teaching of critical race theory and African American history or defunding diversity, equity, and inclusion programs.

While some of these may seem to be isolated cases, most are part of a larger, ongoing movement to reshape the education of America's children and to remake America's schools. Well-funded political action groups are providing parents with ready-made lists of books to challenge and with strategies to employ. For instance, the Heritage Foundation provides a guide titled "How to Identify Critical Race Theory" that alerts parents to be on the lookout for words like "equity" and "systemic" that signal a curriculum supposedly meant to teach America's children to "work to dismantle laws, traditions, norms, institutions, and free-market enterprise—the entire American system itself."[19] Similarly, state legislatures are passing laws using boilerplate language and lists of objectionable books provided by political action groups. For example, the group "Moms for Liberty" provides members with book lists and endorses candidates for school boards. Their mission statement is "Moms for Liberty is dedicated to fighting for the survival of America by unifying, educating and empowering parents to defend their parental rights at all levels of government."[20] They view themselves as "joyful warriors" working to protect America's children from the decadence of the Left and the threat of "woke" ideology, but through their mission statement, the group emphasizes the rights of the parent rather than the rights of the child, and connects national identity to "parental rights," a term used on the Right to signal conservative, patriarchal family values.

The Child, universal and perpetually innocent, is a powerful political symbol. Children, who have very little real power in the political realm, are invoked rather than addressed in political discourse about what is best for the Child. As children's literature scholar Robin Bernstein asks, "How did childhood acquire so much affective weight that the exhortation to 'protect the children' seems to add persuasive power to almost any argument?"[21] Because it carries so much cultural weight, the Child in need of protection can become a justification for oppressive laws. In *No Future: Queer Theory and the Death Drive*, Lee Edelman argues that the concept of the universal, eternal Child can be used to impose restrictions on an entire populous: "On every side, our enjoyment of liberty is eclipsed by the lengthening shadow of a Child whose freedom to develop undisturbed by encounters [. . .] terroristically holds us all in check and determines that political discourse conform to the logic of a narrative wherein history unfolds as the future envisioned for a Child who must never grow up."[22] The Child, as a concept, never grows up—that's what actual children do—but our conception of the ever-innocent Child matters because protecting and controlling it affects the lives of actual children, and adults as well.

Advocates of recent book bans, policies, and prohibitions repeatedly claim that they are protecting innocent young people from danger. For example, conservative activist Ian Prior argues that parents "are worried for the safety of their daughters, who might find themselves in bathrooms and locker rooms with biological males with bad intentions."[23] Trans girls are depicted here as dangerous predators so that parents can view themselves as protectors of their heterosexual, cisgendered girls, rather than as transphobic. Activist parents working to ban books with LGBTQ+ characters worry that their child might become confused if they learn about gender, or pronouns, or even, in a few cases, rainbows and unicorns. Similarly, many parents and politicians also claim that they are protecting children from feeling guilt or shame when learning about US history, especially subjects such as settler colonialism, slavery, Jim Crow, and the civil rights movement. As journalist Benjamin Wallace-Wells notes, "the emphasis in the text of the bills, in Texas and in other states, is often on ensuring that white students not be made to feel racist, and that conservative ones not be made to feel isolated by their views."[24] It seems as though parents might just be projecting their own feelings of guilt or shame onto their children and, as is often the case, other people's children.

In all of these cases, the innocent white Child in need of protection has been marshaled as a symbol that comes to carry the weight of adults' fear of change and their need for order, conformity, and tradition. In "Childhood Innocence and Other Modern Myths," cultural theorist Henry Jenkins writes that, "within the Republican ideology of family values, the innocent child is most often figured in relation to the past, threatened by the prospect of unregulated change, endangered by modernity, and denied things previous generations took for granted."[25] By invoking the Child in this way, adults empower themselves to challenge teachers, professors, intellectuals, and liberal elites who threaten to disrupt existing hierarchies. Adult anxieties about a changing world are made manageable: a parent has no control over a Supreme Court ruling that legalizes same-sex marriage but they can protest a children's book that features gay parents, at which point their homophobia feels justified because they're taking on a protective role.

At what point does protecting the ideal of the Child do harm to actual children? And whose children are being protected, rejected, ignored, oppressed, or privileged? The Child being invoked as in need of protection in the scenarios above has a particular set of characteristics: It is the white child who might be made to feel guilt or shame upon learning the history of Jim Crow, the heterosexual and cisgendered child who might question their sexuality if they read about LGBTQ+ characters in a novel, and the Christian child who needs their faith affirmed in school. The idealized Child under neofascist ideology represents a fear of change and loss of control, as well as a nostalgic longing to return to a mythic past that informs fascistic visions of a utopian future. In their collection *The Nation in Children's Literature* Kit Kelen and Björn Sundmark argue that the concept of the Child is central to nation-building. "It is the sanctity of the nation's dead and the innocence of its children—the national past and future—which give the nation's sentient—the citizens—their raison d'être," they argue, explaining that national identity "depend[s] very much on these two nonvoting parties—those departed whose deeds are represented as nation-making and those for whom the deeds were (and continue to be) done, those to whom the nation will be given in trust. It is this passing of the baton that makes the nation eternal (or rather gives it such an appearance)."[26] In this way, nationhood is conceived of as being generational, defined by the socialization of the Child, which, in turn, influences the ways in which history is constructed and the future is imagined.

In *How Fascism Works: The Politics of Us and Them*, Jason Stanley explains that the goal of a fascist education is "to instill pride in the mythic past": "For the fascist, schools and universities are there to indoctrinate national or racial pride, conveying for example (when nationalism is racialized) the glorious achievements of the dominant race."[27] This focus on "the glorious achievements of the dominant race"—an emphasis the Right euphemistically calls "Western civilization"—means teaching young people about Columbus but not residential schools for Indigenous children, about the Emancipation Proclamation and not the Middle Passage, and about World War II but not the internment of Japanese Americans or Jim Crow apartheid. Education, in this scenario, is centered on withholding information from young people rather than sharing it, on narrowing children's imaginations rather than expanding them. In her book *The Children's Table: Childhood Studies and the Humanities*, Anna Mae Duane argues that, "The study of children, often seen as peripheral to the important work of understanding social, political, national, and ethnic structures, allows us to rethink the very foundations underlying these structures'."[28] When we study attitudes toward and policies regarding the Child, we gain an understanding of the way power is structured in a given society. As I'll argue below, the Child, in need of protection from knowledge that reveals the contradictions, gaps, and suppressions necessary to construct our fragile myth of American exceptionalism, is an essential element of neofascist ideology.

Authoritarian Attitudes and the Child

Children, specifically the white Child, have been important to efforts to create or maintain authoritarian systems before, especially in Nazi Germany, where the Hitler Youth were a vital part of public education, a nationalized school curriculum trained young people to become fascist citizens, and *Mein Kampf* influenced the education of most children. Schools were required to teach a standardized, pro-Nazi curriculum. As Susan Bartoletti explains in her nonfiction children's book, *Hitler Youth: Growing Up in Hitler's Shadow*, "It was important to Adolf Hitler that all Germans shared the same outlook on the world. This was called Weltanschauung, or 'worldview.'"[29] She continues, explaining that, "For Hitler, education had one purpose: to mold children into good Nazis. As soon as the Nazis came to power, they took control of the public schools. . . . They rewrote the curriculum from top to bottom, so that it only taught Nazi-approved ideas."[30] Children were to be shielded from "divisive" ideas and unified under one cohesive ideology. The Child here is viewed as an empty vessel to be filled so that it will carry a nationalistic, fascistic mythology forward into the future. Indeed, the "utopian" future central to fascism depends upon (re)education of the Child, who must be protected from influence by liberalism or communism and must learn to conform to the shared worldview that is central to fascist ideology.

The Child is so central to one's political beliefs that researchers in political science use adults' attitudes about children and child-rearing to determine whether an individual leans toward or against an authoritarian mindset. For example, in early 2016, well before Trump received the Republican nomination for US President, most media pundits were fixated on factors like social class or level of education as they tried to explain the candidate's bewildering popularity. Political scientist Matthew MacWilliams took a different approach: he conducted a survey of Trump supporters' authoritarian tendencies using four questions that assess one's attitudes about child rearing. His January 2016 article, "The One Weird Trait that Predicts Whether You're a Trump Supporter," cites a study of 1,800 registered voters that he conducted in late December 2015: "Running a standard statistical analysis, I found that education, income, gender, age, ideology and religiosity had no significant bearing on a Republican voter's preferred candidate. Only two of the variables I looked at were statistically significant: authoritarianism, followed by fear of terrorism, though the former was far more significant than the latter." MacWilliams predicted that Trump would get his party's nomination because "conditions are ripe for an authoritarian leader to emerge. Trump is seizing the opportunity."[31]

According to MacWilliams and other social scientists, one's views of the Child and the relationships adults should have with children align closely with their views about governance and the structure of society. The correlation between attitudes about child-rearing and political ideology is so direct that some researchers who study authoritarianism use a set of four questions about child rearing to measure whether a person leans toward or against an authoritarian mindset.[32] Respondents are asked to identify which attributes they find the most desirable in children: independence versus respect for elders, self-reliance versus obedience, curiosity versus good manners, and being considerate versus being well-behaved. The more often a respondent picks the latter choice, the more likely they are to favor authoritarianism and vice versa. In their 2009 book *Authoritarianism and Polarization in American Politics*, political scientists Marc J. Hetherington and Jonathan Weiler also draw a direct link between authoritarianism and one's views about the corporal punishment of children. They note one survey that asked respondents whether they "approved or disapproved of various forms of physical discipline for children, such as spanking them or washing their mouths out with soap."[33] Their unsurprising conclusion is that authoritarians are more likely to spank their children than non-authoritarians. People who think children should be obedient tend to think citizens should be obedient as well. People who see families as a rigid hierarchy seek a similar sort of order in their society.[34]

This set of questions about child-rearing beliefs was developed as a way to measure authoritarian tendencies without aligning them to specific issues or affiliating them with left- or right-leaning political viewpoints. Hetherington and Weiler explain that, "This correlation is suggestive of the potential to tap into authoritarianism by relying on measures clearly untainted by any ideological leanings, or any subsequent attitudes or behaviors."[35] In other words, these questions work as a relatively apolitical assessment because many people may not view parenting as informed by and informing political beliefs. Child-rearing and childhood are largely understood as natural, personal, religious, familial, and universal concepts that are, or at least should be, untouched by politics. The reality, though, is that the Child features prominently in adults' political and cultural beliefs and as an important figure in debates about the future direction of the United States.

The maintenance of a neofascist mythology, the idea that America can be made great again by "draining the swamp," removing impurities, and suppressing complex histories, has taken the form of culture wars and battles for the minds of our nation's young people, who are constructed as perpetually "pure" and "innocent" and under siege by liberalism. Recent book bans are only a small part of a gradual authoritarian takeover of our public schools and universities that has been underway for half a century. In her book *Democracy in Chains: The Deep History of the Radical Right's Stealth Plan for America*, historian Nancy MacLean argues that educational reform has been central to the Right's decades-long efforts to dismantle democracy: Theirs, she argues, is a long game. Just as groups on the Right have been steadily, methodically, and relentlessly chipping away at reproductive rights, voting rights, unions, and civil rights for decades, they have also been working steadily, methodically, and relentlessly for just as long to "turn state universities into dissent-free suppliers of trained labor" and to privatize our nation's schools, which they contend are "the most socialized industry in the world."[36]

One of the more publicized battles on this front involves dates. The 1619 Project,[37] (inaugurated by a 2019 magazine-length essay of the same name[38]), which developed a school curriculum that invites us to center the African American experience, is an especial affront to American neofascists because it disrupts a foundational myth symbolized by the date 1776. As backlash against The 1619 Project, the first Trump administration formed the 1776 Advisory Commission, which produced *The 1776 Report*, a jingoistic document that calls for nationalistic education in America's schools.[39] The focus on the year 1776, which emphasizes our rebellion against England and de-emphasizes our history of settler colonialism and slavery, constructs both the Child and the nation as "innocent" as it works to maintain the fragile mythology necessary to fascist ideology. While the 1776 Commission was disbanded after Trump left office in 2021, the rhizomic movement undergirding it remains. For instance, in the spring of 2023, in Woodland Park, a small town in Colorado, parents were protesting at school board meetings, but these protests were different from others around the nation. Parents there were not seeking to ban books or critical race theory. They were protesting a conservative school board and superintendent gone rogue. Even though it was rejected by Colorado's state board of education, this school district was the first in the nation to adopt a new civics curriculum called "American Birthright."[40] The curriculum was created by the "Civics Alliance," which is under the umbrella of a group called the "National Association of Scholars," which used to be called the "Campus Coalition for Democracy" back in the mid 1980s when it was founded as part of a national backlash against multicultural education at public universities. Its consistent goal, then and now, is to preserve Western heritage.

The "American Birthright" curriculum is an example of one small tendril in a rhizomic right-wing network of affiliated think tanks, political action committees, and academics working to remake America's schools and universities. The curriculum adopted by the Woodland Park District includes a reading list that looks like something Holden Caufield would have read at one of the prep schools he failed out of. The list includes foundational texts of Western civilization, the "important" civilization, the one that "matters," and, the one that we all must share as part of a coherent, cohesive nationalistic identity. The curriculum emphasizes primary sources, sacred documents that young people should revere. It inculcates American values like patriotism and individualism. One turn of phrase that particularly stood out to me was that teachers must "instruct students that it is individuals who make history, not impersonal forces."[41] In other words, young people must be kept ignorant of the systems that shape history and ideology, lest they begin to think critically about them.

In the pages that follow, I make a case for books for young people that teach about and challenge neofascist ideology in the United States. I focus specifically on books that reveal "impersonal forces," the ideologies and social systems that shape history, inform politics, and structure our institutions. While there are plenty of books for young people that reproduce and reinforce elements of fascist myth-making, there are also many that reveal the contradictions, omissions, and suppressions necessary to the maintenance of neofascist ideology. Furthermore, I argue that anti-fascist books for young people are ones that address their readers as active participants in our democracy, as fellow travelers and fellow learners, and as companions in a multigenerational struggle to preserve and improve our multiracial democracy.

Books for Beginners

In his book, *Theory for Beginners: Children's Literature as Critical Thought*, Kenneth Kidd considers the idea of books for beginners, not just for children but for readers of all ages. "Beginners, of course, are not always children, any more than children are always beginners," he writes, explaining that books for adult beginners can resemble children's literature in "their methods of education" and "enthusiasm for learning."[42] Timothy Snyder's *On Tyranny*, for example, is a book for beginners that educates readers about fascism and authoritarianism.[43] It's a small, 126-page book broken into twenty brief chapters. It has a lot of white space, is written in clear, jargon-free language, and it assumes an audience of readers who may not know very much about the history of authoritarianism or its contemporary iterations. With its squat size and thin spine, it could fit neatly on the shelf alongside my early reader books for newly-literate children, which also have short chapters, lots of white space, and clear language. Indeed, it's a book I would recommend to a teenager or college student.

The lines differentiating literature for adults and for young readers are blurry. Plenty of adults read young adult novels and lots of older children read books meant for adults, families watch all-ages films and series like *Star Wars* together, and there are even quite a few "children's books" that are actually written for an audience of adults. Michelle Ann Abate chronicles this trend in her book *No Kids Allowed: Children's Literature for Adults*, writing that, "Children's literature for adults encompasses some of the most commercially successful narratives released over the past few decades in the United States. Both *Goodnight Bush* and *Go the F**k to Sleep*, for instance, were *New York Times* best sellers."[44] The implication of this publishing trend, she argues, is that the definition of children's literature, "long defined by its intended audience," is being expanded in ways that challenge our conceptions of what a children's book is or is not, as well as what a book for adults is or is not. Kidd's work troubles these distinctions as well, though from a different angle, as he examines children's books that engage young readers in adult subjects like philosophy and theory. He writes that, "As children's literature is drawing nearer to adult fiction, resembling such in complexity and aesthetic sophistication, it is also drawing nearer to adult critical discourse."[45] Ideas that were once considered "for adults" are increasingly making their way into books "for children" in ways that sometimes unsettle those adults who believe young people should be kept ignorant for as long as possible.

I agree with Kidd that we should be sharing philosophy and critical theory with young people, and that there are a number of books for young readers that address these modes of thinking, that invite the reader to question and to actively participate in the meaning-making process. Literary theorist Terry Eagleton noted that "children make the best theorists, since they have not yet been educated into accepting our routine social practices as 'natural,' and so insist on posing to those practices the most embarrassingly general and fundamental questions, regarding them with a wondering estrangement which we adults have long forgotten."[46] Eagleton makes a good point here about childhood wonder, the usefulness of remembering what we knew before we were "taught better" and of asking an endless series of "why" questions. Adults socialize children, in part, by placing limits upon their ability to imagine and by foreclosing their questions, sometimes because of exasperation at not knowing the answers ourselves. When an annoyed adult says "because I said so" as a way to end a child's questioning, they assert authority over a child's imagination, saying "that's just the way things are. Don't question." Critical theory, like that annoying child, asks the "most embarrassingly general and fundamental questions" as it tries to ascertain not just why things are the way they are, but also how our perceptions of "the way things are" and the "obvious," are shaped by an intricate system of discourses and power relations.

Gender Queer, by Maia Kobabe, which is one of the most banned in the nation, is a good example of a book for beginners that presents theory in accessible ways and blurs the lines between literature for younger and older readers (see Figure 1). It's a memoir told in the form of a graphic novel that chronicles the author's journey of self-discovery as a non-binary person. It includes frank discussions, with accompanying illustrations, about bodies, genders, sexualities, periods, and gynecological exams, details that have led censors to claim that it is pornographic. It is not pornography though, as none of the material is meant to arouse. Instead, it educates the reader about various gender identities and sexualities, the use of pronouns, and ways to be an empathetic ally to people who are questioning or coming out. It anticipates questions that readers, especially those exploring their own identities, might have.

Because of its frank discussions and illustrations, it is not a book that should be taught in primary school classrooms. It is, however, a book that could be helpful to a young person who is questioning their gender and/or sexual identities or to a cisgendered young person interested in being a supportive ally. Is *Gender Queer* a book *for* adults or *for* teens? I think it's both, and that this blurring of lines—between male and female, child and adult—is precisely what so troubles the adults who want the book removed from school and public libraries. If the innocent Child invoked as part of neofascist ideology is anything, it is relentlessly asexual while simultaneously being tacitly heterosexual and cisgendered. This universal Child embodies, through its "innocence," identities that are meant to go unmarked and unnamed in a dominant worldview. When "heterosexual" and "cisgender" go unnamed, they can be constructed as natural, taken as a given, classified as common sense, as "just the way of things." *Gender Queer* is a threat because it challenges a foundational binary, giving a name and voice to an Other whose very existence unsettles existing hierarchies.

Gender Queer is also meant to instruct the reader. Various vignettes teach how to talk about things like gender identity and pronouns in thoughtful ways. In one scene, for example, Maia has a discussion with eir[47] parents explaining, "Female pronouns didn't bother me when I was younger, but now they do. I know switching isn't easy, but please try. Getting called 'she' feels like discovering a rock stuck in my shoe. Or getting scratched by the tag at the back of my shirt. A small spike of solvable discomfort."[48] By depicting this conversation, the book instructs readers about why using preferred pronouns is a kind thing

Figure 1. The cover of *Gender Queer: A Memoir* by Maia Kobabe.

to do. In the field of children's literature studies, however, overt didacticism is often considered a negative quality: No one—child or adult—wants to feel preached at, pandered to, or patronized. Part of the fun, after all, of reading, viewing, or playing a text is the pleasure that comes from figuring things out on your own. That's why we enjoy mysteries and don't want to hear "spoilers"—it ruins the fun. But, as I read *Gender Queer* for the first time, I found myself wanting to learn more, eagerly turning pages and feeling grateful for the way it answers questions that I didn't know I had. As Perry Nodelman and Mavis Reimer note in *The Pleasures of Children's Literature*, "pleasure is not the opposite of thinking . . . thinking is a pleasure."[49] In other words, learning can be a joyful experience and books, both fiction and non, can help us to educate ourselves. They can be part of an informal education when formal education is lacking.

Books for beginners, many written for children or young adults, help my college students, most of whom are still young adults themselves, to educate themselves about a variety of topics. I don't need to translate archaic or opaque language for them because they're able to read and understand the books on their own, which means that teaching can take the form of a dialogue among fellow readers rather than a lecture from the instructor. Books for beginners can present abstract ideas in concrete forms and distill dense and difficult concepts so that they are comprehensible to a broader audience. This isn't to say, however, that books for young readers are transparent or simple, or that they have one easily discernible meaning. As I'll discuss in Chapter 1, books for young people are as complex or as simple as any other texts we read, and can be studied as objects of art and as cultural artifacts that reveal which values a culture or subculture thinks are important enough to pass on to the next generation. As tools for socialization, they can also reflect differing attitudes about the relationship between adults and children, and the role of the child as political actor.

Power and the Child Reader

Although age categories blur, most of the stories we consider children's or young adult literature address young readers in particular ways, especially when they are overt in their function as texts *for* young people. For instance, while all stories are meant to teach, the stories we share with young people are often more direct about this function of literature. Children's books, after all, are one way that adults pass on lessons they have learned, including lessons about democracy, patriotism, nationalism, and citizenship. You can tell a lot about a book if you can figure out its lessons, which isn't always as simple as it might seem. Didactic texts for younger readers can end with a heavy-handed moral—don't steal, be kind to animals, appreciate your family—but most books aren't that straightforward. Books mean multiple things to multiple readers, their meaning changes over time and in different contexts, they might not mean what a writer intends, and oftentimes they mean contradictory things. Language is a tricky tool, and books are filled with allusions, intertextual references, puns, homonyms, figurative language, and gaps that all work to confound and complicate meaning. It's a wonder we're able to communicate at all. The point is that children's literature is complicated in the same ways literature for adult readers is complicated. But books for young people, for the most part, are also complicated in one unique way: They are books defined by the lessons that one group—adults—is passing along to another group—children and teenagers.

This largely unequal relationship between the adult author and the child reader includes other adults as well: the parent who reads aloud to a child each night before bed; adults in the publishing industry who edit, publish, and sell books; the adults who buy them to put into classrooms, living rooms, and onto library shelves; and adults like me who study texts for younger readers and teach them to adults of various ages at universities. It's no wonder that the field has spent decades focused on analyzing adult-centered conceptions of the Child in books for young people. Debates in the field of children's literature in the late twentieth century focused on interrogating adult motivations in writing for young people, but this emphasis has since shifted. Jacqueline Rose held sway over the field for decades with her Freudian analysis of the adult author/child reader relationship in *The Case of Peter Pan: The Impossibility of Children's Fiction*. She asked, what "do we mean by talking to, or addressing, the child—what are we asking *of* the child in doing just that?"[50] Children's books, she argued, "colonize" the child, make them an "Other" to the book that's been written for them. Rose's theory has been challenged since the turn of the century by scholars who consider the child reader as an active co-creator of meaning in a multigenerational conversation.[51]

An important thread in this decades-long discussion is an emphasis on the workings of power, how it is central to relationships among characters in the fictional world depicted on the page, how it's infused into the production process, in adult chaperoning[52] of children's books, and in the ways the implied child reader is hailed by the author as a passive receptacle, as empty container, or as an active co-creator of meaning who brings their own set of knowledge and skills to a text. Even when books are meant to empower younger readers, they can work against this goal by reinforcing existing social structures. For instance, Roberta Seelinger Trites writes about young adult literature that, "[w]hen we investigate how social institutions function in adolescent literature, we can gain insight into the ways that adolescent literature itself serves as a discourse of institutional socialization."[53] This reproduction of existing social structures can also lead to books that do not address all young readers equally. Books for young people exist within, reflect, and influence institutions—schools, libraries, the publishing industry, the family—and these contexts further shape the power relationships involved in reading or consuming a book as product, as teaching tool, as recreational pastime, or as banned object.

In *Power, Voice and Subjectivity in Literature for Young Readers* Maria Nikolajeva argues that, because of its unique character, children's literature requires a theory of its own. She builds upon Michel de Certeau's concept of heterology to discuss the power relations inherent in works of children's literature, where the implied child reader is often constructed in terms of their alterity. Nikolajeva uses the term aetonormativity to characterize the adult-centric nature of children's and young adult literature.[54] Similarly, in his book *The Hidden Adult: Defining Children's Literature*, Perry Nodelman develops a definition of children's fiction as a literature that, for the most part, addresses an adult readership. Adults, after all, buy children's books and read them alongside or on behalf of the child, a situation that creates books that center adult perceptions of childhood. Because they address adult readers in this way, most children's books' "defining characteristics can be accounted for by conventional assumptions about and constructions of childhood."[55] In other words, he argues that children's books often reproduce what adults in a particular time period, place, and culture believe the Child should be or should become, which means they participate in the cultural construction of childhood as a concept.

The field's emphasis on the Adult has led a number of scholars to question the usefulness of discussions among adults about the adult/child binary, discussions focused on the Child as imagined by some theoretical Adult, itself an abstract concept and a construction. The Adult who writes for the Child, after all, is not a monolith any more than the Child is. And, as Wayne Booth argued, just as a literary text constructs a reader, it also constructs an author.[56] It's interesting to think about categories of age and how they shape our subjectivity, but theorizing about a generic Child in a generic children's book written by a generic Adult also runs the risk of normalizing the concept of the "universal" white, cisgendered, heterosexual, male, Christian Child, the same "universal" Child, it so happens, who is at the center of neofascist ideology. I think, for example, this is especially the case in Rose's Freud-influenced assessment of the adult author/child reader relationship, which leaves factors like race and sexuality as unmarked even as it focuses on *Peter Pan*, a text about white British children, boyhood, and imperialism. Significantly, this emphasis on a "universal" adult/child binary assumes that adult/child relations are the same across cultures rather than acknowledging cultural differences. Katharine Capshaw, a scholar of African American children's literature, writes for example that,

> Black children's literature is not at the center of critical discussions in children's literature studies. It remains an alternate in our theorizations, which draw not from Black critical recognition of the permeability and mutability of forms and audiences but from a fixation on the divide between child and adult, between what is us and what is them. It remains an alternate on our syllabi and in our classrooms, in what

we ask our students to value. The reason is plain and must be stated loudly and often: our field is grounded in white supremacy.[57]

Capshaw argues that books that center the Black child can help us to think about the adult/child relationship differently, focusing less on the arbitrary binary between the two and more on the common humanity that adults and children share. In other words, our current thinking about the generic adult/child, author/reader relationship is itself grounded in Western schools of thought that need decolonization.

Capshaw's critique invites scholars to carefully consider which texts they study and the ways in which books address the children (as opposed to the Child) for whom they are written. It also urges the field to move away from an obsessive attention to stories such as *Harry Potter* to studying works written about and for children in minority cultures. This means that, while it is important to study the mainstream, popular texts that shape and reflect dominant ideology so that we can gain a better understanding of our world and the way in which hegemony works, it is equally as important to recover, elevate, and amplify through scholarship those texts and those scholars whose work addresses the margins of the field and the marginalized child. Indeed, as I'll discuss in upcoming chapters, the literature created by and for groups that have been marginalized under American authoritarianism is an invaluable resource for learning about our current systems of power, often by providing readers with a view from the bottom, the side, or the closet, spaces that highlight the effects of our current systems of power.

It's a point of view that Toni Morrison depicted in *The Bluest Eye*, also currently one of the most banned books in the nation, a novel about a child aimed at an adult readership. The novel, published in 1970, is about a girl who is Black, female, poor, pregnant, and a child, a human existing on the bottom rungs of the white supremacist patriarchy in the United States. Morrison shows, by focalizing the story through multiple characters in one community, how the white supremacist patriarchy works as a system, as an ideology, and how it is maintained through a matrix of intersectional oppressions that work together to form a hierarchy. Significantly, Morrison explained in an afterword to the novel that she had regrets about centering her depiction of systems of oppression on the character of Pecola Breedlove, whom she worried had been "smashed" by the story. By the end of the novel, Pecola's only access to agency is to retreat into madness. Morrison's concern was that, as a result, readers would "remain touched but not moved," that they would experience "the comfort of pitying [Pecola] rather than an interrogation of themselves" and their complicity in the system that oppressed her.[58]

The Bluest Eye is a curious case: a book about a child that is often taught to teenagers in US high schools, but which is considered a book *for* adults, not suitable for teens, the main reason given for banning it from classrooms and libraries. Young people in the United States are regularly taught texts with adult themes, Shakespeare's plays for example, which are not challenged or banned. What *The Bluest Eye* has in common with other books on the most banned lists is its emphasis on the Black child and its critique of the white supremacist patriarchy. It is a book that makes tangible the devastating effects of racism, sexism, and poverty on the most vulnerable members of its community. It maps a system. The book's censorship reveals several conundrums: the arbitrary line that separates literature for adults and young people, the worry that educating about larger systems runs the risk of obscuring the humanity of the very people a text is working to humanize, and the fact that young people experience things in their everyday lives that we do not allow them to read about in a book. I wonder what *The Bluest Eye* would have looked like if Morrison had written it *for* children, centering a child like Pecola as its reader rather than its subject.

While much late twentieth-century scholarship in the field of children's literature studies focused on the role of the adult author, newer scholarship redirects our attention to the young people reading books, most especially in ways that acknowledge that young people are not empty receptacles nor passive participants in the meaning-making process. Marah Gubar, for instance, notes that, despite Rose's arguments to the contrary, some Victorian authors "carefully acknowledge the tremendous power that adults and their texts have over young people, while still allowing for the possibility that children—immersed from birth in a sea of discourse—can nevertheless navigate through this arena of competing currents in diverse and unexpected ways."[59] Similarly, Richard Flynn, in his essay, "What Are We Talking About When We Talk About Agency?," argues that scholars in a field focused on books for the young must acknowledge that, "Children are not merely passive recipients of culture; they also learn to become active participants in that culture."[60] If, as social scientists have argued, authoritarians value strict social hierarchies that place children at the bottom and relegate them to passive, obedient positions, then anti-fascist books might be ones that, through their modes of address, encourage young readers to think critically and independently, to view themselves as co-creators of meaning. Most of the books I discuss in upcoming chapters are ones that acknowledge shared affinities between adults and young people rather than depicting the adult/child relationship as a rigid binary.

For example, Kelly McDowell notes that a conservative book like *Little House on the Prairie* depicts the adult/child relationship as strictly hierarchical.

She quotes Pa telling Laura to "Do as you are told and no harm will come to you," noting that "classic works function on a didactic trajectory, which serves to instill the proper values of childhood, created by adults, in the errant child characters and, in turn, in the intended child reader."[61] The adult/child relationship depicted is similar to that imagined by the "authoritarian minded": a child must obey the patriarch of the family rather than thinking creatively and independently. The primacy of western expansion, white supremacy, and the patriarchal family in the Little House books are ideologies interwoven with depictions of child rearing and the text's attitude toward its child readers.

In contrast, McDowell analyzes Mildred Taylor's novel *Roll of Thunder, Hear My Cry*, a book about the Jim Crow South written shortly after the civil rights movements of the 1950s and 60s. Taylor's novel, written in part to compensate for a lack of African American history instruction in public schools, emphasizes "the necessity of child agency as a form of resistance for oppressed cultures" (215). McDowell argues that Taylor, as an adult author, acknowledges that, "In a racist society, African Americans, young and old, are denied agency. Regardless of age, they are robbed of the power associated with adulthood and, in essence, infantilized" (223). The adults and children in the novel are depicted as fellow travelers navigating a treacherous terrain together. Both the child characters in the book and the child reader are given information, but they are expected to "work as active agents, just as their elders do" (224) and, most significantly, they are "encouraged to question authority" (225). As Capshaw notes in her critique of the field, centering a text from a minority culture challenges the generalizations critics make about adult/child relationships and the adult/child binary.

Radical Children's Literature

Literature for young readers, more so than literature for adults, is a tool of socialization, a way to pass on to the next generations a set of values, modes of thinking, ways of reading the world, and lenses for understanding the self and others. In her book *Radical Children's Literature: Future Visions and Aesthetic Transformations in Juvenile Fiction*, Kimberley Reynolds writes that, "at decisive moments in social history children have been at the centre of ideological activity [and] that writing for children has been put to the service of those who are trying to disseminate new world views, values, and social models."[62] Authors on the Left work to inculcate liberal values in the same way that authors on the Right work to instill conservative values, but their modes of address and constructions of childhood differ. Just as there are books that educate about social justice, racial inequalities, or queer identities, there are also books that re-enforce "traditional family values" and conservative points of view, not all of them fascistic. For example, in *Raising Your Kids Right: Children's Literature and American Political Conservatism*, Abate documents the late-twentieth-century development of a niche market of right-leaning books aimed at America's young people. She discusses titles like William Bennett's *The Book of Virtues* that are meant to instill values through a "series of moral maxims that are as neat and tidy as they are impractical and unrealistic."[63] The conservative notion that children should be obedient, well-mannered, and submit to authority is echoed in the structure of such books, which construct the child reader as a passive receptacle of morals, rather than as an active participant in the meaning-making process.

Ideally, then, an anti-fascist, pro-democracy literature for younger readers can do more than educate about neofascism or authoritarianism; it can also construct the reader, child or adult, as a fellow human rather than as a container for ideology. It can invite the reader to think about larger systems, to theorize, to engage in dialogue and knowledge construction. Children's literature scholar Jack Zipes characterizes "radical children's literature" as literature that, "wants to explore the essence of phenomena, experiences, actions and social relations and seeks to enable young people to grasp the basic conditions in which they live."[64] Books cultivate a radical imagination when they encourage readers to see beyond stories of individuals, to understand the larger systems at work in a culture, and to observe the construction of ideology. According to Reynolds, in these ways, certain works of children's literature can be a site "where new ways of thinking are explored, given shape, and so made part of the intellectual and aesthetic currency of that generation of child readers."[65] Significantly, she notes that children's literature has been a fertile site for experimentation partially because it is often underestimated and overlooked.

Julia Mickenberg makes a similar argument to Reynolds's in her study of American radical children's literature from the mid-twentieth century. She notes that in 1941 members of the Antifascist League of American Writers were considering the question, "How do we educate our children so that they will be antifascist and not fascist?" She explains that they discussed the way that children should not be given "economic treatises, nor sermons about class injustices" and focused instead on educating children about racism, labor, and imperialism, asking "How to cultivate children's imaginations, their critical thinking abilities, and their sense of history?"[66] Like Reynolds, she speculates that writers of anti-fascist children's texts in the mid-twentieth century may have benefitted from an environment where children's books received little public attention.

In the 2020s, however, at least so far, books for young readers in the United States are very much on the nation's radar. They are under scrutiny as their pages are searched for evidence of "grooming," critical race theory, and unflattering histories. In response to these threats of censorship and efforts to mandate school curricula, some educators and authors have claimed that critical race theory or theories about gender are far too complex for a second grader or middle schooler to comprehend, that of course these are not ideas we share with children. This defensive stance is justified in an environment where educators' jobs are on the line and librarians are being threatened with arrest, but I make the case in upcoming chapters that we should be teaching critical race theory, gender theories, and various other critical theories to young people in ways that are clear, accessible, and applicable to their lives. Furthermore, theory can highlight the narratives that are necessary to the maintenance of a fascist ideology, which is formed, in part, through a collection of stories that work together to create an overarching worldview, a mythology. We, adults and children, need stories that counter fascist storytelling, narratives that reveal neofascism as a larger fiction, that expose the wires and pull back the curtain of fascist mythmaking, and that give voice to the stories neofascists are working to suppress.

As I'll discuss in upcoming chapters, some works of anti-fascist children's literature focus on the nature of story and thus emphasize the ways in which stories are constructed to persuade, how they shape our collective worldviews. Literary theorist Peter Brooks argues that our contemporary culture is saturated with story. He uses the phrases "overabundance of story" and the "narrative turn" to characterize our contemporary rhetorical situation, in which almost all of our information comes to us in the form of story.[67] Convergence culture narratives, those multi-media stories that crisscross the various screens that populate our current media environment, are so entwined with our everyday lives that they accumulate over time to form myths, all-encompassing worldviews, and that, "on the basis of such fictions become myths we erect theologies."[68] This narrative-driven climate, which is a fertile breeding ground for fascist ideology, is fostered by new media technologies, which are redefining how narrative works and which have created an environment where narrative is intricately interwoven with our everyday, mediated, plugged in lives.

Because of this story-filled context, I focus a lot of attention in upcoming chapters on the way anti-fascist literature for young readers can highlight how stories work to create meaning. In her influential 1988 work, *How Texts Teach What Readers Learn*, Margaret Meek argued that the best works of children's literature teach young readers how they want to be read, how to read and think critically, and how to embrace ambiguity. Most significantly, what such texts teach is that "words mean more than they say," that "the rules can be broken," and that meaning-making is a dialogue between author and reader.[69] Meek wrote specifically about children's literature that, "books not only support children in reading words, but also guide children into learning how stories work and, importantly, that stories have meaning that the reader constructs."[70] In other words, books, and children's books especially, teach readers how they are meant to be read, and how to read other texts as well. A main purpose of children's books is, after all, to teach beginning readers how to read, use, and understand language, something I'll discuss in greater detail in Chapter 1.

Works of fiction also introduce readers to the concept of story. In their simplest forms, they teach that stories have beginnings, middles, and ends, and that stories are supposed to teach us something, that they have a "moral." As they progress, according to the age or experience of the reader, books move children from being read to, to reading on their own, to fluency with reading. Along the way, they provide young readers with scripts that help them to make sense of new texts they encounter. In *Language and Ideology in Children's Fiction* John Stephens explains that because children's stories establish the rules of how narrative works, they can "affect how the mind understands and structures the world."[71] Meek and Stephens highlight the reader's active role in the meaning-making process. They acknowledge that meaning-making is not straightforward and, instead, involves complex interactions between a text, its author, and its readers, which young readers must learn to navigate.

In these ways, certain books for children and young adults can teach about narrative literacy, an understanding of story and the ways that story works to construct our perceptions of the world. Citizens in a democracy need narrative literacy because fascist leaders are adept at creating narratives, at telling compelling stories that inspire followers.[72] Political theatre, after all, is a collection of stories, as is history, as is ideology. Narrative literacy for people living in a world where democracy is under threat means understanding the ways in which our hopes, fears, beliefs, identities and relationships with one another are all shaped, at least partially, through the stories that we tell and are told. Narrative literacy is an awareness of the ways stories are constructed at both micro and macro levels, from individual words and the gaps between them to larger narrative structures to the broader context in which stories are told. It involves an understanding of rhetoric and the ways it is used to persuade or to bamboozle. There's a reason fascists ban and sometimes burn books for young readers: It is because some books can provide the intellectual tools that young people need to question and combat fascist ideology.

Texts for young readers that help to cultivate anti-fascist thinking do so through their subject matter, story structure, their address to the child or teen reader, and through the kinds of thinking they encourage. Kidd explains that works of children's or young adult literature can help young readers to think philosophically, theoretically, and critically, and that, "That is especially true when philosophy is built into the narrative structure of children's books rather than spotlighted as a topic or concern."[73] Significantly, he points out, emotion is also key to developing sophisticated ways of thinking: "It is important to remember that philosophy and theory model and encourage wonder, as well as analytical thought."[74] Wonder is a difficult quality to define, but it is also a quality that distinguishes authoritarian and nonauthoritarian worldviews because the emotions that keep us from feeling wonder—cynicism, skepticism, pessimism, and disdain—are ones common to authoritarian-minded individuals.

Snyder explains that mass skepticism is key to maintaining an authoritarian worldview. Authoritarians often work to sow confusion, to muddle what is true or not true so that no source or institution can be fully trusted: "To abandon facts is to abandon freedom. If nothing is true, then no one can criticize power, because there is no basis upon which to do so."[75] Skepticism may feel like wisdom, but mass skepticism—large numbers of people doubting every fact, assuming all sources of information are equal and equally worthy of suspicion—is deadly for democracy. Wonder, on the other hand, demands intellectual curiosity, the joy of learning or creating something new, and embracing those moments that refuse to let cynicism take hold. Wonder is a sense of awe characterized not by fear but by a desire to learn more; it is the pleasure we feel when our intellectual curiosity is rewarded, not by simple answers, but by narratives that create intricate and challenging puzzles readers are eventually able to master.

Because we accept and even expect a certain level of strangeness in works for children—Harold creates whole worlds with his purple crayon, Alice moves across a chessboard landscape with living, talking game pieces—authors and illustrators of works for children and young adults are able to tell strange, boundary-pushing stories. Books for young readers can run with the grain of dominant ideology or against it, helping to reify it or to expose it as a construction. While some might consider neofascism, authoritarianism, or late-stage capitalism to be ideas that are too complex for children's books, scholars and authors of children's and young adult literature recognize that these are indeed topics that can and should be the focus of texts for young readers, who, as is the case with we adults as well, need to learn to understand and live in the world as it is now.

How This Book Is Organized

In the chapters that follow, I consider books for young people that focus on anti-fascist and pro-democratic ideals; emphasize critical thinking and narrative literacy; address the prejudices and acts of oppression that result from fascist ideology; and construct the child, as fictional character and as reader, as a fellow traveler in our collective quest to preserve and improve democracy. The books I've chosen to discuss are influenced by my teaching, and they are meant to serve as examples, not a definitive list. I focus mostly on texts that hail the reader in particular ways: they encourage active meaning-making on the part of the child or adolescent reader and they assume a young reader able to understand and participate in larger social structures.[76] Because fascism, as an ideology, is a collection of stories, I emphasize books focused on how stories work, how they make meaning, and how they shape our sense of self and community. Some books I discuss are part of the children's literature canon and some are newer. There are pitfalls to using any one text as an example: A canonical text is recognizable to most readers but also works to reify a canon in need of decolonization. My hope is that my arguments can be applied and adapted to discussions of other texts, most especially non-canonical ones that I might have overlooked.

The critical lens I am using to analyze these works of children's and young adult literature is one I've assembled by combining research about fascism and authoritarianism with research from the interdisciplinary fields of child studies, literary criticism, cultural studies, and the study of books and other texts for young readers. Social scientists have laid out a set of characteristics that appear repeatedly in individuals who are "authoritarian-minded" and, thus, susceptible to fascist ideology. Historians and philosophers have documented how fascist leaders amplify, through simple messaging and repetition, a set of ideas that can lead a people to support and vote for an authoritarian government. Some of these attitudes include a fear or disgust for scapegoated Others, those defined as being on the margins of a culture; political rhetoric meant to baffle citizens with bullshit[77]; a selective, mythologized history of nationhood; a re-assertion of patriarchal systems of power; and mass cynicism and skepticism. Each chapter examines works of children's and adolescent literature that challenge fascistic thinking by encouraging empathy for Others, presenting complex histories, promoting critical thinking, and challenging the racism, colonialism, xenophobia, transphobia, ableism, heteronormativity, and sexism that are characteristic of American neofascism.

Chapter 1 focuses on storytelling as rhetoric, how fascists use stories to create a mythology, a worldview, and how some books can highlight this function of narrative. Brooks writes that we need to bring "attention to the ways that narrative works as system and as rhetoric—that is, as means of persuasion."[78] Our political realities are increasingly shaped by stories that take the form of ever-breaking, continuous news, "reality" narratives with casts of recurring characters in roles as heroes and villains. We are surrounded on all sides by stories: There are ones that soothe us and take our minds off of the terrible news that comes to us on every screen, some meant to enrage us or make us afraid, and some that make us think about the world in unexpected ways. Storytelling that teaches about the rhetoric of storytelling can help us to recognize the ways stories are used to construct particular realities and to shape belief systems.

Chapter 2 explores books that directly address and challenge the foundational, nationalist mythologies necessary to American authoritarianism. Because fascism requires an adherence to a mythic history, anti-fascist thinking and activism must be grounded in an honest engagement with our past and the ways it informs our current policies, attitudes, and institutions. Neo-fascists are working at full speed to ban education and literature that teaches about the legacies of slavery and settler colonialism. This is because myths of American exceptionalism and Manifest Destiny are central to US neofascism, which relies upon a vision of America as a once great nation that has been diminished by diversity of people and opinions. Young readers need books that flip this script, that put neglected histories first, and that allow us to interrogate our democratic values and how we have failed to live up to them. A genuine engagement with the ways our nation has always practiced authoritarianism in our treatment of Indigenous people and people of color can challenge the foundational mythology undergirding calls to "make America great again."

In Chapter 3, I focus on the role of the patriarchy in establishing and maintaining fascism. The conservative Christian family, with the father at its head, is vital to authoritarianism, which venerates the strongman leader as father of the nation. Fascism, especially, has at its center the hard-bodied, muscular man who serves as the protector for (mostly) white women and their children. The governing patriarch fortifies the nation's borders as he protects it from enemies within as well as without. This hard-bodied man is at the center of much popular culture in the United States, which venerates its action heroes. Within these patriarchal narrative structures, women, girls, and members of the LGBTQ+ community are viewed as threats, especially when they speak up against the status quo. Books for children and young adults can provide counter-narratives that critique patriarchal values and reveal the harm they cause to women, girls, people in the LGBTQ+ community, and boys and men as well.

Chapter 4 focuses on Others. The characteristic of fascistic thinking researchers consistently list as being most important to establishing an authoritarian regime and to maintaining power is fear. Fascist leaders (and their surrogates) tell stories that stoke fear. Indeed, there is no shortage of things that can be seen as threatening to authoritarian-minded individuals: immigrants, racial diversity, challenges to traditional gender roles, change, uncertainty, and ambiguity. Scapegoats are created so that fears of difference, the Other, the abject, or the loss of a solid-seeming sense of identity take on tangible, concrete forms that a demagogic leader promises to vanquish. Fear-mongering works especially well because authoritarian-minded individuals "find the world a threatening place" and "perceptions of threat are a relative constant for them over time and place."[79]

Simply put, a major characteristic of fascism is that it is a system in which a population is divided between insiders and outsiders, "us" and "them." Children's books can work to codify such distinctions between a dominant group and Others or they can work to create empathy, affinity, and awareness of the causes and effects of othering. In this chapter, I discuss books for children that do both. Researchers studying individuals with an authoritarian mindset list a number of characteristics that they share, a major one being a fear of outsiders, immigrants, and minority groups. Amanda Taub explains that, "People who score high in authoritarianism, when they feel threatened, look for strong leaders who promise to take whatever action necessary to protect them from outsiders and prevent the changes they fear."[80] Authoritarian leaders stoke this fear of the Other as a way to gain or maintain power, often by creating scapegoats that can serve as motivating common enemies while also carrying the blame for societal ills. For example, Trump famously promised to build a wall along the border that the United States shares with Mexico as a way to keep "invading swarms" of South American refugees out of the United States. In his 2024 re-election campaign, he promised mass deportations of migrants. Nonauthoritarians, on the other hand, have a "particular notion of fairness that favors outgroups."[81] This chapter examines sample works of children's and young adult literature focused on the experiences of cultural outsiders, those constructed as Other. Fascism, in the United States and elsewhere, is typically characterized by racism, xenophobia, transphobia, sexism, and homophobia, which means that books that directly address issues of social justice can help to challenge and redefine dangerous constructions of Others.

Finally, I conclude with a focus on story and myth, the way that stories can shape authoritarian mythologies and the way some books can make the construction of such mythologies visible. I focus on epistemic narratives, stories that depict systems and that show how such systems are maintained through ideology as well as through institutions. Stories about systems can shift our gaze from the personal to the political. They can move the background to the foreground. By showing the way narrative works to shape our social systems, such stories can reveal the gaps and contradictions necessary for the construction of neofascist and authoritarian mythologies. Fascism is a belief system, a web of stories connected together to form an all-encompassing worldview. We must counter fascist storytelling, not only with counter-stories, but also with an awareness of how fascist storytelling works.

1
Stories about Stories: Reading Fascistic Rhetoric

> Children's books seem to function primarily as explanations of what adult texts often claim is ultimately inexplicable.
> —ADRIENNE KERTZER,
> *My Mother's Voice: Children, Literature, and the Holocaust.*[1]

Books for beginners introduce readers to abstract concepts. Those familiar cardboard books for toddlers that teach things like shapes, colors, letters, and counting are even called "concept books." The most important abstract concept that children's books teach is language, the idea that there exists among humans a set of symbols with agreed-upon meanings that we use to communicate with one another. When an alphabet book in English features an illustration of a shiny red apple next to the word "apple," it teaches that the combination of letters "a-p-p-l-e" (and the drawing as well) represent a particular object. When the word is read aloud, often by an adult reader to a child listener, the sounds the word makes come to represent the thing as well. Repetition of this lesson, covered across multiple texts and conversations over a period of time, cements the platonic ideal of "apple," a symbol that stands in for a thing or set of things.

Cultures have to agree upon the general meaning of symbols in order to function as a cooperative society. That's why adults teach language to children and why children are eager to learn it. Language opens up the world for a child. For example, when a toddler spies an apple in a fruit bowl that is out of reach on a tall table they can apply their newly acquired understanding of the sounds the word makes. When the child speaks the sounds and imploringly points, a nearby adult reaches for the fruit that the child cannot and hands it down to them. In a sense, then, the child has moved an object using language. When

I think about books for very young children, I try to imagine how powerful language must feel to someone who is a beginner. Imagine it: All of a sudden, you're able to magically make an inanimate object come within your reach by uttering a simple incantation, a word.

Many people assume that children's books are simple—perhaps because they don't stop to think about them very much—but that can't be so because language is far from simple. We are all, adults and children, constantly learning language together from the moment we are born and all throughout our lives. We learn it from the world around us, from other people, from the portable screens we carry with us everywhere we travel, and from the various texts we read, which include but are not limited to books. Our knowledge of language accumulates over the years as we loop our way upward through incrementally expanding spirals, each of which builds upon the knowledge, skills, symbols, and meanings learned earlier. Books for children seem simple because they break this ongoing process of acquiring literacy down into parts, but they are actually quite complex because, in so doing, they must anticipate what a reader does not yet know, what a reader already knows, what that reader needs to know, and how to get them there. Children's books work on a continuum as they present information in manageable bits so that the child gradually moves from being read to by an adult, to reading with help, to reading independently, to reading fluently. In the process, books teach readers how to make meaning from symbols and that the meaning-making process is an intricate dance that happens in the space between the text, its author, and the reader. The abstract concept of language, the Symbolic Order, the agreed-upon meanings attached to the many symbols we use, requires that we come to understand other abstractions as well: What is up? What is 2+2=4? What is family? What is love? These seem like simple ideas until you stop to think about how complex each one actually is, how contested its meanings, how dependent on perspective and existing knowledge.

For example, before we can know what the sentence "Eve bit into an apple" means we have to possess a lot of knowledge already. We have to know that the letters "a-p-p-l-e" represent a fruit and that "bit" is an action, something someone does. While the word "Eve" could mean "evening," the context lets us know that this sentence is about a person, possibly a girl or woman, who has taken a bite out of a piece of fruit. Most experienced readers, however, know that is not the full meaning of the sentence. That's because readers bring outside knowledge to the text with them, which allows them to make deeper meaning by filling in the gaps between the words. Readers familiar with the Judeo-Christian tradition will immediately recognize that Eve is a specific person who bit into a very specific apple in a particular time and place, and that her action of biting into that apple carries with it a distinct set of meanings important to a variety of belief systems. In other words, there is a whole set of stories behind that simple sentence, which we take to be common knowledge, something an author can safely assume does not need to be explained. Unless, of course, the reader is a beginner.

Kenneth Kidd theorizes texts that introduce beginning thinkers to complex concepts, describing books that make philosophy and theory "child-friendly, as well as beginner-friendly."[2] Books for beginners, he argues, can make the most complex concepts accessible by distilling them or breaking them down into smaller, manageable bits. Furthermore, thinking about books as being for "beginners" instead of readers in particular age categories opens up a space to consider books based on the way they convey ideas rather than on the constructs of Adult and Child discussed in the Introduction. And, as is the case with Eve and her apple, each individual story, fragment of story, or referent exists within and contributes to a larger framework, a matrix of meaning, that is maintained through repetition, intertextuality, and accumulation.

Stories help us to explain and organize our lives. They help to shape our shared sense of community, our sense of self and our place in the world, our subjectivity. Karen Coats, for example, begins *Looking Glasses and Neverlands* with a focus on the role of story in identity formation:

> The only way we come to make sense of the world is through the stories we are told. They pattern the world we have fallen into, effectively replacing its terrors and inconsistencies with structured images that assure us of it manageability. And in the process of structuring the world, stories structure us as beings in the world. We begin to tell our own stories, fashioning a self out of the stories and narrative patterns we have received from our culture.[3]

Works of fiction teach the concept of story to beginners by telling stories, short and straightforward ones at first. For example, a picture storybook based on a common tale like "Red Riding Hood" can teach that stories have a beginning, middle, and end; that they have patterns that are similar to those found in other stories; that they are populated by fictional characters; and that stories mean something—they represent an abstraction, a moral, a lesson, a larger idea that the reader is supposed to glean from reading them.

Stories also order things. They spell out the social order and provide rules for living within it. The stories we share with children often provide clear-cut instructions for existing within a social order: Look out for wolves along on your path, obey authority figures, or, in the case of Eve, don't seek knowledge that isn't meant for you. In this way, books open up the world but they also foreclose it, they expand imagination but also limit it, and, in the case of children's literature, they often withhold information that adults have decided young people shouldn't possess, at least not yet. For example, we reserve Holocaust education for older children, usually teenagers. We protect younger children from knowing about the horrors of the Holocaust until they are old enough to "handle" more information, old enough to wrap their heads around the concept of genocide, as if that's something any human, adult or child, could ever fully grasp. Many schools in America don't teach about the Holocaust at all and those that do will often include a Holocaust "unit," a set of lessons delivered all at once to middle or high school students over the course of a few weeks. Because there is little room in most US school curriculums for reading, teachers will often choose just one book—Anne Frank's diary, Lois Lowry's *Number the Stars*, Eli Wiesel's *Night*—to serve as *the* singular story to explain the concept of modern genocide, the extreme end-result of fascism fully realized. The problem, though, is that there exists no single story to teach an idea as large as genocide, its causes, its effects, and how a "civilized" society can devolve into a brutal, murderous dictatorship. Ideally then, Holocaust education should happen on a continuum, with books for younger readers breaking larger ideas into smaller manageable bits, so that gradually, over time, the stories accumulate to form a larger narrative, a fuller picture, about something that is, ultimately, always already incomprehensible, even to adults, even to people who have spent a lifetime studying it. In other words, learning is a process that continues through childhood and into adulthood. Adulthood does not mark the end of learning, which is why adults need books for beginners too. But, where to start with a concept so complex as neofascist ideology?

Some authors of fiction for younger readers have tried to make abstract concepts like fascism, totalitarianism, and the oppression that results from them comprehensible to beginners by using allegory. For example, Voldemort and his followers embody fascist ideals: They believe some people are simply better than others and deserving of more rights, they are obsessed with the purity of the wizarding race, they bully and oppress cultural outsiders and those considered to be less than human, and, when they gain power in the wizarding world, they enforce a strict social hierarchy maintained through the threat of violence. The young heroes of the *Harry Potter* books recognize the threat of fascism long before the general wizarding population, but they are not believed by a public convinced that the threat no longer exists in the present. The wizarding newspaper is far more interested in publishing salacious gossip than in investigating and reporting on the return of Voldemort, and the institutions in the wizarding world are easily commandeered by the Death Eaters when they take control of Hogwarts school and the Ministry of Magic. In other words, the reemergence of fascism in the wizarding world mirrors the reemergence of fascism in our world in the ways that it draws upon existing belief systems, institutions, and old prejudices, and in the ways it is not taken seriously as a threat until it is too late. While the allegory in *Harry Potter* is undermined by the racial makeup of the novel's characters, by inconsistencies, and by the celebrity author's public promotion of prejudice, it does make the abstract concept of fascism tangible in its depictions of the Death Eaters and their obsession with "pure blood."

Lois Lowry's *The Giver* also uses allegory to convey the dangers of fascism. The characters in this novel live in a dystopian world where differences among humans have been suppressed and where historical memory has been repressed. The society seems utopian at first, though bland. Gradually it is revealed that conformity to a strict, hierarchal social order is being enforced through violence, euthanasia, and a denial of basic human rights. Rules and rituals keep the population in a state of obedience and ignorance, language is strictly controlled, knowledge of history is forbidden, and behavior is monitored through surveillance and punishment. Even though it's a work of science fiction, *The Giver* is sometimes taught as part of Holocaust lessons for two reasons: It demonstrates the importance of preserving historical memory and it makes concrete the "utopian" world envisioned by fascism, a uniform, ordered society devoid of diversity, one in which everyone knows their place and no one questions the order of things. Allegories like these, however, may be too general to speak to the specificity and complexity of twenty-first-century neofascism in the United States.

What collection of stories, then, can introduce beginners to a concept so complex, so intertwined with our everyday, mediated lives as contemporary American neofascist ideology? In order to develop a definition of an antifascist literature for young people, I first need to define fascist storytelling, the kinds of stories fascists tell, and the way that our contemporary multimedia environment is a hospitable breeding ground for fascist storytelling. The stories we tell and are told exist within a complex, global multimedia environment, which experts from various fields say is degrading our ability to pay attention and to discern between fact and fiction. We are, as Peter Brooks notes, living in a world "saturated with story."[4] If fascist ideology is created through storytelling, then books focused on the nature of story, especially the way stories work to persuade, may provide critical tools for reading the world around us.

Neofascist Storytelling: Message and Medium

Fascist leaders and their surrogates tell very specific kinds of stories in particular ways. The narratives they weave to ensnare their followers replace facts with feelings as they engage in "a systematic attempt to dismantle any notion of truth"[5] urging their followers to become both naive and cynical at once, believing everything yet nothing. Through storytelling, fascists build fictional, self-contained worlds that pit "us" against "them," a dark mythology based on fear of the Other and fear of change, obsolescence, disorder, corruption, and dissolution. Fascists tell stories about dangerous enemies working to corrupt society from within, forces determined to upend "Western civilization" and the patriarchal, white supremacist status quo. In "The Nazi Myth," Philippe Lacoue-Labarthe, Jean-Luc Nancy, and Brian Holmes note that fascist myth is not simply a set of ideas or stories, it is a total explanation: "This totality signifies that the explanation is indisputable, leaving neither gaps nor remainders."[6] Fascist storytelling works to form a tightly sealed ideological bubble, a self-contained storied world. As I discussed in the Introduction, the totalizing narrative central to fascist ideology is also achieved by suppressing counter-narratives, especially those that reveal its construction and its shaky foundations.

Historian Timothy Snyder explains that authoritarian leaders present "inventions and lies as if they were facts,"[7] they rely on repetition "to make the fictional plausible and the criminal desirable,"[8] they embrace contradiction and "magical thinking," and they deify themselves, making their pronouncements "oracular."[9] Donald Trump's social media posts offer ample evidence of each of these rhetorical moves, ideas that hold sway among his followers despite repeated attempts to challenge the accuracy of his claims. After all, fact-checking is ineffective when worldviews are shaped through belief and disbelief, by feeling something in one's gut, or by outrage, fear, or other strong emotions. In *How Democracies Die*, Steven Levitsky and Daniel Ziblatt argue that, because of these appeals to emotion, "voters are now deeply divided by race, religious belief, geography, and even 'way of life'" and that, "being a Democrat or a Republican has become not just a partisan affiliation but an identity."[10] In this atmosphere, challenging disinformation, contradictions, and even outright lies is ineffective because these can be viewed as a challenge to one's very sense of self and one's most closely held convictions. In other words, you can't fight ideology with the facts.

This is especially so in our contemporary multimedia environment where public and private, fiction and reality, and personal and political have become indistinguishable, where our identities have become intertwined with story.

Someone sitting at their laptop chatting with like-minded people over social media may feel they are in an intimate setting and, if they are alone with their device in a cozy corner of their home while doing so, that may well be the case. Staged drama on a reality television show may feel as real or as concocted as staged drama on a Sunday morning panel of professional political pundits. Engaging in heated political discussions online can make one feel as if they are actively involved in national politics and decision-making, even if they are simply posting on social media while sitting in a recliner, wearing pajamas. The line between reader and writer, consumer and creator, is blurred as well. Posting and reposting links to articles or TikTok videos feels like a creative act, like freedom of choice, or even like empowerment. Our brave new world of social media and integrated programming immerses and consumes us as we consume and are immersed in it, and much of this engagement involves feelings and storytelling.

This is an environment hospitable to fascist mythmaking. Neofascist mythology is continuously created through the "convergence culture" narratives[11] that populate our media landscape, which means that young readers, and older readers as well, need to cultivate slow, careful close reading and critical thinking skills that can help them to recognize and understand the ongoing construction of narratives and the ways in which these are meant to persuade. I imagine anti-fascist stories for young people as being ones that encourage this sort of agency by engaging readers in a metafictional conversation about storytelling, by focusing on the ways we all shape and are shaped by the stories we tell and are told.

Ideologies are gradually shaped, over time, through repetition, an accretion of detail and set of habits—and our habits have changed dramatically over the past few decades. We're not just saturated in media, we are also saturated in story. With so many media companies, channels, and streaming services vying for our attention 24/7, "content providers" must provide captivating, continuous narratives, long involved story threads that keep viewers and readers tuned in over time. Additionally, the internet attention economy thrives on outrage, fear, and anger, all emotions that keep readers plugged in, engaged, and enraged.[12] And, because we're all watching events happen in real time, scrolling through articles with clickbait headlines and YouTube videos with "hot takes," getting instant and ever-updated social media posts and CNN punditry, and reading the toxic comments section on YouTube or the Fox News website, none of it feels quite real. It feels instead like we're all watching a reality television show.

Ben Rhodes succinctly explains how contemporary fascism is wired and global while still retaining characteristics of twentieth-century nationalism and authoritarianism: "The right wing has embraced a nationalism characterized by Christian identity, national sovereignty, distrust of democratic institutions, opposition to immigration, and contempt for politically correct liberal elites" and they have fomented these ideas using new media technologies that "transformed the way that human beings consume information before we were prepared for the problems that would arise when people began living in self-contained bubbles, leaving data trails of their likes and dislikes, a vast blueprint for advertisers, propagandists, and authoritarians."[13] With the help of right-wing media, targeted marketing, and misinformation, Rhodes argues, American democracy is being disrupted "from within," turning our nation into "the ugliest version of itself,"[14] not so much by spreading fascist propaganda (though that is part of it) but by creating distrust, uncertainty, and a kind of mass skepticism and cynicism that assumes every politician, media outlet, and institution is untrustworthy and suspect, and that language has lost its ability to gather us together through agreed-upon meanings.

Adolf Hitler, who also understood that distrust of existing institutions would buoy his populist movement, used the technologies of his day to communicate with and motivate his followers, to wage war, and, eventually, to imprison and murder millions of people. Contemporary fascists still draw upon populist fears and still subvert democratic norms, but the communications technologies available to today's wannabe dictators work in ways that are both more subtle and more profound. They rely on the ubiquitous use of electronic media that has become so much a part of our mundane, everyday lives that—as with any successful technology—it has become invisible.

Henry Jenkins coined the term "convergence culture" to describe storytelling that moves across a web of multiple platforms and mediums. Throughout much of the past century, most stories were told using one medium—a book, a film, a television show—and on one platform—print, television, newspaper, cinema. There were, of course, examples of texts that crossed platforms and mediums—dolls with accompanying books, toys based on films, radio programs with fan clubs—but the narrative aspect of a text, the story, was usually tied to one medium. Over the past few decades, though, as media conglomerates have become larger and fewer, and as they've learned the monetary value of integrated content, stories have become so spread out across multiple sites that in order to understand the entirety of a narrative, consumers must venture out into various platforms. In this way, stories become diffused and meaning-making is spread out.

Convergence culture stories are made up of lots of small, ordinary, everyday things that don't seem like much until they accumulate. For example, when we talk in my children's literature courses about whether Disney's *The Little*

Mermaid affects children's sense of self, students sometimes say, "It's just a movie for kids. We're reading too much into it." But, I ask, what if it's a movie that a child has watched dozens of times? Everyone usually nods in agreement because that's what kids have been able to do for the past few decades, watch a film or show over and over again until they know each song and line by heart. And, what if that same child wore an Ariel outfit for Halloween and slept in a *Little Mermaid* sleeping bag hugging a stuffed Sebastian toy? How might this spreading out and repetition of story affect that child's identity and worldview? Ours is a culture of accumulation, and meaning is created not just through linear plots but also through an accretion of detail as bits of story are woven throughout our everyday, material practices.

The themes of a convergence culture narrative come to us in bits and fragments, through a repetition of icons, characters, stories, visual elements, and familiar tropes. In neofascist propaganda, the repetition of commonly recognized and mythologized symbols—the American flag, the Child in need of protection, the red MAGA hat, the morally corrupt city, the cross—invites us to fill in narrative gaps in very specific and intertextual ways that work together to create and reinforce a mythology, an overarching web of narrative that can become a worldview. In this way, over time, fascist propaganda attaches a set of agreed-upon meanings to symbols: It teaches us the language of fascism, which is a very particular kind of language based in strict binaries and mythologized meanings. This fascist language offers itself up in opposition to the confusing, overwhelming, multivocal nature of our media environment, even as it relies on and uses that environment to tell stories. Fascism dictates meanings for a set of mythologized symbols at the same time that it deconstructs the language of its opposition: It creates an "us" versus "them" distinction by claiming that "we" have the answers and can provide meaning in an otherwise chaotic environment.

According to Roland Barthes, this particular use of mythologized symbols is a speech act performed in a distinct rhetorical situation. A word or object is mythologized, for a time being, when its significance is informed by historical meanings, often tied to emotion. The meaning of a mythologized word or symbol is already filled in for us, which means we needn't work to create our own meaning. It is unambiguous. It presents as icon, brand, ritual, dogma; a symbol that has been simultaneously infused with meaning and drained of it. The mythologizing process happens in the space between signifier and signified when those gaps we fill in with our readerly repertoire are already filled in for us by the weight of myth: Barthes uses the example of a nation's flag draped over the coffin of a soldier killed in combat, a symbol infused with a particular, predetermined set of meanings. Myth, Barthes explains, "is a peculiar system, in that it is constructed from a semiological chain which existed before it [. . .] the materials of mythical speech (the language itself, photography, painting, posters, rituals, objects, etc.), however different at the start, are reduced to a pure signifying function as soon as they are caught by myth."[15]

Fascist leaders are especially adept at mythologizing. We all watched as Trump made red hats and the masks we wore during the Covid pandemic into divisive political symbols, as he turned his body, hair, and clothing into an easily recognizable brand, and as he redefined words, names, and objects so that the name Hillary was always preceded by "crooked" and the image of a wall being erected on our southern border came to be seen as a remedy to a collective fear of immigrants, disease, the Other, and the alleged "replacement" of the white race by people of color. Trump's ability to mythologize has been aided by convergence culture storytelling and a media ecosystem where one platform links to and reinforces another, where global conglomerates pass bits of news and entertainment up, down, and across television programs, commercials, billboards, radio programs, rallies, and multiple other texts and platforms. Convergence culture storytelling, combined with our addiction to attention-diverting devices, works to blur the already porous lines between fiction and reality, public and private, author and reader in ways many people may not recognize as narrative, as storytelling.

Eddie S. Glaude Jr. explains that in America our nationalist mythology of a pure and noble history, also a collection of stories, is made possible only through collective acts of repression.[16] In order to hold on to our nation's "innocence," white America must continuously tell stories that repress and cover over what he calls "blasphemous facts," those aspects of American history that reveal the myth of American exceptionalism to be just that. In order to mythologize, to enforce one agreed-upon meaning upon a symbol, fascists prohibit other meanings. For example, we can only "make American great again," if we believe in the myth of American greatness, which means that stories that expand or trouble that characterization must be suppressed. Reality must be shaped, through stories, in such a way that it doesn't conflict with the wholeness of fascist ideology. Hannah Arendt noted that a closed narrative with restricted sets of meanings is central to fascism, which is "a society whose members act and react according to the rules of a fictitious world."[17] Fascist leaders, she wrote, craft storied worlds that their followers inhabit: "Before they seize power and establish a world according to their doctrines, totalitarian movements conjure up a lying world of consistency which is more adequate to the needs of the human mind than reality itself."[18]

Reality in our struggling, multiracial democracy, is messy, contradictory, and multivocal. The freedom of expression allowed in a democracy creates a cacophony of stories that defy categorization and organization, which can be overwhelming. Significantly, political scientists note that authoritarian-minded individuals are bothered by complexity and ambiguity and seek simplicity and order. They long for stories that provide simple and consistent explanations, ones in which "blasphemous facts" that expose contradictions or hypocrisies have been removed, repressed, or smoothed over. Most importantly, these tidy stories must feel true and natural, which means that their construction must be continuously concealed. Fascists create a mythology, an all-encompassing worldview, by telling and retelling a set of stories that work together to unite people into a like-minded social body. They also borrow from stories that already exist in a culture that are useful to their ends, especially ones that turn a population against itself.

In *How Fascism Works*, Jason Stanley explains that, "The most telling symptom of fascist politics is division. It aims to separate a population into an 'us' and a 'them'."[19] He lists several other characteristics of fascist storytelling, writing that:

> Fascist politicians justify their ideas by breaking down a common sense of history in creating a mythic past to support their vision for the present. They rewrite the population's shared understanding of reality by twisting the language of ideals through propaganda and promoting anti-intellectualism, attacking universities and educational systems that might challenge their ideas. Eventually, with these techniques, fascist politics creates a state of unreality, in which conspiracy theories and fake news replace reasoned debate.[20]

In order to keep followers in a "state of unreality," neofascists in America are banning books and attempting to do away with education that teaches a nuanced understanding of our culture and history. This is because a thinking public is a threat to fascism, which relies on dualistic thinking, spectacle, unquestioning obedience, and fear of the unknown or of difference. As I'll discuss in upcoming chapters, neofascism in the United States is also largely characterized by othering, dehumanizing groups of people who are seen as a threat to the dominant group: Muslims, Jews, immigrants, feminists, intellectuals, people of color, people with disabilities, Indigenous people, and members of the LGBTQ+ community. Fascism is also patriarchal and hierarchal. In the United States, especially, it is white supremacist and has a long history of racist extremism and state-sanctioned violence. This dangerous "us" versus "them" narrative, created through a tapestry of stories, is constructed in a global, largely unregulated media environment that is blurring the lines between what is real and what is fiction as it constructs storied worlds readers fully inhabit.

Convergence Culture World-Building

We, adults and children, live in a mediated story-filled world that is governed not only by national, state, and local governments, but also by a global economy. Twenty-first-century capitalism does not need national borders or democracy in order to survive and flourish. Indeed, in many cases, democracy is at odds with capitalism's goals. Economist Shoshana Zuboff outlines the contours of a contemporary media ecosystem and economy that we are only just beginning to understand: She calls it "surveillance capitalism" and describes it as a global phenomenon that thrives on the internet and in our daily lives through a complex network that keeps us wired, plugged in, recorded, and catalogued at both macro and micro levels. Cameras in public places recognize our faces, algorithms record our every click, pause, and keystroke, and marketers of products and political ideologies target us in order to monitor and shape our most intimate desires. "Surveillence capitalism is profoundly antidemocratic," Zuboff writes. "But its remarkable power does not originate with the state, as has historically been the case."[21] She likens the purveyors of surveillance capitalism to the robber barons of the late nineteenth century as she meticulously outlines the ways they are subverting and influencing, not only the laws being made to regulate their industries but also the political leaders who make those laws.

Surveillance capitalism may also be shaping the ways in which we read and think. In *Stolen Focus*, Johann Hari argues that the reading environments created through the attention economy are robbing us of our ability to read and think in careful, critical ways. "Facebook makes more money for every extra second you are staring through a screen at their site, and they lose money every time you put the screen down," he writes.[22] "YouTube also has an algorithm—and it too has figured out that you'll keep watching longer if you see things that are outrageous, shocking, and extreme."[23] These social media companies and advertisers manipulate our emotions in order to keep us scrolling, and in the process, they wear down our attention spans and our ability to read slowly and to think deeply. Just as books teach us how to read books, social media teaches us how to read social media. It does this by giving us small and continuous rewards for our participation, positive reinforcement that teaches us to learn new ways of reading and thinking. Links move us from one platform to the next as ads blur together with news stories, entertainment, and personal conversations to create an endless stream of ever-evolving content from a variety of sources.

This sea of stories and bits of stories, with its sheer volume, contradictions, and multitude of perspectives, can overwhelm. Zac Gershberg and Sean Illing argue that, "Fascism rises within and against the backdrop of the structural conditions of an open communication environment afforded by democracy."[24] In other words, rhetorical spaces that welcome a diversity of opinions, a plurality of stories, can be overwhelming, and fascism provides a cohesive narrative that creates an appearance of order, that shapes our mediated, postmodern existence into a unified set of stories that "make sense" of the world. Neofascism is thriving in a media environment that dissuades deep, complex, nuanced, and sustained thinking because fascist mythologies provide a simple, totalizing explanation, an antidote to the cacophony.

Another way that our contemporary media environment is fueling authoritarianism is through the polarization it creates for users who are consuming narratives told within carefully curated ideological bubbles. In their prescient 2009 book *Authoritarianism and Polarization in American Politics*, political scientists Marc Hetherington and Jonathan D. Weiler noted several trends in US politics and culture that are creating a cycle of authoritarian thinking.[25] Increased polarization, they argue, is being fueled by increased authoritarianism, and increased authoritarian thinking further fuels polarization. The result of this dangerous feedback loop is that "Americans are now divided over things that conjure up more visceral reactions,"[26] which means that a growing number of people feel actual disgust or fear about people on the other side of the political divide. They note that by the early 2000s, these trends were making the swing of the political pendulum wider. As non-authoritarians work to counter the policy changes of the right wing by, say, passing laws to legalize same sex marriage or promote police reform, authoritarians feel even more threatened and retreat even further into ideology-confirming bubbles. This is a cycle that is accelerating and is being fueled by full-time political pundits, some of whom make a tidy profit from telling stories that promote division, fear, and outrage.

Polarization is also driven by "narrow-casting" or niche marketing, which creates narrower and narrower in-groups of like-minded consumers who share opinion-confirming media among themselves. While many Americans on both sides of the political divide have come to inhabit ideology-confirming bubbles, individuals with an authoritarian mindset may be more susceptible than others to such media bubbles because they have "(1) a greater need for order and, conversely, less tolerance for confusion or ambiguity, and (2) a propensity to rely on established authorities to provide that order."[27] Research on authoritarian personalities has demonstrated that people with an authoritarian worldview are "less politically informed, and less likely to change their way of thinking when new information might challenge their deeply held belief."[28] Our current media environment is one that encourages authoritarian habits of thinking because it creates bubbles of like-minded individuals who share information from the same limited set of sources that are fed to them by algorithms that tailor to their existing tastes: we all participate in the maintenance of the narrative world(s) we inhabit.

The targeted marketing of products, media, and ideas that characterizes surveillance capitalism means that users must actively exert effort to move beyond the bubble that has been custom-made just for them. They must seek out sources of information that do not conform to their existing worldview, something that Hetherington and Weiler argue, authoritarian-minded people are less likely to do: "Once they are introduced to a threat condition, authoritarians subsequently [become] much less interested than nonauthoritarians in seeking information that [is] balanced in its approach, and much more interested in pursuing one-sided information that [reinforces] existing beliefs."[29] In other words, if people with an authoritarian worldview are reluctant to seek out sources that challenge their beliefs, then our current polarized media ecosystem is an ideal space in which to avoid contrary viewpoints.

Understanding and analyzing the convergence culture stories—fictional and nonfictional—that populate our multimedia ecosystem means thinking about narrative frames and world-building, the ways in which whole bodies of stories work together to create an overarching narrative construction of the world. World-building creates a "universe" that characters and readers inhabit. In the *Lord of the Rings* universe, for example, Middle Earth is the fictional world built by J.R.R. Tolkien through thousands of details that work together to form a consistent, contained fictional place. He created languages, maps, illustrations, histories, genealogies, and a mythology that hold the fictional world of the series together, that make it feel like a world big enough for readers to inhabit as well.

Every work of fiction imagines a world for its characters to inhabit and a set of rules to govern that world, but we read convergence culture narratives differently than we read a single story. An individual story has a beginning, middle, and end. It has a set starting point and typically provides closure when it wraps up, untying the knots of the narrative. Convergence culture texts, though, are made up of multiple stories, all woven together into a web. There are two sorts: ones that are based on one original text and ones without one story of origin. The *Harry Potter* world, for example, started with an individual novel, *Harry Potter and the Philosopher's Stone* (*Harry Potter and the Sorcerer's Stone* in US versions). As the series grew, fan clubs formed, and fans connected over the internet. Then came academic papers, college courses, fan fiction, a series of films, theme parks, and even a play. In this sort of convergence culture narrative, even though the stories continue to spread out, they are still anchored in one original story, that depicted in the books, which fans call "canon."

The other sort of convergence culture narrative does not have one central story. Good examples of these sorts of texts are MMORPGs (massive multiplayer online role-playing games), which involve dozens of storylines and characters, multiple points of entry, and varying levels of engagement. There is no original, individual narrative that serves as a foundation and no main character with whom we "identify." Instead, the user (or reader) becomes the main character. What holds this sort of convergence culture narrative together is the fictional world that has been created for users to inhabit. For example, the fictional world of an all-ages MMORPG like *Runescape*, which has been running since 2001, is built through a collection of thousands of details, places, characters, actions, and stories that are part of the fictional world users inhabit. Players can choose to dip into the world now and then or they can spend years diving into its intricacies, becoming an expert. There are wikis and Discord groups where players share tips and strategies for playing, which makes the construction of the world collaborative and participatory. As is the case with individual works of fiction, convergence culture texts are also intertextual. Both *Harry Potter* and *Runescape* are filled with allusions to mythology, fairy tales, and to other works of fantasy literature, an intertextuality that bolsters the construction of the fictional world by linking it to narratives that already exist.

It is important for readers, young and old, to understand convergence culture narratives, the concept of world-building, and the ways these work in multimedia environments because this is now the predominant narrative form in contemporary American popular culture. Convergence culture narratives are used to depict fictional worlds, but the form is also used to tell stories that are nonfiction or even news. Through the horizontal and vertical integration of massive global media corporations and the proliferation of niche marketing, whole immersive "worlds" can be created by collections of stories that thread their way through various platforms. The 24/7 infotainment industry manufactures, amplifies, and repeats interconnected narratives that capture our attention and that are meant to shape our worldview. For example, in the months leading up to the 2024 election, we here in Michigan were inundated with image after image of threatening "invading "immigrants. One ad depicted a map with a spreading black blob making its way up through Central America, then Mexico, and then across our "weak" border, and up into the continental United States. Others depicted immigrants as criminals, gang members, and rapists. Commentators on right-wing programs added stories to the mix, further fueling fear. Together, these stories and bits of stories accumulated to create a larger narrative, the fascist myth that Others are invading, and that we are in danger and in need of protection. The ideological "bubbles" we inhabit are the result of such convergence culture world-building, an accumulation of details that weave together to build an intertextual, believable reality.

Convergence culture stories, like all texts, require that readers fill narrative gaps with their repertoire in order to create meaning: readers use what they already know about story in order to understand new stories. But the difference between reading a convergence text and a single-platform text, like a book, is that a book is finite and contained, while a convergence text is open, malleable, diffused, and linked to myriad other texts. Popular convergence stories like *Harry Potter, Runescape, Lord of the Rings,* or *Star Wars,* that spread out across multiple platforms and mediums, resemble the real-life political dramas we follow because they contain intricate subplots and large casts of characters, they encourage active fan participation, they involve learning minute details about the lives of authors or characters/performers, they span years in content and storytelling, and they become metafictive through constant, often instant, analysis and interpretation from various "experts," who themselves become part of the narrative. If the lines between fiction and reality seem blurred, it is because they are.

Because our multimedia environment creates electronic subcultures, whole communities of like-minded readers can have their worldview continuously confirmed by inhabiting what Arendt described as a "lying world of consistency which is more adequate to the needs of the human mind than reality itself."[30] The world-building can be self-contained, sealed off from outside influence, because convergence-culture narratives are large and sprawling enough to hold an entire fictional world. Through convergence culture narratives, white supremacists can build a subculture, a discourse community with their own literature, vernacular, symbols, and agreed-upon mythologies. QAnon, the conspiracy theory that pedophilic "elites" are kidnapping children, is a participatory, interpretive community with its own language and set of meanings. The right-wing Fox News network carefully builds its narrative world by featuring a cast of recurring characters, news personalities, commentators, and politicians who make frequent appearances on the network as they weave in and out of various stories that create "us" versus "them" narratives. There is a cast of villains: Dr. Anthony Fauci, who became a symbol of pandemic lockdowns; "The Squad," women of color who serve in Congress; "illegals," brown-skinned immigrants "swarming" across the southern border; and "the woke," liberal "elites" who are brainwashing children with "gender ideology" and critical race theory. Stories about these villains, cast as recurring characters, thread their way through time and across multiple platforms, always in ways that reinforce the rules that govern that particular narrative universe. There isn't just one story, for example, villainizing women in positions of power. There are multiple stories, told over and over, meant to create an overarching narrative thread that women, especially women of color, shouldn't be in positions of power at all. The ideology being cemented through this particular repetition of stories, through this accretion of details, is that of the white supremacy and the patriarchy, a worldview that is central to fascism.

Ideological bubbles are created when readers take on the constructed world as their personal worldview, when the fictional world built by the convergence culture narrative becomes their "real" world, the language they use to construct their reality and identity. Brooks writes that in a world saturated with story, we must "remain critical of the all-encompassing claims of story" and we must "oppose critical and analytical intelligence to narratives that seduce us into the acceptance of dominant ideologies. We need as listeners and readers to resist a passive narcosis of response."[31] In other words, readers need to become aware of the way that we are taught to make meaning through story, the way we are instructed to attach particular meanings to particular symbols, and the way that stories appeal to our emotions as they work to persuade. Stories that teach about storytelling and about the nature of story may provide tools that can lead to meta-awareness: They can help us to consider not just what a story is about but also the way in which it is being told and how it invites us to make meaning.

While the entertainment and political industries have stayed up to date on our reading and viewing habits, many academics and teachers struggle to keep up. Vavrus argues that, "Because the teaching of critical media literacy as a part of a civic education is rare, along with an absence of anti-fascist education, young people can become more susceptible to distorted information that leads to far-right fascist politics."[32] As I'll discuss in upcoming chapters, narrative literacy, an understanding of how stories work, is essential to maintaining an educated, questioning electorate. While the need to better educate citizens about civics, history, scientific method, media literacy, logic, and ethics is an urgent one, the ability to tell fact from fiction is most especially urgent.

Post-Truth Rhetoric, Mindful Reading and "Bad News"

Our current, multimedia rhetorical context makes learning various literacies a challenge. In *Post-Truth Rhetoric and Composition*, Bruce McComiskey describes our present rhetorical situation as "post-truth." A post-truth rhetorical context is one in which "objective facts are less influential in shaping public opinion than appeals to emotion and personal belief."[33] In a post-truth landscape the lines between fiction and reality blur and mass skepticism, the perception that all politicians are liars or all media sources are suspect, creates cynical readings of every narrative. Language becomes a "purely strategic medium. In a post-truth communication landscape, people (especially politicians) say whatever might work in a given situation, whatever might generate the desired result, without any regard to the truth value or facticity of statements."[34] Fact-checking alone, then, may not work to counter authoritarian convergence stories because one major difference between the functioning of narrative in a liberal democracy versus an authoritarian system is that we can no longer assume that people take a text's claims to be the truth. Slavoj Žižek argues that, as a result of this undermining of truth under authoritarian systems, "the prevailing ideology is that of cynicism; people no longer believe in ideological truth; they do not take ideological propositions seriously."[35] As they seek to gain power, fascists sow confusion and work to encourage mass skepticism. They foment distrust of existing institutions and promote a cynical worldview that undermines democracy, which requires faith in democratic institutions. Our multimedia environment is a space particularly well suited for this dangerous relativism, which is why we need to counter authoritarian convergence culture narratives with ones that encourage critical thought and slow reading. This means that cultivating narrative literacy—noticing the ways story shapes reality, learning to recognize various story structures, rhetorical situations, and strategies—is vital in helping us to learn to weigh and discern the credibility of various stories amidst a cacophony of information, much of it persuasive rhetoric.[36] Knowledge of the rhetoric of story might help to make our rhetorical situation less overwhelming and make neofascist rhetoric less appealing.

In their textbook, *Ancient Rhetorics for Contemporary Students*, Sharon Crowley and Debra Hawhee argue that knowledge of rhetoric can "free its students from the manipulative rhetoric of others."[37] Similarly, Brooks argues that analysis of story involves understanding the ways stories are meant to persuade, which means paying "attention to the ways that narrative works as a system and as rhetoric."[38] In order to resist the lure of neofascist storytelling, readers need to grasp how narratives are constructed in the rhetorical space of our media-saturated environment where traditional tools for analysis do not always apply. For instance, readers can learn to question the source of an article published by a news site: Is the author reliable? Are they an expert? Was their work vetted by a reputable editor? Is the source dependable? But these same questions don't apply to the many "unauthored" memes that float across the internet. A meme can be fact-checked but its origin is free-floating, especially when it is shared across various platforms, interest groups, and relationships. Furthermore, the rhetorical situation of the internet blurs the lines that once separated public discourse from private and consumers of content from creators. For example, in *The World Made Meme*, Ryan M. Milner writes that internet memes appear to be "authorless." He says of memes that, "finding their creator and site of origin is largely impossible, and arguably inconsequential when considering how they resonate."[39] Memes, like other portable bits of popular culture, are shared mainly to convey affinities and identity: When our online friends like a meme we shared, they are acknowledging a kinship, they are saying they feel the same way about an issue or that they also find a joke funny. They pay attention to us, which matters a great deal in a rhetorical space where attention is the currency we exchange. The simple act of sharing an ideology-confirming meme makes the reader an active participant in the story-telling process as they read and then share a small ideology-confirming detail to the convergence culture narrative.

Because internet memes are so ubiquitous and simple-seeming, just bits of information, fragments of story, it is easy to dismiss them as meaningless. But their meaning, as part of a larger mythology, comes from accumulation and repetition, their pathos from the collective act of sharing. Most memes are intertextual. They often put two or three separate texts into dialogue by remixing them: Photos, phrases, film clips, and turns of phrase are reused and recombined with other found pieces circulating on the web, which means that their pleasure comes from the meaning readers are able to assemble on their own. Their intertextuality grounds them, weaves them into the larger narrative, the sea of referents, of which they are a part. When memes are used as part of an online conversation, they can become witty retorts, ad hominem attacks, clichéd insults, or creative analysis depending on the rhetorical skills of the poster. As with other texts, critical thinking and reading require discernment, an ability to assign weight to arguments and to recognize the individual meme as one small part of an interrelated web of texts. In order to recognize narratives meant to work as propaganda, users need literacies focused on rhetorical strategies that are specific to online spaces, and they need to learn to see themselves as active, contributing participants.

One creative educational text that helps readers to understand information in a post-truth rhetorical situation is the online game "Bad News," which was designed for players fourteen years or older. Researchers have found that teens struggle to distinguish between reliable and unreliable information online: One study found that, "Only about 3% of students realized, for example, that a website purporting to deliver legitimate information about climate change was run by the fossil fuel industry. More than half believed a misleading video supposedly showing ballot stuffing in a U.S. election. (It was a video from Russia.)"[40] Young people, and adults as well, strain to discern fact from fiction amidst the cacophony on the internet. By showing the creation and maintenance of a "fake news" account from the point of view of the account creator, the game highlights tactics used to lure followers: "Fake an official Twitter account or impersonate someone important," the game instructs, "Start by using Twitter to vent. Post a frustrated tweet."[41] As the player progresses through the game, they create a fake news site and bots to respond to their posts, both of which create a veneer of respectability through the appearance of engagement: if other users like this, then it must be true.

Stephanie Pappas explains that, "The goal of the game is to expose the tactics and manipulation techniques that are used to mislead people and build up a following. 'Bad News' works as a psychological 'vaccine' against disinformation: playing it builds cognitive resistance against common forms of manipulation that you may encounter online."[42] Players take on the role of an unscrupulous content creator and learn how appeals to emotion can build a following. The first prompt explains that, "I am here to guide you in your quest to becoming a disinformation and fake news tycoon."[43] As players go through a series of prompts, the game makes visible the way participatory convergence culture narratives are carefully crafted over time. Players earn badges in six categories as they progress through the game: impersonation, emotion, polarization, conspiracy, discrediting, and trolling. Posts in the game illustrate ways users' emotions, especially anger and outrage, are manipulated in order to create engagement. Psychologist Zara Abrams explains that, "Psychological research backs several methods of countering misinformation. One is to debunk incorrect information after it has spread. Much more effective, though, is inoculating people against fake news before they're exposed—a strategy known as 'prebunking.'"[44]

The game teaches readers how stories on the internet are constructed, providing insider information they need to successfully navigate online spaces. It promotes a kind of mindfulness while reading, posting, and sharing. Propaganda works because it appeals to emotion, which means readers need to become aware of their emotional responses to what they read and see: Why did I feel anger, outrage, or fear about a social media post? What piqued my interest enough that I clicked on a link? If we're scrolling past dozens of posts, memes, video clips, and news stories in a matter of minutes, these blend together on our feed so seamlessly that they all seem equal in weight and import. Mindful reading, though, is about discernment, about stopping to weigh different sources in an environment that encourages the very opposite. Such slow and close attention to reading is difficult because the internet discourages careful and

STORIES ABOUT STORIES: READING FASCISTIC RHETORIC   51

slow reading and because fluency means being able to read without stopping to think about how to read, without stopping to ponder each gap we fill in order to make meaning. Furthermore, the internet is governed by an attention economy where conflict, anger, fear, and disgust are considered quality engagement because they generate the most clicks by keeping people engaged and online. This means that learning to read and think critically involves swimming against a very powerful current of information meant to keep us moving quickly and seamlessly from one story to another, from one platform to the next.

Hari notes that "the average child between the ages of 13 and 17 in the United States was sending one text message every six minutes they were awake" and that these continuous interruptions "cause a deterioration of people's abilities to focus and think clearly."[45] The thesis of his book is that, due to multiple factors, we are losing the ability to focus our attention for long periods of time, which means that we're not thinking deeply or in a sustained way. "Reading books trains us to read in a particular way—in a linear fashion, focused on one thing for a sustained period," but scrolling down screens and following links trains us to read "in a manic skip and jump from one thing to another."[46] Hari quotes Anne Mangen, a literacy professor, who claims that "this scanning and skimming bleeds over. It also starts to color or influence how we read on paper."[47] Online reading is focused on speed. Scrolls of information update instantly and continuously so that we're always chasing the latest, freshest bit of news. On the other hand, reading in a careful, mindful way means that the reader has to slow down. "Life is complex," writes Hari, "and if you want to understand it, you have to set aside a fair bit of time to think deeply about it,"[48] a set of habits that books can encourage.

Reading the Margins: "The Amnesia Machine"

One example of a story that teaches its readers to slow down and think is Shaun Tan's "The Amnesia Machine," a two-page story in his illustrated collection *Tales from Outer Suburbia* (see Fig. 2). Tan is another writer for children who skirts the border between writing *for* children and *for* adults. His books, like *The Arrival*, are rich, beautifully illustrated texts that require deep attention to detail and multiple re-readings, a complexity which makes them perfect picture books to share with young people. Picture books, after all, are texts that have to stand up to multiple re-readings and to close inspection. As is the case with much of Tan's work, the layout and design of "The Amnesia Machine" reward careful reading, looking, and thinking by encouraging readers to pay attention to a larger ecosystem of meaning-making. Tan has illustrated the story as if it were a cutout from a newspaper: It is laid out in columns like a newspaper story

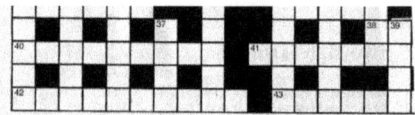

Figure 2. *Tales from Outer Suburbia* by Shaun Tan. Reprinted with permission from Scholastic.

and fills a two-page spread. The story's unreliable narrator tells us that they read an article about "the recent election result, an unsurprising government victory, and some other stories about media ownership, missing government revenue, corruption, and so on, [which were] all quite boring."[49] Ultimately, the narrator is easily distracted from the news of the day and from suspicious events in his own neighborhood by an offer of free ice cream. In the illustration that accompanies the story there is a large machine (presumably the amnesia machine) hovering over a neighborhood, but people seem not to notice it as they walk below it to an ice cream truck.

As is often the case in Tan's work, the meaning of the story only emerges from an assemblage of visual and textual clues that require the reader to pay close and careful attention and to explore the margins. The cut-off newspaper stories along the margins of the page are the "boring" stories our narrator has chosen to ignore in favor of an ice cream treat. After reading the main story, the headline below it, "Truth overrated, explains Minister," is the next image to catch the eye, and in this story we learn that, "The Minister for Public Denials yesterday issued a press statement ahead of a government inquiry into government corruption, anticipating finding that no such thing exists."[50] The remnants of the story next to this one, "Meltdown not so bad," begin, "As the nation faces its most devastating environmental crisis in history, the federal government has been quick to assert that unemployment is at an all-time low" and that "Interest rates are also at their best since the last time they reached an equivalent level."[51] After careful inspection of the stories surrounding the center story, it becomes clear that the amnesia machine is meant to divert people from dire news stories about environmental disasters and government corruption. Through their language, these marginalized stories turn our attention to the double-speak of politicians. Furthermore, the physical layout of the pages calls our attention to the physicality of the book as we strain to make sense of words cut off by the margins of the page, which makes the text even more interactive. It creates a puzzle for curious readers to assemble.

The margins on top of and to the sides of the story all contain bits of information that the narrator ignores but that clever readers can spot: for instance, the "thought for the day" under a Sudoku puzzle is from Saul Bellow: "A great deal of intelligence can be invested in ignorance when the need for illusion is deep."[52] Vertically cut-off stories along the side of the page contain fragments of words and phrases: "weapons of mass . . . distraction," "public ignorance," "war against terror," "omission of facts," and "[i]t is vitally important . . . that we find new enemies . . . in order to maintain . . . greater political . . . over our citizens"[53]. The meaning of this collection of snippets of stories, bits, and fragments, which the reader must actively assemble, is ambiguous and multifaceted.

It takes significant work on the part of the reader to glean meaning from these fragments, but a careful reader is rewarded for their attention with surreptitious knowledge: They are able to recognize the larger media ecosystem that eludes the story's adult narrator. Ultimately, this is a story about the stories we see and those we ignore, about a government's use of bread and circuses to distract from dire news, and about media focused more on entertainment than information. The meaning of the story—what is an amnesia machine, how does it work, and why would it be used?—amasses in the spaces among the different elements on the page and must be assembled by the reader. This is a story that takes its readers seriously and constructs them as co-creators of meaning by rewarding careful observation with deeper meaning.

Laurie Finke and Martin Shichtman, in an essay about the medieval imagery and iconography commonly used in white supremacist memes and propaganda, argue that young people need to be educated on how images create meaning: "Teaching students to read for form (close reading, or what art historians call slow looking), slows down the speed encouraged by digital browsing and provides a means of unpacking the tactics of alt-right medievalism."[54] "The Amnesia Machine" not only slows down the reading process; it encourages readers to "unpack the tactics" of malignant rhetors, to read for form, to stop and think about what information is included and what is not, and to assemble seemingly disparate fragments into a larger perspective that focuses on how and why information is shared or withheld.

Bullshitters, Demagogues, and Dragons: *Bone*

In his book *On Bullshit*, Harry Frankfurt defines bullshit as a particular rhetorical stance. According to him, a bullshitter is not the same as a liar because it doesn't matter to a bullshitter whether his words are true or false. "His eye is not on the facts at all, as the eyes of the honest man and the liar are, except insofar as they may be pertinent to his interest in getting away with what he says. He does not care whether the things he says describe reality correctly. He just picks them out, or makes them suit his purpose."[55] Because a bullshitter doesn't care whether he is lying or telling the truth, "bullshit is a greater enemy of the truth than lies are."[56] In a post-truth rhetorical situation, the bullshitter succeeds because of "various forms of skepticism which deny that we can have any reliable access to an objective reality, and which therefore reject the possibility of knowing how things truly are."[57] Such mass skepticism is an important factor in building and maintaining fascist ideology: If no one can be trusted, if all news stories are fake and all politicians are liars, then citizens need not put in the effort required to discern between a truth teller, a liar, and a bullshitter. According to McComiskey, in post-truth bullshit, "even the audiences have no concern for facts, realities, or truths, thus relieving speakers from the need to conceal their manipulative intent. Post-truth audiences accept bullshit as the norm in public discourse without objection because post-truth audiences, like bullshit rhetors, are now disassociated from the epistemological continuum."[58]

As is the case with Hans Christian Andersen's "The Emperor's New Clothes," children's literature has the potential to reveal bullshit. This is certainly the case in Jeff Smith's all-ages comic *Bone*, an epic fantasy narrative that follows the adventures of three Bone cousins who find themselves entangled in major events in a fantasy world called The Valley. One of the cousins, Phoney Bone, is a classic huckster who is constantly coming up with various schemes to swindle people out of their money. Because we see his behavior repeated throughout the book, readers learn not to trust Phoney Bone. They see him trick the same people, the citizens of Barrelhaven, on more than one occasion, which means that the reader is in a position where they are wiser than the gullible townspeople. As the townspeople fall deeper under Phoney's spell, he transforms from mere huckster into charismatic leader. In one episode, for instance, Phoney uses ginned-up fears of an Other to convince the people of Barrelhaven that they should hire him to be their dragon slayer, even though dragons are no threat to the town of Barrelhaven. Child readers following the story know that a dragon is aiding the protagonists in their quest, which means that Phoney's description of dragons as a danger to the town is suspect: "You say you've seen shapes in the woods, heard bumps in the night. You say it's not safe to go outside after dark. Yessir, I've seen these symptoms before. Oh, you think it'll never happen in a nice little quiet town like this . . . but you can't stop 'em. They're here to stay."[59] Phoney convinces the townspeople to build a makeshift wall and gate around their town and they uncritically follow his orders, even when these make very little sense. When we witness our heroes barred at a makeshift gate, Phoney's sway over the townspeople is made tangible: "According to the boss, anybody who's not inside is a stranger. Strict orders! Afraid there's nothin' I can do."[60] Because the text features both characters who fall for Phoney's schemes and those who see through them, readers are able to see Phoney's statements and the unquestioning belief of the townspeople as equally ridiculous.

As the story progresses, Phoney embraces his new role as demagogue: "I am this village's sworn dragonslayer! Everything I do, I do to protect the people of Barrelhaven!"[61] He convinces the townspeople that hoarding valuables attracts dragons, and the solution is that they must give all of their valuables to him. We see one of the novel's protagonists roll his eyes as Phoney tells the townspeople, "We must root out this moral decay in our midst before it's too late! Go to your homes and get every single thing of value that you own, and bring it here immediately."[62] Before Phoney can abscond with all of their valuables, the townspeople capture the dragon who has been aiding our protagonists. In this moment, Phoney's storytelling has gotten the best of him and, more significantly, we witness the very real harm he is causing: While the townspeople have been following Phoney Bone, the real enemy has attacked Barrelhaven. As their town is overrun by an invading army and set on fire, they realize too late that they have been duped. "What have we done?"[63] asks one townsperson. Through the use of dramatic irony, young readers are included in on the rhetorical analysis because they witness the storytelling techniques, rhetorical strategies, and bullshit Phoney uses in order to effectively sway the townspeople. Just as Phoney is revealed to be a bullshitter, *Bone* also reveals the gullibility of the people of Barrelhaven who fall too easily under his sway.

Jinnie Spiegler suggests that schools should teach students about the power of propaganda, a strategy that proves effective because, "in some ways, there's nothing teenagers hate more than feeling like they're being manipulated and used."[64] Texts like *Bone* and "The Amnesia Machine," which hail younger readers as co-creators of meaning, may be effective means for this because, instead of simply telling about the effects of propaganda, they require the reader to piece together the meaning of larger systems on their own. In *Bone*, this means reading Phoney's words in the context of the facial expressions of those around him, the slack-jawed acquiescence of the townspeople, and the incredulity of the protagonists who witness his pronouncements that become more and more untethered from reality and, as a result, more dangerous. Texts like these can introduce beginning readers to the rhetorical strategies bad actors employ by depicting a larger rhetorical situation: The game "Bad News" gives players a chance to play the role of a bad rhetor, someone using the tools of social media to manipulate the opinions of others. The government in "The Amnesia Machine" diverts citizens' attention away from important matters, as does Phoney Bone. While one story implicates an uninterested populous, the other focuses on the gullibility of townspeople too willing to believe tales about threatening Others. The next two books I discuss depict larger, more complex rhetorical situations, specifically the ways in which our everyday lives are interwoven with our multimedia environment, and the way that the technologies we use, or are used by, influence our everyday lives, communities, and identities.

"All you have to do is want something and there's a chance it will be yours": *Feed*

M.T. Anderson's young adult novel *Feed* depicts the complex rhetorical situation created by the internet, surveillance capitalism, and neoliberal policies. It is set in a dystopian future where the planet is dying but the novel's main characters don't notice because, as is the case with "The Amnesia Machine," they are distracted.[65] The novel's protagonist and unreliable narrator, Titus, is a wealthy teen surrounded by a group of equally wealthy, equally superficial friends. As the story progresses, we learn that Titus and friends have had the feed their entire lives: Since birth, they've been hooked up through bodily implants to a steady stream of electronic media, news, pop songs, inane sitcoms, and advertisements. This relentless stream of information—even in one's sleep—has made these young people dim-witted, enthusiastic consumers of a seemingly endless array of disposable products.

Their addiction to the feed also keeps them from being politically engaged. Education scholar Henry Giroux writes that under American authoritarianism, "the public is treated to a range of distractions and diversions that extend from 'military shock and awe overseas' to the banalities of a commodified culture industry and celebrity-obsessed culture that short-circuits thought and infantilizes everything it touches."[66] Our attention is split, fragmented, spread out, consumed by distractions that keep us from understanding the larger social structures governing our lives. In George Orwell's 1984, government workers simplify language in order to control the population, but in Anderson's dystopia this simplification is led by the culture industry with the goal of creating docile, uncritical consumers of disposable products.

Anderson prevents easy emotional identification with the novel's protagonist by frequently interrupting the plot of the story in ways that intrude into Titus's first-person narration and our experience of the text: ads, news stories, song lyrics, speeches from politicians, and text messages continuously weave their way in and out of Titus's fragmented thoughts. The result, as my students tell me, is that readers can't "identify" with Titus because they are emotionally distanced from him. Bertolt Brecht called emotional distancing from a story "verfremdungseffekt." He argued that when readers or viewers identify with a character or get caught up in the plot of a narrative, that they lose the ability to think critically about the larger societal systems being depicted.[67] A story like *Feed* that aims to highlight the effects of our media ecosystem creates distancing through the ways in which Titus's narration is continuously disrupted. In this way, the book highlights the feed and its effects, and not the character or plot. It brings the background of our mediated lives to the foreground in order to critique it.

Titus's feed, much like the algorithms that track what we purchase or view on the internet, uses his thoughts, purchases, and interactions to send him advertisements specifically tailored to him. Much in the way that the narrator of "The Amnesia Machine" is distracted by ice cream, the feed diverts Titus's attention from any musings he might have about the nature of his world and converts them into a consumer desire for merchandise. Elizabeth Bullen and Elizabeth Parsons write about the novel that, "Readers are thus given the provocative narrative position of experiencing the world of the story through Titus, and simultaneously having to reject and critique that world-view, while they are looking through it."[68] Because the reading experience is fragmented by sporadic intrusions, our sense of Titus's identity becomes fragmented as well, and we're not certain where the advertisements and his thoughts separate. Furthermore, after his feed has been hacked and malfunctions, we're no longer sure whether the news he sees is a government- and industry-sanctioned version of events or if Titus is receiving subversive snippets of information broadcast through a digital version of something akin to Radio Free Europe. Either way, when Titus finally begins to pay attention to the world beyond his feed at the novel's end, it is too late for him and for the dying planet around him to recover, but readers are left to contemplate our own reliance upon our feeds, which are increasingly attached to our cyborg bodies as we carry them throughout the day and as they keep us in constant contact with global consumer culture.

As is the case with "The Amnesia Machine" and *Bone*, *Feed* also focuses attention on the shape of political rhetoric. In between advertisements, Titus's feed occasionally includes statements from the US president and fragments of news stories. For instance, people are inexplicably getting lesions—the book never explains why but hints that these are the result of pollution or perhaps the feed itself—and the president denies any connections to industry saying,

> It is not the will of the American people, the people of this great nation, to believe the allegations that were made by these corporate "watch" organizations, which are not the majority of the American people, I repeat not, and aren't its will. It is our duty as Americans, and as a nation dedicated to freedom and commerce, to stand behind our fellow Americans.[69]

It is clear in this and other snippets that words like "freedom" are being used by political leaders to distract citizens from manmade disasters that are poisoning the environment and making people ill. Significantly, even as the characters in the novel are not able to resist the feed, Anderson imagines readers who know more than his characters and who are able to assemble a fictional world from fragments of story.

Feed was published at the turn of this century, long before social media became ubiquitous, iPhones became appendages for most Americans, and surveillance capitalism became a worldwide practice. In *Twilight of Democracy*, Anne Applebaum argues that authoritarian ideas have been taking root over the past few decades partially because "we are now living through a rapid shift in the way people transmit and receive political information—exactly the sort of communication revolution that has had profound political consequences in the past."[70] The most profound technologies are the ones that become a "natural" extension of our cyborg bodies: pens, glasses, implants, iWatches, pads, and phones; the way our eyes know to scroll down a screen; how we type "T-i-k-T-o-k" without thinking the letters or noticing when they are automatically filled in for us; and the way we click our way to yet another screen before we stop to think where we are going or why. We may even come to view these rhetorical spaces, shaped by the intimate relationships among humans and machines, as comfortable and nurturing: Our feed meets our every need by showing us products we might like, ones that fit our consumer profile, or by auto-correcting that difficult-to-spell word we are searching for. In *The Age of Surveillance Capitalism: The Fight for a Human Future at the New Frontier of Power,* Shoshana Zuboff explains, "This process can be accomplished successfully only in the presence of our unrelenting hunger for recognition, appreciation, and most of all, support."[71] Just as fascist world-building manipulates emotions, the attention economy preys upon humans' need for acceptance and affirmation, even as it feeds upon negative emotions like anger and fear.

Surveillance capitalism and the attention economy tap into basic human, emotional needs in order to create consumer desire or political ideologies. They manipulate our longing for love and acceptance, our need to be part of a community, at the same time that they separate us from one another via a culture of individualism and technologies that keep us isolated. As Applebaum explains, "The issue is not merely one of false stories, incorrect facts, or even election campaigns and spin doctors: the social media algorithms themselves encourage false perceptions of the world,"[72] and these false perceptions work to amplify authoritarian thinking.

Anderson's novel depicts this relationship between our current rhetorical situation and our collective imagination. For instance, when our narrator Titus enthusiastically explains to us that "the braggest thing about the feed, the thing that made it really big, is that it knows everything you want and hope for, sometimes before you even know what those things are. [. . .] so all you have to do is want something and there's a chance it will be yours,"[73] he demonstrates how his imagination is being constructed and constricted by consumer culture. Desire is created and satisfied in an instant, and then created again in an endless loop to keep the economy running. Titus and his friends, shaped by the institutions in their culture, are spoiled, wealthy American teenagers who devote much of their time and energy to consuming disposable products that quickly become obsolete. They are unlikeable, self-centered, superficial young people who lack self-awareness. Titus's disjointed narration, marked by constant interruptions, depicts his cyborg subjectivity and the story he is trying to tell about himself as inextricable from the neoliberal culture that is destroying the dystopian landscape he inhabits.

As is the case in "The Amnesia Machine," we are encouraged by the text to read the world around the characters by focusing on the information popping up in the margins, on the edges of Titus's narration, in the spaces between what he knows about his world and doesn't. For example, Titus and his friends are not oblivious to critiques of the feed, they just acquiesce and rationalize:

> Of course, everyone is like, *da da da, evil corporations, oh they're so bad*, we all say that, and we all know they control everything. I mean, it's not great, because who knows what evil shit they're up to. Everyone feels bad about that. But they're the only way to get all this stuff, and it's no good getting pissy about it, because they're still going to control everything whether you like it or not.[74]

Titus demonstrates here the numbing effect of cynicism, often a response to an overabundance of contradictory information. Zuboff argues that new technologies are initially met with resistance, but that changes are occurring at such frequency that, "People habituate to the incursion with some combination of agreement, helplessness, and resignation. The sense of astonishment and outrage dissipates. The incursion itself, once unthinkable, slowly worms its way into the ordinary."[75] She describes this process of submission as characterized by "profound psychic numbing"[76]: we acquiesce, give up attempts to understand or critique. Arendt explained that through a "mixture of gullibility and cynicism," citizens in authoritarian regimes "reached the point where they would, at the same time, believe everything and nothing, think that everything was possible and that nothing was true."[77] Here, Arendt links cynicism to gullibility. Cynicism is a response that can make someone feel clever but it is actually a defensive stance against complexity and ambiguity: We dismiss what we are unwilling or unable to work to understand. Much like its cousin disdain, cynicism is intellectually lazy. It's easier to say, "all politicians are crooked" than it is to discern among them, easier to view all media as suspect rather than to read critically.

Anderson's novel critiques the cynicism of its teenage characters and, in the process, shows how being plugged into the feed is one factor that makes them so cynical. By the end of the novel, Titus learns from his girlfriend, Violet, to read against the grain of the feed, to tune out its steady stream of advertisements, and to actively seek out news reports of global unrest, government corruption, and climate disasters. At the book's end, he's able to pick out "little pieces of broken stories"[78] that reveal terrifying glimpses of the world beyond the feed that had not been visible to him at the book's beginning. *Feed* is a novel that teaches its readers to read beyond the text and to consider the ways the rhetorical context of the internet shapes our perceptions, but it is not a novel that creates a lot of agency for its characters. The last novel I look at for this chapter is one that situates its young protagonist as a rhetor, as a young person able to use technology to talk back.

"The Khalil I know": *The Hate U Give*

While the characters in *Feed* lack agency, *The Hate U Give* chronicles its protagonist's movement toward agency as she finds her voice and is able to use our multimedia ecosystem to tell stories of her own. Books that reveal the process of storytelling, the ends of rhetoric, can also help readers to imagine themselves as storytellers, as contributors to the larger conversations around them. As Coats notes, as we learn more and more about stories, "We begin to tell our own stories, fashioning a self out of the stories and narrative patterns we have received from our culture."[79] Readers of all ages are not merely passive recipients of story; they actively participate in storytelling and in the construction of meaning. And, just as fascists tell stories, there are also those who tell counter-stories that combat fascist ideology, that reveal it as constructed, that highlight its inconsistencies and gaps, and that open up possibilities beyond the ideological bubble created through fascist mythmaking. In their book *By Any Means Necessary: The New Youth Activism*, Henry Jenkins, Sangita Shresthova, Liana Gamber-Thompson, Neta Kligler-Vilenchik, and Arely M. Zimmerman focus on the ways young people use the internet to engage in activism. They explain that, "Young people are rarely addressed as political agents, [. . .] and [they] are not consulted in the political decision-making process, whether local, state, national, or global."[80] Despite this, there are many young people who are politically and civically engaged. To be clear, not all engagement is pro-democracy. There are some young people who are recruited into alt-right groups or radicalized in online spaces. There are plenty of young people who support the MAGA movement, but there are also many young people who focus their attention on social justice issues, protecting the environment, and other forms of pro-democracy/anti-fascist activism:

> Young people are most apt to become politically involved if they come from families with a history of citizen participation and political activism, if they encounter civics teachers who encourage them to reflect

on and respond to current events, if they attend schools where they are allowed a voice in core decisions, and if they participate in extracurricular activities and volunteerism that gives back to their community.[81]

Young people are also influenced by narratives that invite them to participate in their society. Stories can inspire activism, expand possibilities, and help us to imagine possible futures we can work toward.

Marah Gubar argues that there are works of literature that invite young people "to view fiction not as a set of marching orders from an omnipotent author but as a shared playing field."[82] This conception of the child reader is an anti-authoritarian stance that challenges the hierarchy of adult/child and author/reader. In other words, the differences in attitudes about child-rearing that I discuss in the Introduction are reflected in the texts that authors create for child readers. Does an author write a book that assumes young people should be obedient and well-behaved or do they create a story that encourages them to be independent and curious? Is a book imparting rote lessons or is it creating a space for its readers to develop their own responses and interpretations? Books focused on helping young readers to understand and use rhetorical strategies may provide tools that those readers can use as they navigate the world around them.

One such book is the young adult novel *The Hate U Give* by Angie Thomas, which depicts its protagonist Starr Carter learning to find her voice after a close childhood friend is murdered by a police officer. Right after witnessing the murder, a shocked Starr explains, "They finally put a sheet over Khalil. He can't breathe under it. I can't breathe. I can't. *Breathe.*"[83] Her internal monologue, with its repetition of the word "breathe," is a direct reference to the 2014 murder of Eric Garner, who died after being choked by a New York City police officer. Starr lives in a Black community but attends a mostly white school in the suburbs, where she learns that the media's negative portrayals of her friend and his murder directly influence the attitudes of her classmates. A white friend of Starr's notices that Starr, who hasn't told her friends about the murder, is acting strangely and asks, "Does this have something to do with the police shooting that drug dealer in your neighborhood?"[84] Starr realizes that, while the media depicts the police officer who shot Khalil in humane ways, Khalil is depicted as a "thug," an image some of her white classmates accept uncritically.

In response to these negative media depictions, Starr uses the internet to counter the media's characterization of her friend: "I started a new blog—*The Khalil I Know*. It doesn't have my name on it, just pictures of Khalil." She captions the photos and tags them with Khalil's name. For instance, she captions a photo of four-year-old Khalil in a bathtub with "The Khalil I know loved bubble baths as much as he loved his grandma."[85] In this way, she uses the skills and mediums available to her in order to humanize her friend by telling stories about him. "In just two hours, hundreds of people have liked and reblogged the pictures. I know it's not the same as getting on the news like Kenya said, but I hope it helps."[86] Where Titus is an unlikeable and unreliable narrator, Starr is self-aware and able to model learning, healing from trauma, and active resistance against a racist system. Through protests, both online and in person, Starr learns by the end of the novel to construct herself as a speaking subject with important stories to tell.

As is the case with many characters in civil rights stories, Starr does not upend the oppressive system she inhabits. She lives to fight another day in an imperfect world. What she has gained is a new-found power, her voice, the ability to use words in a public space as a means of persuasion, the ability to make oneself heard using whatever means are available. She counters a steady stream of dehumanizing narratives by creating counter-narratives, matching story with story. Audre Lorde famously said, "The master's tools will never dismantle the master's house,"[87] but what if those are the only tools we have available to us? The lesson of *The Hate U Give* is that we need to fight fascist storytelling, not with facts, but with anti-fascist storytelling.

What kinds of stories count as anti-fascist storytelling? An easy and simple answer is: The ones neofascists are trying so very hard to suppress. *The Hate U Give* is one of the most banned books in the nation because it educates about "blasphemous facts," the epidemic of police brutality against young Black men and women, and boys and girls, that reveals the racism embedded in our system of law enforcement. It is an anti-fascist narrative because it depicts a complex system, not a simple dichotomy. Starr's uncle is a police officer and her boyfriend is white: Her relationships are intersectional and multigenerational as she moves between white and Black communities, a liminal identity that expands her perspective, and the reader's as well. Anti-fascist stories don't traffic in "us" versus "them" narratives, they problematize the very notion of "us" versus "them" and the idea that we are on "different teams," that we are groups of people who are so very different from one another that we can't possibly find a single thing we have in common. That can't be so, though, because humans are complicated and multifaceted. We are more like than unlike, and children and adults of all ages share affinities, even if they're not always evident in a mediated environment that separates rather than unites us. While Starr should never have had to humanize her friend, that's what works of literature, stories populated by fictional characters that we care about, can do: They can humanize "Others" by highlighting shared affinities, by challenging "us" versus "them" stories, and, as I'll discuss in the next chapter, by shifting our perspective.

2
The Order of Story

> Stories have been used to dispossess and to malign. But stories can also be used to empower, and to humanize. Stories can break the dignity of a people. But stories can also repair that broken dignity.
> —CHIMAMANDA NGOZI ADICHIE, "The Danger of a Single Story."[1]

Born on the Water is a picture book created as part of the 1619 Project.[2] It frames the history of slavery in the United States through the perspective of a Black girl whose teacher asks students to "Trace your roots. Draw a flag that represents your ancestral land." The girl is not able to complete the assignment because she does not know her family's ancestral land and is ashamed, so she asks her family for help. Her grandmother helps her understand her ancestry by telling her a story, a history of slavery beginning with the lives of free people in western Africa who were captured by European slavers and brought to the colonies in 1619, "a whole year before the *Mayflower* arrived." The picture book depicts the grim conditions of the Middle Passage, the indignity of being sold, the unpaid labor that built much of early America, and the persistence and resiliency of Black Americans. The grandmother's story ends on a decidedly patriotic note: "And because the people survived / and because the people fought, / America began to live up to its promise of democracy. / It is the people who fight for this democracy still."[3] The last page of the book, subtitled "Pride," depicts the girl drawing an American flag: "I draw the stars and I draw the stripes / of the flag of the country that my ancestors built, / that my grandma and grandpa built, / that I will help build, too." *Born on the Water* defines patriotism as derived from an unblinking and nuanced understanding of history: Enslaved people were forced to labor but they also resisted; their culture was taken from them so they created a new culture; family bonds were broken by the slave trade but they built families nonetheless. The girl's pride springs from this ancestral knowledge passed down from her grandmother who explains to her, "Never forget you come from a people of great strength."

It is ironic that a story that instills patriotism, respect for one's elders, and pride in one's ancestors is being attacked by the American Right as un-American. Indeed, attacks from the Right on The 1619 Project, a set of texts and a curriculum that center the African American experience, range from the banal to the downright bizarre. For instance, in an essay titled "'1619' Pulitzer Will Boost Socialist Teaching in Schools," Heritage Foundation fellow Mike Gonzalez argues that teaching that slavery was connected to capitalism will "indoctrinate young minds on how America and its capitalist system are racist to the core. Its goal: destroy our present institutions, economic system and ways of thinking, and replace them."[4] The word "replace" is commonly used by white supremacist groups who fear that white people and white culture (Western heritage) are being replaced by immigrants, minorities, and minority cultures. The word, connected to the racist, xenophobic concept of the "great replacement theory," signals fear of losing the white majority in the United States and of losing a central place and dominant voice in the histories we construct about ourselves. The threat posed by The 1619 Project is an existential one for neofascists because this new, unfamiliar date "replaces" a date that has been mythologized. Instead of viewing history as additive, evolving, multivocal, and collectively constructed, the Right must hold firm to a whitewashed understanding of history that smooths over and denies the contradictions inherent in our founding. The "us" versus "them" narrative central to neofascism presents the public an either/or choice that signals one's political orientation: One is *for 1619* or one is *for 1776*.

The 1619 Project, launched by *The New York Times* in 2019, seeks to re-center American history by challenging what Chimamanda Ngozi Adichie calls the "single story," a dominant cultural narrative. The year 1619 marks the date when about twenty enslaved Africans were sold to colonists. It is the moment America established itself as an economy built by slavery and "the moment that its defining contradictions first came into the world."[5] In many ways, the project is a thought experiment: What if we reimagined our understanding of US history from a different perspective? How might our understanding of our institutions and founding values change as a result? Nikole Hannah-Jones, creator of The 1619 Project, explains that, "Doing so requires us to place the consequences of slavery and the contributions of black Americans at the very center of the story we tell ourselves about who we are as a country."[6] When those on the Right criticize the project for challenging our widely accepted construction of US history, they're not wrong. It does. It moves to the foreground what has long been in the background, adds new perspectives, highlights the neglected stories of people long excluded from American democracy and from the stories we tell about ourselves, and it asks us to weave those stories into a broader, more inclusive collective understanding of history and nation. In other words, instead of asking us to choose 1619 *or* 1776, The 1619 Project asks that we consider 1619 *and* 1776 together, and in dialogue with one another.

In this chapter, I focus on books that, like The 1619 Project, challenge the unified, whitewashed version of American history that is central to a fascist mythology of nationhood. This mythology, as I discuss earlier, can only be maintained through the deliberate erasure or cover-up of "blasphemous facts," perspectives like those in The 1619 Project that reveal the gaps in the carefully crafted fictional worldview required to maintain neofascist ideology. Our history of slavery and settler colonialism is so central to our national identity that erasing, denying, or downplaying it requires willful ignorance, cognitive dissonance, and deliberate denials. As Cornel West writes, "We are exceptional because of our denial of the antidemocratic foundation stones of American democracy. No other democratic nation revels so blatantly in such self-deceptive innocence, such self-paralyzing reluctance to confront the nightside of its history."[7] Neofascists ban discussions of, books about, and education about The 1619 Project and critical race theory because these offer a critical lens that makes visible the construction of an important set of lies and cover-ups necessary to fascist mythology. Neofascist mythmaking works to construct a cohesive narrative about the grand achievements of the "master race" in order to justify white supremacy. American authoritarianism is, at its core, racist, but no one, except members of white supremacist or neo-Nazi groups, wants to think of themselves as being a "racist." Therefore, they must maintain a "self-deceptive innocence," a fragile worldview that must be continuously reinforced. In order to maintain the fiction that America is not, at its core, a racist and imperialist nation, they must smooth over the contradictions inherent in our founding and that are still present in our systems and institutions, which involves suppressing stories that, simply through their existence, challenge nationalistic mythologies of nationhood.

In 2020, the Trump administration responded to the blasphemous 1619 Project by creating their own President's Advisory 1776 Commission, whose task it was to present "a definitive chronicle of the American founding, a powerful description of the effect the principles of the Declaration of Independence have had on this Nation's history, and a dispositive rebuttal of reckless 're-education' attempts that seek to reframe American history around the idea that the United States is not an exceptional country but an evil one."[8]

The Commission, which was disbanded by President Biden on his first day in office, produced *The 1776 Report*, which remains as a chilling document chronicling the Right's deliberate and ongoing attempts to whitewash history and civics education in America's schools. The executive order that formed the commission explains that, "Despite the virtues and accomplishments of this Nation, many students are now taught in school to hate their own country, and to believe that the men and women who built it were not heroes, but rather villains."[9] The report vilifies the work of scholars and educators, and instead advocates for a uniform education focused on maintaining patriotic myths of America's founding so as to create a generation of like-minded young people.

Stanley explains that, "While fascist politics fetishizes the past, it is never the actual past that is fetishized. These invented histories also diminish or entirely extinguish the nation's past sins. It is typical for fascist politicians to represent a country's actual history in conspiratorial terms, as a narrative concocted by liberal elites and cosmopolitans to victimize the people of the true 'nation'."[10] In other words, history is an important site where authoritarian and non-authoritarian worldviews are constructed, which is why challenges to the myth of American exceptionalism are viewed by neofascists as challenges to their core beliefs. Fascism requires portable symbols laden with predetermined meaning that work together to form a larger mythology: the Rebel flag, the Boston Tea Party, the year 1776. Complex multivocal histories, though, cannot be reduced to these mythic functions because they require an active and open dialogue with the present, an acknowledgement that history is never simply over and done with, and an understanding that there are multiple US histories, multiple, sometimes conflicting, stories we tell about ourselves and our founding.

An authoritarian version of history also requires unity: unity of identity, sameness of thought, and unquestioning loyalty, which is why, in the last few months of Trump's presidency, his administration was focused on ridding education—for both children and adults—of "divisive concepts." In an executive order, the Trump administration defined "divisive concepts," in part, as teaching that the United States is "fundamentally racist or sexist" and that "an individual, by virtue of his or her race or sex, is inherently racist, sexist, or oppressive, whether consciously or unconsciously."[11] The executive order bans instruction that might make individuals "feel discomfort, guilt, anguish, or any other form of psychological distress on account of his or her race or sex," or that implies that "an individual, by virtue of his or her race or sex, bears responsibility for actions committed in the past by other members of the same race or sex."[12] The order, which was revoked by President Biden just hours after his inauguration, claimed to "promote unity" by purging adult education for federal employees or contractors of the "pernicious and false belief that America is an irredeemably racist and sexist country." Similarly, the authors of *The 1776 Report* claim that the goal of education should be to provide children with a common identity and worldview. According to the authors of the report, love of country is foremost and educators who teach a less jingoistic, more accurate version of history and civics are unpatriotic or, worse, are working to actively undermine the nation. Both of these documents, the executive order and the report, with their emphases on avoiding "divisive concepts" and "factional ideologies," attempt to promote "national unity," which values uniformity over diversity of opinion and uncritical patriotism over nuanced, multivocal considerations of history, civics, and culture.

Even though the Trump administration's efforts were stymied, this same language is making its way into legislation being passed at the state and local level in multiple states. In *Education Week*, Sarah Schwartz reports that, "Since January 2021, 42 states have introduced bills or taken other steps that would restrict teaching critical race theory or limit how teachers can discuss racism and sexism."[13] She also noted that, "The same language echoes throughout much of the legislation, from bans on 'divisive' or 'racist or sexist concepts,' to provisions that require teachers to present contending perspectives on 'controversial' issues."[14] The Heritage Foundation is one group that provides language for state lawmakers to use when seeking to ban the teaching of critical race theory in public schools. As part of their mind-bogglingly convoluted argument, they claim that because "slavery, legal racial discrimination, and racism are so inconsistent with the founding principles of the United States" that "means that America and its institutions are not systemically racist."[15] This statement defies logic, but it is included in a "model bill" published by the foundation that has been adopted in multiple states and is published under the deceptive title, "Protecting K–12 Students from Discrimination." In a list of concepts that should not be taught in elementary or secondary schools, they explain that no "individuals, by virtue of race, ethnicity, color, or national origin, bear collective guilt and are inherently responsible for actions committed in the past by other members of the same race, ethnicity, color, or national origin."[16] Adults who feel threatened by histories told from the point of view of minority cultures invoke Child innocence as a way to express their own discomfort at being made to feel "responsible for actions committed in the past." The Child, specifically the white Child who might be made to "bear collective guilt," is being used as a symbol in discourse surrounding legislation being passed in multiple states. Childhood innocence is defined here as unwavering belief in the myths of nationhood that many of us were taught as children, belief that is "corrupted" later in life when the myths are revealed as myths.

These restrictions are also an example of how neofascism in the United States is rhizomic, springing as much from local and state governments as from national mandates.

Adults who are banning books and challenging school curricula "on behalf of the children" are trying to control the narrative, the set of stories that work together to create a mythology of nationhood. Peter Brooks argues that recent debates about removing statues of Confederate war generals are an example of the importance of narrative to our culture. Various protests focused on removing or maintaining Confederate statues, some of them ending in violence, are evidence that, "controlling the narrative, in this case the narrative of who we may be as a people and a nation, is of vital importance. The battle over representations of history makes manifest how crucial the stories we tell can be in our claims to identity and to self-knowledge."[17] Recent debates about the stories we share with or withhold from young people are largely centered on maintaining our nation's innocence.

For example, under a recent law restricting what is taught in Texas classrooms, teachers are required to teach that slavery was an aberration, an exception to otherwise just laws, not something central to the founding of the United States. Texas has banned teaching of The 1619 Project and instead has created an alternate 1836 Project meant to teach a patriotic history that begins with Texas's independence from Mexico. According to the *Texas Tribune*, "Some critics have pointed out that Texas' independence didn't apply to all of those living in the state at the time, such as slaves and indigenous groups. The Constitution of the Republic of Texas, passed in 1836, legalized slavery and excluded indigenous groups from gaining independence."[18] Texas's new laws ensure a willful forgetting, a deliberate and harmful erasure of the histories of non-white people.

Journalist Anne Applebaum explains that, for authoritarian-minded individuals, accurate, complex, and unflattering histories can lead to "decay, of a loss of purity, a loss of innocence."[19] Complete and nuanced histories can be a personal afront to individuals who base their political identities on nationalistic fictions. "Many of them don't recognize their fictions about the past for what they are," she writes. "They don't acknowledge that the past might have had its drawbacks. They want the cartoon version of history, and more importantly, they want to live in it, right now."[20] She explains that individuals with an authoritarian mindset are "bothered by complexity. They dislike divisiveness and prefer unity. A sudden onslaught of diversity—diversity of opinions, diversity of experiences—therefore makes them angry."[21] This anger has been on full display in the early 2020s at school board meetings around the nation where citizens, often spurred on by television pundits and organizations like the

Heritage Foundation, have demanded an end to the teaching of critical race theory,[22] a focus on racism as a system embedded in our laws and culture.

Laws that restrict teaching about systemic racism are an example of systemic racism. Attorney and civil rights activist Angela Glover Blackwell argues that, "[s]uppressing racial history allows right-wing politicians and their sympathizers to insist that persistent inequalities are the result of the failings of Black, Indigenous, and racially marginalized people—not the consequence of past and present racial discrimination and the selective generosity of government-based investments that uplifted white people for generations."[23] The histories we share with one another, or don't, shape current laws, institutions, attitudes, and behaviors. An honest engagement with US history and the systems we have inherited involves working to change those systems, but authoritarian-minded individuals fear and resist change. Neofascist histories centered on upholding unchanging, solid-seeming myths tell a single, fixed story, a unified and coherent construction, a fiction that is maintained by excluding counter-narratives. A pro-democracy understanding of history, on the other hand, is multivocal and additive, and open to change when new perspectives or discoveries are revealed. Non-authoritarian, anti-fascist histories reveal rather than conceal their construction.

Anti-fascist education, and by extension anti-fascist works of literature for young readers, engages with complex, contested histories. If democracy requires a population of informed and engaged citizens, then uncritical patriotism based on a whitewashed history is an enemy of the democratic process. Henry Giroux and Ourania Filippakou argue that, "at a time when fascists across the globe are disseminating toxic racist and ultra-nationalist images of the past, it is essential to reclaim critical pedagogy as a form of historical consciousness and moral witnessing. This is especially true at a time when historical and social amnesia have become a national pastime, particularly in the United States."[24] They argue that "a democracy cannot exist or be defended without informed and critically engaged citizens" and that "schools have a central role to play in fighting the resurgence of fascist cultures, mythic historical narratives, and the emerging ideologies of white supremacy and white nationalism."[25] Books for young readers that present history as contested, multivocal, and in progress can counter neofascist mythmaking as well.

Learning about our long history of American authoritarianism—freedom and franchise for some but the oppression of Others—can help us to understand American neofascism, which is grounded in centuries of white supremacy and imperialism. For instance, in his book *We Charge Genocide! American Fascism and the Rule of Law*, Bill V. Mullen describes the history of the "dual state," a two-tiered US legal system that targets people of color. Fascism, he argues, depends upon the "constant legal production of a dangerous internal enemy challenging state power whose suppression rationalize[s] the state's own preservation."[26] In this way, US fascism predates European fascism, which it inspired. While fascism is a system born out of conditions in the twentieth and twenty-first centuries, it roots itself in history, old prejudices, and existing myths. Just as fascism in Germany relied upon centuries of antisemitism, neofascism in the United States relies upon centuries of white supremacy. In his book *Teaching Anti-Fascism*, Michael Vavrus notes that, "Fundamentally, the anti-racism of multicultural education is inseparable from overall goals of anti-fascism."[27] He continues, writing that "Anti-fascism in the late twentieth and early twenty-first centuries in the United States and Europe is most recognizable in actions that support anti-racism, decolonization, migrant protection, feminism, and anti-patriarchal policing of sexual and gender boundaries, all of which are bedrocks of critical multicultural education."[28] Instead of teaching a "feel-good history,"[29] educators have a responsibility to practice "a *critical pedagogy* for an anti-fascist civic education. Critical pedagogy is a dialectical process that tests assumptions and assertions for accuracy as part of an ongoing interrogation of political and historical claims, a process that can lead to social justice actions by teachers and students."[30] While Vavrus focuses on instruction, these same ideas can apply to works of children's and young adult literature like *Born on the Water* that illustrate what is at stake in the construction of history and that make that construction a collaborative process between author and reader.

Reordering Stories, Recentering History: 1491

In her TED talk "The Danger of a Single Story" Chimamanda Ngozi Adichie explains that, "The Palestinian poet Mourid Barghouti writes that if you want to dispossess a people, the simplest way to do it is to tell their story, and to start with, 'secondly.' Start the story with the arrows of the Native Americans, and not with the arrival of the British, and you have an entirely different story."[31] The nonfiction children's book *Before Columbus: The Americas of 1491* by Charles C. Mann begins the history of the Americas thousands of years ago. In highlighting the date 1491, Mann is challenging the Eurocentric construction of history that starts with Columbus's voyage in 1492 and that characterizes the Indigenous people of the Americas as "uncivilized." The author explains in the introduction that "almost everything I was taught about early American history was wrong, especially the parts about Native Americans."[32] The book highlights recent discoveries that show that "Native Americans created societies that were older, bigger, and more highly developed than we used to think."[33]

It constructs a history that challenges the myth of Manifest Destiny, the idea that Europeans were settling a vast, empty, "untamed" wilderness.

The history books we read when I was a young person were not to be questioned but, increasingly, there are books for children and young adults that can make readers aware of the way history is assembled and narrated in the present. They make the construction of history visible to younger readers and highlight the ways in which different versions of history can create different narratives about our national identity. For example, at the end of *Before Columbus*, Mann speculates that, "It may be a while before our schoolbooks and TV shows catch up with the fact that the Americas were not a wilderness when European settlers arrived. [. . .] These and other revolutionary new views of the past are still taking shape, as fresh discoveries and discussion add to our knowledge of the Americas before Columbus."[34] Instead of presenting history as a settled collection of facts, the book presents it as a process of discovery and a dialogue.

Another children's book that centers Native American culture and history by highlighting neglected stories is *The Birchbark House* by Louise Erdrich (Chippewa). This work of historical fiction, which Erdrich also illustrated, tells the story of Omakayas, an eight-year-old Ojibwa girl who lives with her family on Madeline Island in the mid-nineteenth century. Readers learn details about life on the island as Omakayas helps her family to tan a moose hide, chase crows away from their corn, harvest rice, and take care of her younger siblings. As Elizabeth Gargano writes, "In *The Birchbark House* the looming threat of white expansion remains muted, allowing Erdrich to describe a relatively self-contained Ojibwa community on the Island of the Golden-Breasted Woodpecker (Madeline Island) in southern Lake Superior."[35] The novel is organized around the seasons to convey the rhythms of what daily life might have been like over the course of a year. As is the case with *Before Columbus: The Americas of 1491*, *The Birchbark House* challenges the American myth of Manifest Destiny by depicting the civilizations Indigenous peoples built.

In a sequel to the novel, *The Game of Silence*, Omakayas and her community are forced to move west after the US government breaks a treaty with the Ojibwa. In *The Birchbark House*, set two years earlier, the incursion of white settlers is already impacting their community in profound ways, the most deadly of which is the spread of smallpox. Omakayas loses her infant brother to the disease and she finds out, at the novel's end, that she was adopted as a toddler when all of her birth family was infected and died: "You were the toughest one, the littlest one, and you survived them all," Old Tallow tells her.[36] As is the case with *Born on the Water*, the novel focuses on strength and survival, presenting these as a source of pride to child characters and readers.

Stories of survival are also passed on to young readers to preserve memory, to bear witness to generations of genocide. In *An Indigenous Peoples' History of the United States*, Roxanne Dunbar-Ortiz places Indian boarding schools within the context of a larger history of centuries of settler colonialism and genocide. She explains how the schools, some of which were open until the 1970s, led to generational trauma. "The experience of generations of Native Americans in on- and off-reservation boarding schools, run by the federal government or Christian missions, contributed significantly to the family and social dysfunction still found in Native communities. Generations of child abuse, including sexual abuse—from the founding of the first schools by missionaries in the 1830s and the federal government in 1875 [. . .] traumatized survivors and their progeny."[37] For example, corporal punishment was not practiced in many Indigenous communities, but children brutalized by it in boarding schools grew up to pass this generational trauma on to their children. "Often punishment was inflicted for being 'too Indian'—the darker the child, the more often and severe the beatings. The children were made to feel that it was criminal to be Indian."[38] Our history about these schools in both Canada and the United States is incomplete, which is why stories from survivors and witnesses are vital.

I Am Not a Number, written by Jenny Kay Dupuis (Nipissing) and Kathy Kacer and illustrated by Gillian Newland, tells the story of Dupuis's grandmother who spent a year in a Canadian residential school for Indigenous children (see Fig. 3). In an afterword, the authors explain that "Irene Couchie Dupuis was among approximately 150,000 First Nations, Métis, and Inuit children—some as young as four—who, for over a century, were removed from their homes and sent to live at residential schools across Canada. [. . .] Children were poorly fed; infectious diseases thrived; many students died alone and far from home."[39] The stated goal of the residential schools, both in Canada and the United States, was to destroy Indigenous cultures by rearing children away from their families and communities. "The [Truth and Reconciliation Commission of Canada] Final Report concluded that the Indian Residential School system was an attempted 'cultural genocide,' but the escalating number of recovered unmarked graves points to something even darker."[40] The current estimate of 4,120 students known to have died in the schools may be only a fraction of the total. Recently, more than 1,300 unmarked graves have been found at the sites of former schools. "Residential school survivor testimony has long been filled with stories of students digging graves for their classmates, of unmarked burials on school grounds, and of children who disappeared in suspicious circumstances."[41] As is the case with stories of the Holocaust, the stories of the

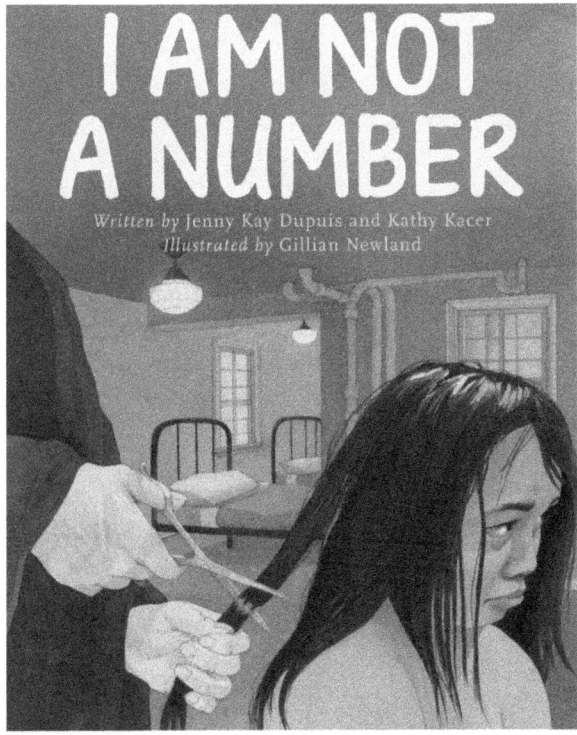

Figure 3. The cover of *I Am Not a Number* by Jenny Kay Dupuis and Kathy Kacer and illustrated by Gillian Newland.

residential schools must be preserved as an act of moral witnessing and in order to pass on memory to the next generation.[42]

I Am Not a Number begins with a frightening scene as an agent comes to Irene's house to take her and two of her brothers away to a residential school. "My mother wrapped her arms around me. 'I won't let you take her.' The man shrugged. 'Give me all three or you'll be fined or sent to jail'."[43] At the school, Irene and her brothers are separated. She is told she is no longer allowed to use her name and must instead use a number: "You are 759," a nun tells her. The nun orders Irene and the other girls who have arrived with her to shower, saying "Make sure to scrub all the brown off." As the story progresses, Irene's hair is cut off and she endures severe punishments. When she speaks her native language, she is physically abused and the nun tells her "That's the devil's language! [. . .] We don't speak it here."[44] Every lesson and punishment is aimed at destroying the children's culture and language and replacing these with Western culture.

When Irene is sent home for the summer, she and her brothers tell their parents about the abuse they've endured, and their parents risk arrest to protect them. When the agent comes to take the children back to the school, their father has them hide in his workshop, an act of civil disobedience that protects his children from further abuse. Dunbar-Ortiz notes that there are stories of resistance from the children who were sent to boarding schools: "Running away was the most common way to resist, but there were also acts of nonparticipation and sabotage, secretly speaking their languages and practicing ceremonies. This surely accounts for their survival, but the damage is nearly incomprehensible."[45] *I Am Not a Number* preserves this history of resistance, gives voice to groups of people who have been constructed as invisible, and documents a history that has been marginalized, and it does so in a way that is accessible to child readers.

Another form of cultural genocide occurred in the mid-twentieth-century United States through forced assimilation. In *Indian No More*, Charlene Willing McManis (Umpqua) and Traci Sorell (Cherokee) tell the story of an Umpqua family that relocates from the Grand Ronde Indian Reservation to Los Angeles after the US Congress passes termination laws and the Indian Relocation Act of 1956, which were designed to integrate Indigenous peoples by moving them off of reservations. Dunbar-Ortiz notes that these acts were meant to end native sovereignty and to "eliminate Indigenous identity entirely through assimilation, a form of genocide."[46] The family at the center of *Indian No More* is one of thousands relocated to urban areas in a program that "gave rise to large Native urban populations scattered among already poor and struggling minority working-class communities, holding low-skilled jobs or dealing with long-term unemployment."[47] In an afterword to the novel, McManis explains that the termination acts, much like the boarding schools, were a way to kill Native identity by severing people from their communities and cultures.

Chapter 1 is titled "The Walking Dead" and begins with the line, "Before being terminated, I was Indian."[48] The narrator, Regina Petit, explains that her reservation was "erased" and that her tribal roll number has been removed. Significantly, she raises an important question for the reader at the chapter's end: "Now I ask you, how can we be dead if we're still walking?"[49] In these ways, the novel addresses the centuries-long genocide of Indigenous peoples, the diaspora of people forcibly removed from their lands, and the effects of generational trauma. It does so in ways that are accessible to younger readers, to beginners who might not know very much about the subject. Regina's grandmother explains that "The president has just signed a bill from Congress saying that we're no longer Indian" to which Regina responds, "But . . . but what if I still want to be one?"⁵⁰

In their new, multicultural neighborhood in Los Angeles, the children make a diverse set of friends and they come into contact with stereotypes of American Indians perpetuated in 1950s media and culture. Neighborhood children play "cowboys and Indians" and are perplexed that Regina and her family don't have a tipi. Regina explains that, "Sometimes Budlong Elementary School felt like the boarding school that Chich's mother had gone to long ago. No one seemed to respect our language, culture or stories. We celebrated Thanksgiving at Budlong, another holiday no one back home in Grand Ronde observed."⁵¹ When the children perform a play about the first Thanksgiving, Regina must wear an Indian costume made of a paper bag covered in crayon drawings of "'Indian symbols [Keith] learned through Boy Scouts," and someone's mother paints Regina's face with lipstick lines. She's made to sit cross-legged on stage and then perform a dance that "didn't look like anything I had heard of or seen back home."⁵² Regina, who has heard the stories from her grandmother about boarding schools where "the schoolteachers wouldn't allow the children to speak Umpqua or sing our songs"⁵³ is shaken by the performance saying, "I wasn't sure I'd ever forget this day or what those stripes felt like."⁵⁴

The creative layout of the book emphasizes stories told by elders, specifically Regina's grandmother, by setting them in a different font and framing them with a pattern in the margin, which calls attention to their importance. In one such story, the grandmother places their relocation to Los Angeles into a longer history of relocation. She explains that the Umpquas were forced to move a century before, when white settlers claimed their land: "So in the winter of 1856, the Indian agent came to our people and said they had to move to Grand Ronde, a reservation some one hundred and fifty miles away. Forced to leave their homes, our ancestors left only with the clothes on their backs and what little they could carry."⁵⁵ In this way, the character and the author(s) participate in moral witnessing by passing on oral stories not contained in history books. "My chich [grandmother] was six years old when she walked that trail. She remembered soldiers shouting for them to keep moving. And she remembered her chich dying one night on the journey when the group stopped to camp. They quickly buried her without any of the proper ceremonies."⁵⁶ When her grandchildren are distressed by the story, she acknowledges that it is sad but that "The story also shows that our people survive. Even in the harshest conditions."⁵⁷

The narrative portion of the book concludes with Regina putting her own story in the context of her grandmother's stories. "We came from survivors. Our ancestors survived being forced to leave our homelands and march to

Grand Ronde in the winter. Her mother overcame the loneliness and abuse in boarding school to return home and grow her own family." She is able to claim her Umpqua identity because she has heard the stories of her ancestors and "because I survived to tell their stories and mine. Like this one."[58] The book continues the narrative beyond the story of Regina, which is based on the author's childhood and family, and it reveals the process through which history is constructed.

Three afterwords included after the narrative portion of the book place the story of an Umpqua girl inside a collection of other stories about individuals, communities, and American history. In an editor's note, Elise McMullen-Ciotti (Cherokee) puts the novel into a larger context, which includes the field of children's book publishing. She explains that, "I had struggled as a Cherokee within the publishing industry. Why couldn't we move beyond marketing Native American books only in November and around the Thanksgiving holiday?"[59] Her afterword shows how and why *Indian No More* is a rare children's book and why it was so important for the author, co-author, editor, cover illustrator, and press to get it right, to be as accurate as possible. "What many non-Natives do not realize is that it is very rare for us to 'get the microphone' within society" she writes. "And when we do, we are very, very aware of all the Native Americans standing behind us. We speak for ourselves as individuals—we all have a voice—but we are never speaking only for ourselves."[60] The afterwords by the author, co-author, and editor highlight what is at stake in the sharing of stories, in the construction and reconstruction of historical narrative. They make that construction deliberate and visible, and they include the child reader in on the stories behind the story. Thirteen-year-old Ashleigh wrote a review of the book for "Indigo's Bookshelf: Voices of Native Youth," much of which focuses on the telling of the story: "All these amazing Native women worked together to bring Ms. Charlene's story to readers like me. I am not Umpqua. This is not the story of my family or community. But I feel like it belongs to me."[61] The authors' openness about the construction of the story creates a space for young readers like Ashleigh to enter into the meaning-making process as an active participant.

The notes from the author, Charlene Willing McManis, who died in 2018 before she could finish her book, her co-author, Traci Sorell, who promised to finish the book for her, and the editor working with them show how important the act of telling stories is. By sharing the difficult process of telling McManis's story, they include the child in on the storytelling process. Joe Sutliff Sanders writes of non-fiction for children that, "When a book declines to polish its presentation of information, the book communicates humility instead of authority; it leaves bare the gaps in understanding rather than presenting a unified front of finished information; it makes plain its vulnerabilities."[62] Such books, he argues, are an "invitation to critical engagement" because they make the construction of story visible. Instead of smoothing over the bumpy parts of storytelling in order to create a unified, whole narrative, they reveal the gaps in the story, the complexity and messiness of storytelling, and the ways historical narratives continuously change over time and why.

Reordering Stories, Recentering History: 1775

M.T. Anderson also writes books that do not pander to or patronize young readers. He assumes a readership that is interested in learning about and participating in the world around them, young readers able to grasp complexities. When asked about his *Octavian Nothing* books, which gruesomely depict the violence of war and slavery, and whether such topics are appropriate for young readers, Anderson said, "If we're going to ask our kids at age 18 to go off to war and die for their country, I don't see any problem with asking them at age 16 to think about what that might mean."[63] The two volumes that make up *The Astonishing Life of Octavian Nothing, Traitor to the Nation* take place during America's revolutionary years. Octavian begins life as the subject of an enlightenment experiment in which he is classically educated and at the same time studied as a lab specimen. He is initially unaware that he and his mother are enslaved, but when the Novanglian College of Lucidity is sold to masters who have no interest in proving that Africans can be educated as well as Europeans, Octavian is cruelly made aware of his status as an enslaved person: He and his mother are whipped and tortured, and his mother dies from smallpox and is dissected for research.

Octavian escapes and, before he is recaptured, spends time working alongside the Sons of Liberty to oppose British rule. He observes that, "The Africans amongst us risked our lives for liberty, and yet had no assurance liberty would be ours; our pay, in many cases, came not to us, but to our owners—for it was reckoned that we belonged to them, and so *our labor was theirs*."[64] Because the narrative is focalized through Octavian, readers are made aware of the profound contradictions inherent in the founding of the United States and their painful effects on enslaved people. In an afterword, Anderson explains,

> It is startling, perhaps, to consider that the continuance of slavery was so thoroughly interwoven with the politics of freedom. In the course of my research for this book, I have come to believe that the American Republic would not have survived its early years—would not have made it through the war of 1812—if it had not been fueled

and funded by two profound acts of ethnic violence: the establishment of slavery and the annexation of Native American land, both of which practices played a major part in the inception and conduct of the Revolution. The freedom—economic, social, and intellectual—enjoyed by the vocal and literate elite of the early Republic would have been impossible if it had not been for the enslavement, displacement, and destruction of others.[65]

By focalizing the Revolutionary period through the point of view of Octavian, Anderson crafts a complex retelling of American history, one which centers the experiences of an enslaved person who is uncertain of his fate, unsure where his loyalties should lie, and painfully aware of his position as Other. When Octavian is able to escape a second time, he joins Lord Dunmore's Ethiopian Regiment. Dunmore offered freedom to any enslaved man who joined the regiment to fight on the side of British, and hundreds of escaped slaves took up his call to arms and his promise of freedom. Anderson weaves several historical documents into his narrative to frame his fictionalized accounts. A letter from George Washington, for example, describes Dunmore's actions as "diabolical schemes" that need to be "crushed."[66]

Through Octavian's narration, readers learn about the contradictions inherent in America's founding, both the promise and the flaws of enlightenment thinking. Because events in the novel are bounded by history, there is no plausible happy ending for the book's protagonist, whose narrative ends as he sets out to find a maroon community, a place to "secure us from the ire and indifference of both England and Colony."[67] In this way, the *Octavian Nothing* books counter the single story of the American Revolution told from the point of view of European colonists. While *The 1776 Report* claims that "the principles of the Declaration [of Independence] are universal and eternal,"[68] Octavian challenges the idea of natural, universal human rights, the laws of nature cited in the Declaration, stating, "Our rights are unnatural, or we should need no government to defend them."[69] Octavian, who is enslaved and studied as the subject of an experiment and who works alongside both the British and the rebels, is acutely aware of his identity as evolving and constructed by social forces. His is a complex history, a perspective that challenges simplistic, jingoistic portrayals of the founding of the United States. West wrote that, "To confront the role of race and empire is to grapple with what we would like to avoid, but we avoid that confrontation at the risk of our democratic maturation."[70] Neofascism works to construct American identity as innocent, but "democratic maturation" involves understanding and addressing the hypocrisy that undergirds our shared values and institutions, the oppressions necessary to maintain our long history of American authoritarianism, and the growth we need to undertake as we aspire to live up to our democratic ideals.

American authoritarianism, freedom for some and oppression for others, weaves its way throughout our history. Rooted in settler colonialism and slavery, the white supremacist patriarchy reasserts its power through periodic backlash against the expansion of civil rights to all Americans. In her novel *Roll of Thunder, Hear My Cry*, Mildred Taylor situates her characters within this long history of progress and regress by portraying a multigenerational Black family struggling to hold onto land purchased from former slave owners, something seen as a threat to white supremacists living in the Jim Crow South. Taylor presents stories about the Logan family from the point of view of a child who is learning about the history of systemic racism alongside the modern reader. For example, Taylor makes tangible the effects of segregated schooling through an accretion of physical details: the Logan children must walk to school while white children ride a bus that runs the Black children off the road while "laughing white faces pressed again the bus windows."[71] The Logan siblings walk past the school for white children, with its two yellow busses and sports field, on their way to the school for Black children with its "four weather-beaten wooden houses on stilts of brick" located near the plantations where Black sharecroppers farm land they do not own. Once at school, Little Man, the youngest of the Logan children, is distressed when he's given a used and worn book that has passed through the hands of white students for eleven years before finally making its way down, in "very poor" condition, to the Black school. After he studies the chart in his book that lists its previous owners, Little Man "[springs] from his chair like a wounded animal, flinging the book onto the floor and stomping madly upon it."[72] While some of his peers have become complacent, Little Man has not and he rages against an unfair system.

The Logan children are regularly terrorized by one of the two big yellow school busses that carries white children to school. Taylor describes it as a monster: "Little Man turned around and watched saucer-eyed as a bus bore down on him spewing clouds of red dust like a huge yellow dragon breathing fire."[73] The youngest Logan sibling, Little Man, is bewildered and naively asks "where's our bus?" The white school has two busses while the Black school has none, a fundamental lack of fairness. The monstrous bus symbolizes multiple facets of racism in the Jim Crow south: its cruel adult driver, its complicit child passengers, the violence it inflicts upon Black children, the injustice of segregation, and the ever-present legacy of slavery. The children in the novel are not protected from the violence of Jim Crow apartheid, which means their elders must teach them survival skills: when they can and should resist and when they must retreat.

On a rainy day, the bus runs the children off the road and into a gully filled with rainwater: "Little Man, chest-deep in water, scooped up a handful of mud and in an uncontrollable rage scrambled up to the road and ran after the retreating bus. As moronic rolls of laughter and cries of 'Nigger! Nigger! Mud eater!' wafted from the open windows, Little Man threw his mudball, missing the wheels by several feet. Then, totally dismayed by what had happened, he buried his face in his hands and cried."[74] Little Man's older brother, Stacey, understands that this is a turning point in Little Man's development, that if he doesn't find an outlet for his pain, frustration, and anger, these will eat away at the boy's sense of self. Stacey plans a small act of revenge against the yellow monster: He and his siblings dig holes in the rain-soaked road, making it appear as if the road has been washed out. The bus driver falls for their trap and runs right into the manmade lake in the middle of the road, which forces the white children to have to jump into the gully to get off the bus. The bus driver tells them, "all y'all gonna be walkin' for at least two weeks" while the bus is being fixed. It's a small victory, but enough to return Little Man's sense of agency and dignity.[75]

As the novel progresses, we see child characters learn from adults how to quietly subvert Jim Crow racism. Mary Logan, the children's mother, is a teacher who practices small acts of civil disobedience meant to instill pride among her students. For instance, for the students in her classroom, she covers over the inside cover of old school books that show how the books were handed down to white students for years. A fellow teacher tells her that Black children "got to learn how things are sometime," to which Mrs. Logan responds, "Maybe so [. . .] but that doesn't mean they have to accept them . . . and maybe we don't either."[76] Mary Logan ends up being fired from her job when school board members witness her teaching about the history of slavery, and her attempts to boycott a plantation store fail, but her acts of defiance are a precursor to the civil rights movement that would follow a few decades later. *Roll of Thunder*, after all, was published in 1976, and is itself a political act. Taylor writes in her preface to the novel that she learned about the history of Jim Crow from her family, and what she learned from them is that her people were strong and resilient: "I learned a history not then written in books but one passed from generation to generation on the steps of moonlit porches and beside dying fires in one-room houses, a history of great-grandparents and of slavery and of the days following slavery; of those who lived still not free, yet who would not let their spirits be enslaved."[77] Black history was not included in most textbooks or school curriculums in the 1970s, which means that Taylor's act of educating through literature was in of itself a form of resistance.

Resistance, civil disobedience, and getting into "good trouble" in the fight for social justice are also at the center of an autobiographical set of books by civil rights activist and US Representative John Lewis. The three-volume graphic novel series *March*, written by Lewis and Andrew Aydin and illustrated by Nate Powell, chronicles Lewis's life and the historical events that influenced and were influenced by his sixty-year involvement in the civil rights movement. *March* chronicles the long, difficult, dangerous work that civil rights activists endured in order to end segregation and get the Civil Rights and Voting Rights Acts passed. It provides an unflinching look at the movement by depicting debates within about goals and tactics, and by depicting decades of violent resistance from law enforcement, political leaders, and ordinary citizens. The text includes transcripts of several speeches that were given by civil rights leaders and opponents of civil rights, including an infamous one by Alabama Governor George Wallace, which contained the notorious phrase "Segregation today, segregation tomorrow, segregation forever."[78] The segment of Wallace's speech that is included uses the words "tyranny" and "freedom" to illustrate how these meant very different things to segregationists than they did to civil rights activists: "It is very appropriate then, that from this cradle of the Confederacy, the very heart of the great Anglo-Saxon southland, that today we sound the drum for freedom. . . . Let us rise to the call of freedom-loving blood that is in us, and send our answer to the tyranny that clanks its chains upon the South."[79] Integration is shown here as being viewed as "tyranny" and a threat to the "freedom" of whites to practice discrimination. This, and other examples, give readers a chance to think about the ways in which political rhetoric is deployed, and to pay close attention to how value-laden words are used to defend authoritarian practices. Shortly after this scene, the story includes the speech that Lewis gave at the 1963 March on Washington, which redefines the word "freedom" and presents a counterweight to Wallace's rhetoric: "Get in and stay in the streets of every city, every village, every hamlet of this nation until true freedom comes, until the revolution of 1776 is complete. We must get in the revolution—and complete the revolution."[80] Lewis redefines "freedom" as "true freedom," a way for the nation to live up to its promise of democracy. In this way, the graphic novel highlights American ideals, the way that we've repeatedly fallen short of those ideals, and the continuous movement toward making them a reality for all Americans. It invokes the iconic year 1776 as part of an unfinished historical legacy upon which we need to build.

The history depicted in March is framed by the 2009 inauguration of President Barack Obama, which weaves its way throughout the series so that events of the past are connected to current events and so that long-term progress, the long arc of justice, is made visible. For example, a full two-page spread features an image of Aretha Franklin singing "My Country, 'tis of Thee" at Obama's inauguration but there are cutout images surrounding her that depict scenes of bloodied activists and Confederate flag–carrying men.[81] It's a visual juxtaposition that highlights the generations of struggle that led to the election of our nation's first Black president. The scene of Franklin singing at the inauguration comes in the middle of a section depicting the attack by hundreds of people on the First Baptist Church in Montgomery, Alabama, in 1961. After the page turn, the lyrics "Oh let freedom ring" follow the same arc as a firebomb being thrown at the church, which was filled with 1,500 people there to support the Freedom Riders. The way in which these images are interwoven works to highlight the importance of music to the movement as a way to instill hope. Lewis explains that after Dr. Martin Luther King, Jr. spoke to the crowd in the church, and as the angry white crowd gathered outside, "we poured our hearts into the music of the movement, songs like 'Ain't Nobody gonna turn me 'round' and 'We Shall Overcome,' to give us strength."[82] These juxtaposed words and images work to create new meaning for the lyrics that Franklin sings at the inauguration: "Land where my fathers died" refers not only to those who fought in the revolutionary war but also those who fought for civil rights.

Today, in the aftermath of a 2013 ruling by the US Supreme Court that weakened the Voting Rights Act of 1964, *March* serves as a reminder as to why the act was fought for and passed in the first place. It depicts obstacles to voting like literacy tests and the harassment of African Americans standing in line to register to vote. In one scene, state troopers don't allow those standing in line to register to have food or water. "If any of y'all leaves that line for any reason—if you have to go to the bathroom, or you're thirsty—any reason whatsoever—you're not coming back, y'hear?!"[83] The graphic novel was published in 2016 so the authors could not have predicted that in 2021 a new voting law in Georgia would prohibit people from giving food or water to people standing on line to vote, sometimes for hours in districts with large Black populations and too few polling places. Indeed, the Right has been chipping away at voting rights at the state and national level for quite some time. Reading *March* in our current historical moment highlights the fact that the battle for civil rights is ongoing, a generations-long process with ebbs and flows of movement and backlash.

The message is that while our history is, at times, a dark one, there are also historical figures and movements that inspire. West argues that, in addition to confronting our troublesome history, we also need to maintain faith that we have made and can continue to make progress. "This is what happened in the 1860s, 1890s, 1930s, and 1960s in American history,"[84] he writes, noting the importance of remembering and learning from past movements for civil rights. Viewing American history through the lens of generational progress demonstrates that we have had several moments of "awakening among the populace from the seductive lies and comforting illusions that sedate them. [. . .] Just as it looked as if we were about to lose the American democratic experiment—in the face of civil war, imperial greed, economic depression, and racial upheaval—in each of these periods a democratic awakening and activistic energy emerged to keep our democratic project afloat."[85] Lewis often spoke about the importance of hope, the need to "keep hope alive," an ideal which the *March* series provides through its portrayal of civil rights history. Rather than teaching young people to feel guilt or shame, an unflinching understanding of our history highlights the strength and moral clarity of generations of Americans who worked to expand the promise of freedom to a broader population. "Never forget you come from a people of great strength" says the grandmother in *Born on the Water*, drawing inspiration from past generations who fought to expand democracy in the United States.

3
Fascism Is the Patriarchy

> I begin with the young. We older ones are used up. . . . But my magnificent youngsters! Are there finer ones anywhere in the world? Look at all these men and boys! What material! With them I can make a new world.
>
> —ADOLF HITLER, quoted in *Hitler Youth: Growing Up in Hitler's Shadow* by Susan Campbell Bartoletti.[1]

In his famous study of the diaries of *Freikorpsmen*, the group of mercenaries who supported Adolf Hitler's rise to power, Klaus Theweleit discovered some curious patterns of thought, especially in their descriptions of dreams, fantasies, and nightmares. Based on these diaries, Theweleit theorized a psychology of fascism, a common set of ideas that these men, who were proto-Nazis, seemed to share. As he mapped their worldview by studying the words they had written, one pattern he found repeatedly was references to floods, swamps, mires, and mud, all fluid landscapes with porous borders. Often, such imagery was connected to women and femininity, or to communism and the working classes. "To the *Freikorpsmen*, the Reds, like individual women, are a nameless force that seeks to engulf—described over and over as a 'flood,' a 'tide,' a threat that comes in 'waves,'" writes Barbara Ehrenreich in her forward to Theweleit's work. "A man must hold himself firm and upright, or be 'sucked in' by this impure sea."[2] The *Freikorpsmen* were obsessed with hard male bodies, flesh made impenetrable through strength of will, and they believed their hypermasculinity was a bulwark, a strong, solid defense against the menace of the femininized Other.

But, Theweleit argued, their repeated nightmares of floods and waves threatening to corrupt and engulf them revealed a deep anxiety, an obsession with masculine borders being breeched, boundaries penetrated. Fearful that they will lose their purity, their wholeness, fascists must continuously erect borders and build walls, both literal and metaphorical. They are "firm and upright" as they enforce and work to reify definitive lines that separate men and women, child and adult, self and other, "us" and "them." By studying the stories this group of fascists recorded, Theweleit pieced together a theory about fascism as grounded in a fear of the feminine Other and obsessed with the maintenance of hypermasculinity. Theweleit's theory helps to make sense of recent patterns in our own culture here in the United States: Donald Trump's easy misogyny, the Proud Boys, Christian nationalism, armed militias, and laws meant to take away bodily autonomy from women and members of the LGBTQ+ community are all connected in the ways they reassert patriarchal values that are under assault by uppity women and queer people. And they're not wrong. Feminists and queer people are challenging the patriarchy because it is a system that oppresses us and a system at the very heart of fascist ideology.

Just as neofascism in the United States grounds itself in white supremacy, it also grounds itself in the patriarchy. It fetishizes hard-bodied hypermasculinity, elevates a strongman leader, emphasizes the father-headed nuclear family, and promotes the traditional feminine roles of wife and mother. For example, vice-presidential candidate J.D. Vance argued that "childless cat ladies" are ruining the country, childless people should pay higher taxes, and postmenopausal women are only useful in their role as grandmothers. In other words, he believes that women should be bound to their reproductive role and contained within the patriarchy. These values take tangible form in laws restricting marriage, bodily autonomy, and LGBTQ+ rights. The availability of safe and legal abortions gives women autonomy over their own bodies, the very existence of trans and queer people challenges heteronormativity and the gender binary, the legalization of same-sex marriage expands the definition of family, and women occupying positions of power subvert male dominance. Neofascism resists these recent changes to gender norms and existing hierarches and promises to bring the nation back to a time before feminist and LGBTQ+ civil rights movements, a mythical past when women knew their place and queer people were invisible. Under the benign-sounding phrase "family values," neofascists in the United States have been working to counter gains in civil rights by restricting the rights of women and LGBTQ+ people, often, ostensibly, on behalf of children in need of protection from decadence and decay. The "magnificent youngsters" of fascism, the future leaders who are white, heterosexual, and hypermasculine, must be protected from corruption because they represent the fascistic future, a neat and orderly patriarchal hierarchy where everyone stays in their allotted place.

In this chapter, I look at the relationship between neofascism, hypermasculinity, and the patriarchy and how this manifests in the stories that we tell to and about boys and men. First, I focus on the role of the patriarchy as a grounding system of fascist ideology. Then, I examine the heated debates swirling around popular, convergence culture, all-ages stories like *Star Wars* or films set in the Marvel Universe, which have been both a site of adulation and a target for criticism from the alt-right, a loosely affiliated collection of white nationalist, neofascist groups and individuals, many of whom self-identify as anti-feminists. While fans of these texts come from a wide range of perspectives, some researchers note that the alt-right has had an outsized voice in online discussions, especially those lamenting that women and people of color are being cast in roles usually reserved for white men. Public debates about popular culture narratives reveal the vital role story plays in shaping and reflecting our collective values. Finally, I examine some texts that offer children and young adults strategies for critiquing patriarchal structures and hegemonic masculinity, and some that offer models of alternative, feminist masculinities.

The Patriarchy in/as Fascism

Guus Kuijer's children's book *The Book of Everything* is set in the Netherlands in 1951 when the country was still "struggling with the consequences of its occupation by Germany during World War II."[3] A historical note at the start of the novel explains that some Dutch people collaborated with the Nazis during occupation while others resisted. Although it's never explicitly mentioned, it is clear that nine-year-old Thomas's father was on the side of the fascists during the war. His father is a rigidly religious man who abuses his family and runs his household as an autocrat. At the start of the novel, Thomas's mother tries to defend him and Father slaps her. "[Thomas] heard the slap smack into his mother's soft cheek. He heard all the slaps Mother had ever suffered, a rain of slaps, as if it was hailing in Jan van Eyck Street and the leaves were being ripped off the trees. He pressed his hands over his ears."[4] Later in the scene, Father beats Thomas with a wooden spoon, and then makes him pray. When Father is confronted about the abuse by his sister-in-law he tells her, "It's simply a fact of life that the man is the head of the household. [. . .] It is the man's task to lead and instruct his wife and children. And if they refuse to listen to him, he has no choice but to [. . .] take severe measures. That is how God has ordained things."[5] The Christian, patriarchal family promoted as the ideal under fascism is depicted in *The Book of Everything* as traumatizing to Thomas, his mother, and sister, as harmful to women and children.

By the book's end, Father—and, by extension, the patriarchy—is diminished by a group of neighborhood women and his daughter, who pulls a carving knife on him at the dinner table: "I don't give a damn what you believe," she says to him. "But there will be no more hitting."[6] Thomas is also helped by the family's neighbor, Mrs. Van Amersfoort, who is a widow because her husband was executed for being part of the resistance. Neighborhood children call her a witch and Thomas's father calls her a communist. In this work of magic realism, she helps Thomas to confound his father with the plagues of Moses, including summoning thousands of frogs to their street. She and other women and children work together to intervene in the abuse Thomas and his mother suffer. When Mrs. Van Amersfoort and other women come to his home for an evening of reading and listening to records, Mrs. Van Amersfoort says to Thomas, "You wanted the plagues of Egypt, didn't you? Not the frogs, not the gnats and not the Bubonic plague, but we are the best plague, we women and children. No Pharaoh can resist us."[7] The women and children in the novel work together to challenge the hierarchy of Thomas's family. By the end of the book, Thomas comes to understand why his father behaves the way he does: "Father was afraid of laughter and joy. He was particularly afraid of ridicule. He was afraid that someone would say that humans are descended from apes. Or that the earth is much older than four thousand years. Or that someone would ask where Noah got his polar bears from. Or that someone would swear. Father was terrified."[8] This realization by Thomas gets to the heart of authoritarian thinking, which is motivated by fear of change and fear of challenges to existing hierarchies. At the book's end, the weakened patriarch of the family retreats to his room as the house fills with the sound of jazz and the laughter of women and children.

As is the case in much historical fiction, stories about individuals are used to personalize larger historical events and movements, but, in this instance, Thomas's family is also a microcosm of fascism. As I discuss in the Introduction, scholars attempting to understand the workings of fascism often connect the structure of authoritarian society with the structure of the patriarchal family[9]: The fascistic leader is viewed as the patriarch of the nation just as the father is patriarch in his home. In *The Mass Psychology of Fascism*, Wilhelm Reich wrote that, "Since authoritarian society reproduces itself in the individual structures of the masses with the help of the authoritarian family, it follows that the political reaction has to regard and defend the authoritarian family as *the* basis of the 'state, culture, and civilization'."[10] The family, as patriarchal and hierarchal, is an essential institution that works to uphold the larger system of which it is a part. "The authoritarian position of the father reflects his political role and discloses the relation of the family to the authoritarian state. Within the family the father holds the same position that his boss holds toward him in the production process. And he reproduces his subservient attitude toward authority in his children, particularly in his sons."[11] The son, who will eventually become a patriarch himself, is expected to reproduce the system once he becomes an adult but, as a child, he must submit to authority hoping to one day in the future to be in a position of authority over others.

A fascist leader imitates the structure of the patriarchal family when he performs a strongman persona, when he takes on the role of hypermasculine protector of his people. In *The Fascism This Time: And the Global Future of Democracy*, Theo Horesh writes that, "The leader portrays himself as a father of the nation, whose primal power is beyond question, and the followers he gathers mythologize his vitality, bolstering themselves through joining in his power."[12] Patriarchal structures, which are often tied to firmly held religious beliefs about the roles of men and women, place the man at the head of the household, the business, and the government. In *Strongmen: Mussolini to the Present*, Ruth Ben-Ghiat explains that strongmen call upon ideas of utopia, nostalgia, and crisis as a way to reassert traditional gender roles that are depicted as under threat by feminized, liberal forces: "the desire for a pristine and perfect community" and their "nostalgia for better times . . . involves the fantasy of returning to an age when male authority was secure and women, people of color, and workers knew their places."[13] The patriarchy is an intersectional system with white, heterosexual, cisgendered men occupying and continuously working to maintain their positions of power over, not only women, but also minorities and members of the LGBTQ+ community and children.

In *Jesus and John Wayne: How White Evangelicals Corrupted a Faith and Fractured a Nation*, Kristin Kobes Du Mez argues that white evangelical Christians in the United States support Donald Trump in overwhelming numbers because he embodies a version of hypermasculinity they want to see in a leader. While many were baffled as to why Christians would vote for a man who cheated on all three of his wives, consistently lied, and bragged about assaulting women, "evangelical support for Trump was no aberration, nor was it merely a pragmatic choice. It was, rather, the culmination of evangelical's embrace of militant masculinity, an ideology that enshrines patriarchal authority and condones the callous display of power, at home and abroad."[14] Kobes Du Mez outlines a decades-long history that culminated with around 80 percent of evangelical or "born again" Christians casting votes for Trump in the 2016 and 2020 presidential elections[15]: "His testosterone-fueled masculinity aligned remarkably well with that long championed by conservative evangelicals. What makes for a strong leader? A virile (white) man. And what of his vulgarity? Crudeness? Bombast? Even sexual assault? Well, boys will be boys."[16] Indeed, the strongman's vulgarity is part of what makes him appear to be virile. Ben-Ghiat explains that the fascist leader speaks the words that his followers feel too encumbered to speak aloud. Strongmen "pronounce clearly what others fear to whisper."[17] In other words, Trump's obvious misogyny and homophobia were reasons to support him, not exceptions.

In many ways, the election of Trump can be seen as a reactionary response to gains in rights for women and people in the LGBTQ+ community. Hillary Clinton posed a threat simply by being a competent woman who wanted to lead, as did Kamala Harris. What, after all, could be a greater threat to the patriarchy than a woman getting her party's nomination for president? Horesh writes that, "[Trump supporters] chanted 'lock her up' not simply because they viewed [Clinton] as a criminal but because they were reasserting their patriarchal right to power."[18] In fascist ideology, the man is the breadwinner, the protector, and the authority, while women take a subservient role, which means that female leaders are suspect. Furthermore, the fascist leader must not be a feminist or effeminate: Men who embrace alternative variations of masculinity, who are gay or trans or who are effeminate in other ways, are seen as threats to the social order as well. "Since fascist politics has, at its basis, the traditional patriarchal family, it is characteristically accompanied by panic about deviations from it," writes Stanley. "Transgender individuals and homosexuals are used to heighten anxiety about the threat to traditional male gender roles."[19] Recent moral panics about schools "grooming" children to become members of the LGBTQ+ community and fears of transgender students using gender-affirming restrooms are also a response to threats to the patriarchy.

Hypermasculinity is fragile. It must be continuously performed and reasserted as a way to (over)compensate for changing social mores. Hypermasculinity also harkens back to a mythic past when social hierarchies were more pronounced. According to Stanley, "In fascist politics, myths of an idealized patriarchal past, threatened by encroaching liberal ideals and all that they entail, function to create a sense of panic at the loss of hierarchal status, both for men and for the dominant group's ability to protect its purity and status from foreign encroachment."[20] This sense of panic comes from a fear of a loss of status for men, as well as from women who believe they benefit from their position within the patriarchy. The order of the social body, hierarchal and rule-bound, must be protected, which is why "strongmen" leaders promise to shore up institutions that preserve "traditional family values."

Fascist hypermasculinity is tied to race and racism as well when white men view themselves as protecting white women from assaults by immigrants or people of color. Fears of scapegoated groups are exacerbated when threats of rape and miscegenation are highlighted as potential dangers. For example, Stanley writes that, "According to Hitler, Jews were behind a conspiracy to use black soldiers to rape pure white women as a means of destroying the 'white race.' This was a conspiracy theory shared by the American Ku Klux Klan in the 1920s, which fantasized openly about Jews intentionally plotting the mass rape of white women by black men to undermine the white race in the United States."[21] Such conspiracy theories are also intersectional in the ways they meld together racism, sexism, and antisemitism to create a convoluted justification for fears of the Other and for aggressive discourse and behavior toward perceived Others. They also work to cement the fascist male's role as protector. As Stanley notes, "Trump famously began his campaign by denouncing Mexican immigrants to the United States as rapists."[22] Just as the white man protects his family, the fascist leader protects the white women of the nation from perceived threats from non-white men. In Trump's case, he promised such protection in the form of a wall between the United States and Mexican border. He expanded this pledge in 2024 when he promised mass deportations of immigrants, which he predicted would be "bloody."[23]

Authoritarian Boys' Clubs

A far-right, male-only group, the Proud Boys became a household name when Trump mentioned them at the September 29, 2020, presidential debate where he told them to "stand back and stand by," which they took to be a sign that the president endorsed the group. A few months later they helped lead the violent insurrection at the US Capitol on January 6, 2021. While they claim to simply be a fraternal organization, the Proud Boys espouse far-right, antisemitic, racist, sexist, and anti-immigrant views and regularly engage in brawls with counter-protesters or with anti-fascist groups. The founder of the Proud Boys, Gavin McInnes, is openly misogynistic, saying, for example, "Maybe the reason I'm sexist is because women are dumb. No, I'm just kidding, ladies. But you do tend to not thrive in certain areas—like writing."[24] The group claims to venerate the housewife and sees women's main role as birthing and rearing children. They view feminism as a threat to the traditional nuclear family and claim it is "de-masculating" men. In response to the perceived threat of the flood of feminism, men in the group perform hypermasculine rhetoric and activities, including initiation rituals. The highest status in the group is awarded to members who endure violence for the cause. Additionally, "all members are banned from watching pornography or masturbating more than once a month because, in theory, it will leave them more inclined to go out and meet women."²⁵ Fascist hypermasculinity stands firm and upright, fetishizing the solid masculine body maintained through self-control, through strength of will. McInnes said he founded the Proud Boys because "There's a real war on masculinity in this country that starts in kindergarten and goes all the way to adulthood. And it's not natural."²⁶ This "unnatural" war on masculinity comes from feminine forces, mothers and teachers encouraging boys to be "soft," feminists promoting "girl power," queer people deconstructing binaries of gender and sexuality. Boys, they argue, need to be rescued from these femininizing forces that seek to engulf them. The group accepts male members as young as 15, and, as is the case with other alt-right groups, it actively recruits young people.

Groups like the Proud Boys seek to appeal to men and boys who feel that they have been denied a status that is owed to them. Susan Faludi chronicled this emotion when she argued in the late 1990s that many men in America felt "stiffed." Although feminism had changed our culture and institutions over the decades, she found that many men had not kept pace with these changes and felt left behind:

> Ask feminists to diagnose men's problems and you will often get a very clear explanation: men are in crisis because women are properly challenging male dominance. Women are asking men to share the public reigns and men can't bear it. Ask antifeminists and you will get a diagnosis that is, in one respect, similar. Men are troubled, many conservative pundits say, because women have gone far beyond their demands for equal treatment and now are trying to take power and control away from men.²⁷

She argued that when boys are reared to expect a higher status in society than girls and women, they come of age with a sense of entitlement that can lead to disappointment (feeling stiffed) or, worse, to a desire to "take back" the power they believe they are being denied. The decades-long trend Faludi described is reproduced through parenting as many Americans are still rearing boys to believe they are entitled to a status that only existed in a mythic prefeminist past. This leads to precarity, a feeling that one's rightful status is being taken away, which creates an "immutable feeling of instability, uncertainty, or the sense that one is at risk of losing something."²⁸ Samantha Kutner argues that groups like the Proud Boys are able to recruit members by amplifying these feelings of precarity: "As a perceived antidote to being seen as effeminate, members maintain their redpilled status through aggressively overperforming masculinity and adopting rigid gender roles."²⁹ She explains such groups advocate for a "radical traditionalism" when it comes to gender roles and that their attempts to curtail women's rights make them "authoritarian at their core."[30]

Michael Kimmel interviewed white men across America for his book *Angry White Men* to try to understand their feelings of precarity and anger. "White men's anger is 'real'—that is, it is experienced deeply and sincerely. But it is not 'true'—that is, it doesn't provide an accurate analysis of their situation." He observes that, "The 'enemies' of white American men are not really women and men of color. Our enemy is an ideology of masculinity that we inherited from our fathers, and their fathers before them, an ideology that promises unparalleled acquisition coupled with a tragically impoverished emotional intelligence."[31] Kimmel uses the phrase "aggrieved entitlement" to characterize the feeling that one is owed something by virtue of their identity. "Angry white men tend to feel their sense of aggrieved entitlement because of the past; they want to restore what they *once had*. Their entitlement is not aspirational; it's nostalgic."[32] If boys are reared to expect the boyhood their father once had—or imagines he once had—they are being set up for disappointment. They become "young men whose inheritance has been seemingly stolen from them. They feel entitled and deprived—and furious."[33]

Authoritarianism can appeal to men and boys who feel aggrieved entitlement because it promises to restore order, to restore their place within the social hierarchy. Fascism, especially, is intently focused on promoting a hyperbolic and nationalized masculinity that promises power to men and boys who feel entitled to it. In a fascist system of governance, male authority extends from the structure of government to the structure of the military and workplace all the way down to the structure of the patriarchal household, which is its foundation. Feminism, in all of its waves over the past century and a half, has, bit by bit, critiqued and challenged male authority and the institutions that uphold it. Neofascist reassertion of patriarchal values is backlash against these gains by women. "Misogynistic post-feminism ranges from a prejudice and dislike of women, especially feminists, to structural and physical violence and overt expressions of hate."[34] Misogyny is not simply a feature of neofascism; it is foundational to neofascist thinking, policies, and organizational structures: Women must be put back into their place, shut up, locked up, and slapped into submission.

Michael Vavrus connects fascist misogyny to white supremacy: "The patriarchal far right in Europe and North America emphasized that the primary role of women should be mothers whose reproduction helps stem the 'replacement' of Whites by an increasingly ethnically diverse population."[35] The role of the white woman, in this scenario, is to maintain both racial purity and the patriarchy—she is the one who reproduces fascist ideology by reproducing. Feminists, who support things like reproductive rights and equal pay for women in the workforce, are a threat to this patriarchal family structure, especially when they ("childless cat ladies") refuse to reproduce it. In addition to feminism, movements for trans and gay rights also challenge the patriarchal hierarchy. The effeminate or feminist man, for example, threatens the idea of "natural" hypermasculinity. As Vavrus notes, "Heterosexual men who reflect a hypermasculine discourse resent and loathe men who fall outside the parameters of this intense form of masculinity and consider such men as effeminate and a danger to society."[36] The hypermasculine man of the far right is a fragile construct constantly under assault, and his masculinity must be continuously and strenuously performed and reinforced so that it appears to be "natural." In "The Fascist Cult of Masculinity," Jared Yates Sexton explains that the hypermasculinity of contemporary alt-right groups stems from an intense feeling of precarity: "An under-discussed aspect of fascism is its reliance on masculine insecurity. The story of authoritarianism is built on the foundation of creating a base of men who feel weak, powerless, and alone, and then co-opting that insecurity in order to fuel a large and violent movement."[37]

Theweleit argued that for twentieth-century fascists, fear of emasculation, of society being engulfed by feminine forces, led to the cultivation of hard, solid-seeming individual and social bodies. "The threat of the 'flood' may be combatted with 'erections': towering cities, mountains, troops, stalwart men, weapons."[38] He also noted an idealization of absent women or asexual nurses and the vilification of what he referred to as "red women": the whore, the open body, the sea that threatens to swallow a man whole. The disciplined troop, he explained, "produces an expression: of determination, strength, precision, of the strict order of straight lines and rectangles; an expression of battle, and of a specific masculinity."[39] The ideal male body of authoritarianism is solid, muscled, and impenetrable. Hypermasculinity emphasizes physical fitness and paramilitary activities as it venerates a virile, strongman leader as the head of state. "Fascist politics are unequivocally patriarchal and hypermasculine," writes Vavrus. "Hypermasculinity amplifies traditional masculinity and ignores differences among men by advancing an essentialized, one-dimensional conception of masculinity."[40] Those who subscribe to dominant masculinity ridicule "beta males," men who don't conform to this essentialized, "natural," masculinity, calling them "cucks," "losers," "soft," and worse in order to enforce gender conformity among all men, to police rigid boundaries between masculine and feminine, and to entrench the binaries central to a patriarchy.

Riot Grrls: *Moxie* and *Speak*

Children's books and toys are still marketed according to gender so that there are books *for* girls and books *for* boys, and reading in general is still viewed as a feminine or effeminate activity. One simple way to encourage boys to "identify" with or feel empathy for girls and women is to encourage them to read books, play games, or watch films with girl protagonists or fully fleshed-out female characters. Another is to share books and films that depict alternative versions of masculinity, ones where boys and men are allies to women and girls and/or ones where masculinity is defined in ways that are not hegemonic. As I'll discuss in the next section, in mass culture, white men and boys can see their perspective represented everywhere in video games, shows, YouTube videos, sports, news stories, and in books, a constant repetition of representation that can affect their sense of self. Because most of the popular stories in our culture are still told from the point of view of white boys and men, everyone else gets used to "identifying" with them, used to seeing the world through their perspective.

But it doesn't work the other way around, which is a shame: White boys in America, going all the way back to our founding, have hardly ever been asked to "identify" with anyone other than themselves in story after story that we tell ourselves about ourselves as a nation and as a culture. As a parent raising a white boy at the turn of the twenty-first century, when almost all of our pop culture heroes were white men—Luke Skywalker, Superman, Batman, Frodo, Neo, and, of course, Harry Potter—I had to work to find books, shows, and movies to share with my son that didn't center the white male experience. I ended up writing about this struggle in my first book, *Boys in Children's Literature and Popular Culture*, where I argued that popular hero stories, like Disney's *Tarzan*, were not preparing boys and young men for a feminist future. Although our culture has changed after waves of feminism, the hero monomyth has hung around, and what it has told generations of boys is that they are the center, the "norm," and that they are entitled to a destiny to fulfill and to a hero's boon.

Stories work to naturalize ideology through their narrative structure, not just through subject matter, which is why things like narrative point of view are important. Boys should be encouraged to watch shows or films or read books where characters like them are not always the focal point and where they can be encouraged to consider other points of view. In other words, if the only stories we share with boys are ones that tell them that they are the center of the story, the protagonist, the reason for every other character's existence, then they will come to believe those things about themselves. If we want to raise boys who don't feel entitled to more than their fair share of power, money, bodily autonomy, and civil rights, then we can't keep giving them a steady diet of stories that repeatedly make them the main character. Boys and men who want to be allies can read books that center a female point of view.

Books with female protagonists focused on the workings of the patriarchy can highlight the tangible effects of an oppressive system. They can help boys to understand their position in the patriarchy relative to others. Additionally, girls and women need books that help them to resist the patriarchy, to feel less alone, and to see their perspective represented, especially since girls and women are most often the principal victims of patriarchal hierarchies, prohibitions, and violence.[41] For example, Jennifer Mathieu's novel *Moxie* is about a group of girls who work together to challenge patriarchal systems in their small-town Texas high school where the football team is given free reign and girls are regularly subjected to sexist dress codes and hallway and classroom harassment. The novel's protagonist, Vivian, finds her mother's Riot Grrl zines from the 1990s and is inspired to create zines of her own, which she leaves in the girls' bathrooms. "I can visualize the Riot Grrls—my mother among them—walking the streets at night in their Doc Martens and their bad haircuts and their dark lipstick, ready to stand up for what they believed in. What they knew was right."[42] When the boys on the football team repeatedly tell girls who speak up in the class to "make me a sandwich," Vivian creates issue no. 1 of "Moxie Girls Fight Back" as a way to connect with other girls in her school. The novel highlights the way that small, everyday acts of aggression against girls accumulate to create an oppressive environment: Girls no longer raise their hands to participate in class discussions because they have been intimidated into silence. The patriarchy is depicted as a system maintained by both individuals and institutions: Boys on the football team, who feel empowered to grope girls in the hallways, are supported by teachers and parents who are football fans and by the institution of the school.

The boys on the football team perform hypermasculine behavior that, at its core, is misogynistic. For example, at a pep rally, one boy takes his football jersey off and underneath it he's wearing a t-shirt that reads, "GREAT LEGS—WHEN DO THEY OPEN." "'Gross,' I mutter. Jason is wearing the shirt in front of Coach Cole and Principal Wilson, but it won't matter. He can get away with it."[43] Most students at the pep rally are laughing as Jason gyrates at girls in the front row, but Vivian notices one girl getting increasingly uncomfortable. "Jason must get Lucy's disgust because he makes a point of gyrating his hips right up near her face, and she just looks away, down at the floor."[44] This event inspires Vivian to create the first issue of her *Moxie* zine, which asks, "Are you tired of the football team getting tons of attention & getting away with anything they want?"[45] The issue asks girls to draw hearts and stars on their hands so that they can "find girls who feel like you."[46] In this way, the zine works to organize individual girls into a loosely affiliated group able to take collective action.

Girls aren't just harassed by boys, they are also harassed by adult men in the school. For instance, the assistant principal enforces the school's dress code by making girls stand up for inspection in the middle of class. Girls found guilty of "wearing an outfit that could distract the boys"[47] must don oversized gym shirts for the rest of the school day. "This is bullshit," says Vivian's friend, Lucy. "Making girls monitor their behavior and appearance because boys are supposedly unable to control themselves? That is one of the oldest fucking tricks in the book."[48] In response to a week's worth of clothing inspections, Vivian uses her zine to organize a protest where girls show up to school wearing bathrobes: "If a teacher asks you why tell them you're playing it safe so you don't distract our poor male students!"[49] The novel models acts of civil disobedience that originate from the girls, a bottom-up, collective resistance.

Moxie depicts hypermasculine boys as harmful, but it also creates a space for boys and men to participate as allies. After a girl is assaulted at a party, reports the assault to the administration, and is rebuffed, she asks students to participate in a walk-out to protest violence against women: "If you support this walkout you support all girls. You support a movement."[50] About half of the school's girls walk out and so do a few of the boys, including Vivian's boyfriend: "When he sees me looking at him, he nods. Then he gives me a thumbs-up, which is the corniest thing he's ever done."[51] In this way, the novel models ways for boys to reject hypermasculinity, to be allies to girls and women, and to help to dismantle patriarchal systems of power.

In *Moxie*, girls build community by making zines and organizing creative protests, and in the novel *Speak*, by Laurie Halse Anderson, girls create community through sports and by writing about their experiences with sexual assault in a stall in the girl's bathroom. The main character, Melinda, was raped by an older boy named Andy Evans. Although she's unable to speak to anyone about her rape, Melinda writes "Guys to stay away from: Andy Evans" on the door of a bathroom stall. Days later other girls have added comments like "Stay away!," "He should be locked up," and "Call the cops": "There's more," Melinda notes when she sees the conversation, "Different pens, different handwriting, conversations between some writers, arrows to longer paragraphs. It's better than taking out a billboard. I feel like I can fly."[52] Being raped silences Melinda, who spends much of the school year hiding in a janitor's closet. Connecting with and communicating with other girls helps her to heal and to find her voice.

Although Melinda must share high school hallways with her rapist and she is harassed by a male teacher throughout much of the novel, there are also male characters who model being mentors and allies. Melinda's art teacher helps her to express and work through her trauma in various art projects, and he is the first adult she is able to speak to about her rape. She also has a friend, David Petrakis, who helps her to find her voice: "The suffragettes were all about speaking up, screaming for their rights," he tells her. "Don't expect to make a difference unless you speak up for yourself."[53] Texts like *Speak* and *Moxie* counter the messages boys and young men receive in a culture that is saturated with hypermasculine constructions of manhood.

Policing the Borders:
The Hypermasculine in Convergence Culture

Andrew "Cobra" Tate is a cigar-smoking, fast-talking internet influencer whose content on TikTok and other streaming sites has been viewed by millions of people around the world. Some of his biggest fans are boys and young men. A former professional kickboxer, he advocates for traditional, hard-bodied masculinity, urges his followers to free themselves from a "slave mentality," and claims that women are less intelligent than men, need to be subservient to men, and are their husband's property. He's been banned from several social media sites and is, as of this writing, facing charges in Romania for sex trafficking, which means his fame and influence may be short-lived. But, in the early 2020s at least, he was a role model for many boys in the United States.

In an article including interviews with several teachers who expressed alarm over Tate's influence over their students, Lindsay Dodgson and Bethany Dawson explain that "Tate's primary audience is impressionable teenage boys, many of whom have started picking up on his sexist statements and views. Tate's influence affects how preteen boys see the world—particularly how they perceive women. And these views have not stayed confined to a TikTok audience; they've been steadily seeping into homes and classrooms."[54] Teachers interviewed for the article report that boys as young as 11 are echoing Tate's catchphrases and philosophies and harassing female teachers and classmates. One teacher said, "Students are being mystified by people like Andrew Tate to believe that the majority of their teachers are useless because they're female."[55] Another article quotes a teacher noting that some of her Tate-influenced eleven-year-olds are telling rape jokes. Madeline Will writes that, "Experts say preteen boys are particularly susceptible to Tate's brand of toxic masculinity. Teachers across the world, including in the United States, have shared on social media that they've seen an uptick in male students repeating sexist vitriol in class to get a rise from their classmates and teachers."⁵⁶ One teacher even said she felt threatened when a student repeatedly asked her about Tate.

It's easy to dismiss Tate's popularity among boys as a passing fad, which it may well be, but it is a significant fad because it is part of a pattern and part of an ideology being created through a web of related texts. There have always been depictions of hypermasculine men in film, literature, and art, but now, in our media-saturated environment, one can consume a steady diet of them. Muscular protagonists punch, kick, and shoot their way through thinly plotted films, series, and video games that are often told in the familiar and comfortable form of the hero monomyth. Even though waves of feminism have significantly affected the roles and identities available to girls in the literature and popular culture created for them, boys are still, for the most part, given texts that depict twentieth-century versions of hegemonic masculinity. In other words, contemporary boys are being prepared to enter a traditionally masculine manhood that exists largely in the past rather than learning to adapt to a culture that's been changed by recent feminist movements.

There's no shortage of muscular heroes in popular culture, especially in action movies and video games that feature hypermasculine protagonists. Kimmel explains the allure and popularity of such power fantasies, writing,

> What if some white guys, moved to righteous anger, can single-handedly halt an alien invasion, a horde of zombies, a crowd of vampires, or a brilliantly coordinated band of terrorists? What if I play some first-person-shooter video game and can wipe out the entire terrorist conspiracy with only my biceps, an assault weapon that never runs out of ammunition, and the ability to jump onto roofs from a standing position three stories below?⁵⁷

Boys and young men are invited through such texts to embody and identify with the hypermasculine hero, who is still at the center of many such narratives. The original twentieth-century stories that serve as the foundation for franchises like *Star Wars, Harry Potter,* and the Marvel Universe are based on the hero monomyth, in which the white, young, male protagonist goes on a quest, surmounts a series of challenges, and defeats an evil foe. Such hero narratives, dating back to Hercules, Gilgamesh, Beowulf, and King Arthur are steeped in patriarchal values and glorify violence and hypermasculinity. In *Deconstructing the Hero: Literary Theory and Children's Literature*, Marjorie Hourihan notes that the men in such narratives perform a stereotypical, exaggerated version of hard-bodied masculinity that "redefine[s] 'male' to exclude virtually all human qualities except strength, violence and aggression. Even in more benign works the conventions of stereotyped masculinity are endlessly reinscribed."⁵⁸

The traditional hero narrative in its various forms, reifies, through repetition, a version of hegemonic masculinity that defines itself in opposition to the feminine, both women and effeminate men. His journey, though, is presented as "universal," as the unmarked norm, as *the* story of man moving into his preordained position as a leader of his people. This may explain why even minor deviations from the traditional hero narrative in pop culture texts are met with resistance and even hostility.

With streaming available in many homes, adults, teens and children often watch the same films and television shows and play the same video games, a number of which are based on the hero narrative. While all of these texts might not be "child appropriate," they are widely consumed by audiences of all ages, especially popular franchises. As a result, the same red, white, and blue circular shield that comes with Captain America Halloween costumes for kids adorns the shelves of adult comics fans. Interestingly, the shield is also a symbol that was worn on T-shirts of adult men storming the US Capitol on January 6, 2021. Dan Spinelli writes about alt-right fans of the Marvel hero that, "Here was a superhero who was conceived as anti-fascist propaganda being appropriated by the supporters of a racist bully who, unable to accept his decisive election loss, had encouraged his supporters to storm the seat of government and stage a putsch."[59] The iconic red, white, and blue shield and the hypermasculine character carry a diverse set of meanings for various audience constituencies, both child and adult. The superhero's role as part of a wide-ranging convergence culture text—fans can access stories about Captain America via films, various fan cultures, or decades' worth of comics—means that the meaning of the character is both iconic and diffused, both set and malleable; he is at once a symbol for democracy and for authoritarianism, the very contradictions inherent in our nation's founding and history.

Members of alt-right groups who are fans of popular culture narratives actively participate in cultural battles in online spaces as a way of either appropriating icons or hijacking popular narratives they deem insufficiently masculine or white. These debates focus largely on narratives that are popular with boys and men: action films, video games, and superhero films that, up until very recently, were stories populated almost exclusively by casts of white men. Because these popular all-ages stories are convergence culture narratives, their repetition is endless: Fans can read comics and books, play video games, watch and rewatch films and spin-offs, participate in fan discussion forums and wikis, and view fan-created videos and memes, all of which can lead to a feeling of ownership of a particular narrative or character. The stories cross multiple platforms as they are retold and expanded in various formats by both media corporations and fans. As parents share their childhood favorites with their children, multigenerational audiences follow multigenerational casts of characters across sequels and prequels as labyrinthian plots intertwine the stories of fictional children, siblings, parents, and ancestors. Depending on one's point of view, adult films have become children's entertainment or adults are indulging in children's texts: the first is sometimes met with alarm, the second with disdain. In reality, texts like those in the *Harry Potter,* Marvel and *Star Wars* universes are for both adults and children; they are "crossover" narratives with layers of meaning aimed at various sets of readers or viewers.[60]

As these decades-long narratives spread out into convergence culture texts that include active and vocal fan communities, battles over interpretation can become ideological battles. For instance, in an *Esquire* essay Dom Nero discusses the ways in which the alt-right has come to dominate debates about more recent films in the *Star Wars* series, which have increasingly diverse casts:

> Since the earliest promos for *The Force Awakens*, members of this testosterone-fueled community have flooded the internet with their regressive criticisms that *Star Wars* seems to no longer be a white male-led franchise. In spite of virtually every movie in the new Disney iteration of the series being headlined by white actors, with white men dotting out almost every frame of the films, many fans feel that there is a "social justice warrior" or "liberal" conspiracy within the new *Star Wars* films.[61]

The alt-right may be a minority in these fan communities, but they are an enthusiastic and vocal minority known for verbally abusing and even threatening female fans and cast members. In an article about sexist attacks on female gamers and fans, Ian Sherr and Erin Carson explain that, "According to the trolls, instead of burning bras or abandoning their homes, as feminists were accused of doing decades ago, an SJW [social justice warrior] wants to force the video game industry to adhere to new, politically correct standards the trolls believe will ultimately ruin everything that makes video games fun."[62] While girls and women are accustomed to and expected to "identify" with male characters, boys typically aren't expected to read books, play games, or enjoy films with female protagonists. Outrage over diverse casts comes from boys and men who are rarely asked to identify with characters unlike themselves.

Members of the alt-right are especially active in defending their favorite heroes against what they see as an incursion of political correctness: women cast in traditionally male roles and people of color cast in roles traditionally held by white actors. Hourihan writes of hero narratives that "one reason for their appeal is their very predictability: The formula to which they conform is so familiar that they present no challenge to the reader's interpretive or critical skills."⁶³ These formulaic texts also don't challenge a reader's ideology. They maintain social order. The hero story presents readers with the comfort of familiarity and the certainty that "good will triumph over evil," however vaguely these are defined. Changes in casting, either in comics or on film, disrupt this comfortable identification. As a result, "Right-wing activists called on moviegoers to skip 'Ghostbusters,' 'Wonder Woman,' 'Black Panther,' 'Aquaman,' 'Mad Max: Fury Road' and the four newest 'Star Wars' films—all films in which the lead wasn't a white man,'"⁶⁴ writes Bethany Lacina. She explains that the alt-right's engagement with popular culture is a way to find new recruits: "Criticisms of popular culture are an entry point to the alt-right, offering fun subject matter and a jokey culture that obscures commentators' far-right politics. People with extreme alt-right ideals build camaraderie with newcomers who do not yet share their views."⁶⁵

Another reason members of alt-right groups complain about their favorite stories being "ruined" is because many of them have co-opted characters or symbols from their favorite franchises. They have invested emotional capital into "identifying" with the hero, who shares and perhaps even represents their values and worldview. According to Corinne Engber, "Since outright display of Nazi symbols is generally frowned upon, neo-Nazis rely on a multitude of coded icons, gestures and objects to indicate their alliance."⁶⁶ Symbols from Norse mythology, American history, and Nazi iconography are combined with icons from popular culture to create makeshift uniforms. "Among the MAGA hats, Don't Tread on Me flags and Trump 2020 banners on display during the January 6 invasion of the Capitol, were also logos and images belonging to various comic book characters. One of the most popular was the Punisher's signature white on black skull emblem, which cropped up on patches, shirts and flags."⁶⁷ The Punisher, a vigilante character who avenges his dead family, is a favorite among members of the alt-right who don his symbol, a menacing skull with long teeth. "The Punisher's mythos (as is the case with many white male characters) originates when he loses his family to organized crime. After an extensive cover-up by the NYPD, the Punisher becomes a vigilante. But, unlike Batman, another brooding figure, the Punisher has no qualms about using violence. It is easy to understand, then, why a violent neo-Nazi movement would be drawn to him."⁶⁸ His loss of family signifies a (temporary) loss of status as patriarch, which he has to earn back through violence. It's a perfect metaphor for men who feel precarious, as if a status they are owed has been taken away from them. In narratives like the Punisher, vigilante violence is justified and celebrated because vengeance is the Punisher's hypermasculine response to being emasculated. In popular culture vigilante justice is often administered by a white man who is avenging a dead woman, family, or, in the case of John

Wick, a pet. In films like *Gladiator* and the original *Mad Max* the dead women who are being avenged are idealized, silent, pure, and frozen in time after their death. The violence that follows is justified as an act of love by a hero who now, conveniently, is unencumbered by feminine influence.

As mentioned above, another favorite of the alt-right is Captain America, a hypermasculine hero of a different sort. The character of Captain America was created more than eighty years ago by Joe Simon and Jack Kirby. In the comic, a skinny, though determined Steve Rogers is transformed into a muscular super soldier as part of a government experiment. "Rogers, the creation of two Jewish comics legends, was an anti-fascist symbol of American might, willing to fight Hitler nine months before the United States even entered World War II."[69] Issue no. 1 featured a cover image of him punching Hitler.[70] While Captain America has been a fixture of Marvel comics through much of the late twentieth century, he was brought back into the popular culture spotlight with leading roles in action films set in the Marvel universe. Aja Romano writes that,

> To the right, the character represents national pride, faithful military service, and American power. To the left, he's a staunch protector of the people, dedicated to fighting fascism and white supremacy. Across the ideological spectrum, inflamed citizens are seeking solace and inspiration, and have held up the beloved superhero as a touchstone for their own values—and their very different views of what America should be.[71]

As complex storylines and characters are watered down and simplified in blockbuster films, they become icons, empty containers that carry a wide range of ideologies. Their status as convergence culture texts makes their meaning malleable so that once they are appropriated in particular contexts and subcultures, their meaning shifts. It may no longer be possible to recoup Captain America or the Punisher from their entanglements with the alt-right. Marvel has tried to assert copyright infringement, but with limited success.

Ultimately, the history and the very structure of hero narratives may mean that these cannot be extricated from patriarchal values. Hourihan challenged the universality of the hero story by marking the characteristics of the hero that go unmarked, his identities as white, Western, male, young, and heterosexual. "Whether it is *The Odyssey*, *Jack and the Beanstalk*, *Treasure Island*, *Doctor Who*, *Star Wars*, the latest James Bond thriller, or *Where the Wild Things Are*, the hero story takes the form of a journey and follows an invariable pattern" where the hero must venture into the wilderness, defeat monstrous others, and return home with a boon.[72] Other characters in the story—companions, the monsters to be defeated, the girl he avenges or saves—are part of the narrative only in relation to the hero, only in the role they play in helping him to achieve his quest. The hero story presents readers with the comfort of familiarity, and it is so engrained in Western culture that challenging it challenges deeply entrenched values, which is why changes to it are met with resistance.

Superman Smashes the Klan But Not the Hero Narrative

Is the hero narrative, because of its history and embedded ideology, a form that can be used to encourage anti-fascist thinking? Does it always, necessarily, reinforce patriarchal values? Because it is so familiar and comfortable, maybe it can also be a site where fascist values can be addressed and perhaps challenged. For example, in an ode to the first issue of Captain America, Gene Yang's 2020 graphic novel *Superman Smashes the Klan* begins with an image of Superman punching a Nazi, a villain named Atom Man who wears a swastika prominently displayed on his chest.[73] The graphic novel begins with this violent and iconic image, starting from the place of the comfortable, recognizable hero narrative. The main plot of the graphic novel, though, focuses on a Chinese American family that moves into a white neighborhood in Metropolis and is terrorized by the Ku Klux Klan. The Klan burns a cross in their yard while the Grand Scorpion says to fellow Klan members, "My fellow knights, I warned you that these non-Americans would not be satisfied with their own filthy corners of our city. Sooner or later, they would crawl out to infest our law enforcement, our government, and our very neighborhoods."[74] The words "crawl" and "infest" are a way to mark immigrants as being less than human and to associate them with vermin. Having these words spoken by a character who is clearly a villain reveals the nefarious way white supremacists construct Others as animal-like and less-than-human.

As is the case with many a comic book villain, the Klan members clearly announce their evil plans and the racist beliefs that fuel their villainy. For instance, a Klan leader tells his nephew, "I'm taking you to a meeting tonight. We're going to make sure that folks like you and me aren't **replaced** ever again."[75] The word "replaced" is in bold, which highlights for readers white supremacists' fear of being replaced by minorities and the racist undertones of a word commonly used on the Right. In a confrontation between Superman and the Grand Scorpion, the Klansman explains that his group's guiding principle is "the conviction that a **strong** America is a **pure** America [. . .] When push comes to shove, you cannot unite a **nation** of people who share neither **blood** nor **history**. And as much as you want to deny it, Superman, you are one of us!"[76] Each word highlighted in bold letters is a part of white supremacist rhetoric:

An authoritarian nation is defined by the unity and purity of its people, who are bonded through a shared blood and shared history. Significantly, the Grand Scorpion is not wrong in noting that Superman is "one of us," a fellow white man. Superman responds, saying he is not like the members of the Klan, and the Grand Scorpion tells him, "You're **living proof** of just how **superior** a **white man** can be!" Superman's response to this announcement is to toss the Grand Scorpion into the trunk of a car without saying anything. He never directly addresses the claim that he, as a character, is indeed an example of the whiteness and hypermasculinity that characterizes most superheroes. On one hand, he models being an ally but, on the other, he takes on the role of "white savior." It's a moment of tension in the graphic novel that is never resolved but, in many ways, Superman isn't the main focus of the story.

The character of Chuck, the nephew of the Klan's Grand Scorpion, is the character who undergoes the most transformation, and he represents an alternative to white hypermasculinity. As his uncle tries to shape him into a Klan member, Chuck resists in small ways. For instance, when his uncle orders him to throw a Molotov cocktail into the window of the Lee family's home, Chuck purposely misses.[77] Chuck also questions his uncle's characterization of the Klan saying, "I-I read about this at school . . . isn't this a group of hateful **bigots**?!" His uncle responds with, "**Lies** perpetuated by **corrupt** newspapers and textbooks! We don't hate anyone, Chuck. On the contrary, we are motivated by love—Love of Our Nation! A nation will crumble to dust unless its people are united as **one**."[78] This exchange performs common talking points for members of contemporary white supremacist groups, who cloak their racism in patriotism and calls for national unity. It also provides an example of a young man, a teenager, who pushes back against the toxic masculine role that is being forced upon him and who challenges the authority of a patriarch in his community.

Throughout the graphic novel, the Klan members repeat the creed, "One race! One color! One religion!," which reveals the white supremacists' need to create a solid-seeming social body that must be protected from diversity. White allies like Superman are mocked for "betraying" their race: "Ha! Ha! You've been **brainwashed** by corrupt newspapers and textbooks, Superman!" the Klan leader says when Superman defends the Lee family. "The Lees aren't '**your own**'! You share no **blood** with them! No **history**! There is literally nothing that binds you together! [. . .] A nation bound by nothing **cannot last!**"[79] Superman responds, saying he is bound to the Lees and other members of their community through shared values, through affinities: "We are bound together by the **future**. We all share the same **tomorrow**."[80] By linking all of our fates together, Superman represents an alternative to the individualism of hypermasculinity and to the conformity required by fascism. He is connected to the Lees by his background as an alien: Through flashbacks, we see him taunted by other children for being different. This experience, the text implies, creates affinities, empathy based in commonalities in experience, identity, and worldview. Superman is still the hard-bodied superhero he's been for more than eighty years but his choice to align himself with people considered to be Other and his rejection of white supremacist ideology mark him, at least in this adaptation, as an ally, someone who uses their position of privilege to dismantle the white supremacist patriarchy rather than uphold it.

As is the case with *Indian No More* (discussed in Chapter 2), the supplementary materials included in an afterword provide significant insight that contextualizes the story and its retelling. An afterword titled "Superman and Me," places the graphic novel within its historical context in mid-twentieth-century America, both in terms of the history of Superman and the history of the Ku Klux Klan. Yang, who worked as a teacher before becoming a cartoonist, uses the afterword to educate young readers about the history of Klan: "These men believed in white supremacy, the idea that people from Western and Northern Europe are just plain better than all other kinds of people."[81] He explains that by the end of the Civil War, Chinese people made up around 10 percent of the population in California, something seen as threatening by the Klan. "The terrorism in the West was never as widespread nor as organized as the terrorism in the South, but it was still terrifying," he writes, citing the example of a mob that "hanged to death between seventeen and twenty Chinese men and boys" in Los Angeles's Chinatown. The graphic novel highlights America's long history of authoritarianism, the way in which non-whites have not had access to the same freedoms or rights afforded to white people, and the ways in which minority groups have often endured violence in a white supremacist culture.

Yang explains how he based his graphic novel on a wildly popular sixteen-part radio story that aired in 1946. To avoid being sued by the Klan, creators renamed the terrorist group depicted in the series "The Clan of the Fiery Cross." For weeks, "listeners across America huddled around their radios to listen as young Tommy Lee, his father Dr. Lee, and his unnamed mother and sister moved into Metropolis and ran afoul of a group of violent bigots. They cheered when Superman leapt to the family's defense."[82] The popularity of the show, Yang writes, may even had led to the downfall of the Klan's public image: "After being portrayed as bumbling, hateful rubes on a children's show, the Ku Klux Klan would never again command the same level of respect it had once enjoyed."[83] By reimagining an anti-fascist story from America's past, Yang highlights the way American popular culture can work both with the grain of dominant ideology and against it.

Non-Hegemonic Masculinities: *All Boys Aren't Blue*

George M. Johnson's "memoir-manifesto" for young adults, *All Boys Aren't Blue*, (see Fig. 4) begins with an introduction titled "Black. Queer. Here," immediately centering the story and the perspective of a male hero who is "Other." In clear and direct language, Johnson describes growing up as an effeminate Black boy. "I was *very* sassy as a little kid," Johnson explains. "A *sissy* is what the kids used to call me back then, before they got older and escalated to the word *faggot*."[84] Johnson was teased because he played with girls on the playground and picked up their mannerisms and language. He cites an example of he and the girls using the word "honeychild." "Adults began to wonder why a boy would be saying a word so 'feminine',"[85] he writes of efforts to police his queer identity. His teacher called his mother to ask her to tell him to stop using the word, which shows how women also participate in the maintenance of hegemonic masculinity. Significantly, he notes that, "I've lived enough to know that today's adults are still uncomfortable with boys who do anything not considered 'masculine'."[86] Johnson reflects, from the distance of an adult looking back, the ways his sexuality and performance of masculinity were constantly policed by adults and by other children too, explaining that, "So the adults in my life dictated what masculinity would look like for me. It was also their responsibility to ensure that the person I was, this 'sissy,' didn't influence other children—as if my being who I was would change who others were."[87] His queerness isn't just an expression of identity distinct to him—it threatens to engulf other children as well, like an infection, a disease introduced to the social body, a rupture that reveals heteronormativity to be the construct that it is.

All Boys Aren't Blue has been near the top of banned books lists in the United States since its publication, which is yet more evidence of adults trying to dictate the gender and sexuality of young people, trying to stave off the flood that threatens compulsory heteronormativity and, by extension, the patriarchy. According to PEN America, 41 percent of banned books in 2022 were about people of color and 33 percent were about LGBTQ+ themes. *All Boys Aren't Blue* is both, which makes it a prime target for censors.[88] As I discussed earlier, what makes these contemporary book bans even more alarming is how they have been coordinated at a national level. Groups like Moms for Liberty provide parents with book lists and sample questions that they can use to ask school authorities about subjects like preferred pronouns or whether transgender girls can use the girls' bathroom. The assumption is that heterosexuality and cisgender identity are the norm, and therefore go unmarked. Representations, like those in *All Boys Aren't Blue*, which go against this norm by challenging rigid gender roles and making their construction visible, are especially

Figure 4. The cover of *All Boys Aren't Blue: A Memoir Manifesto* by George M. Johnson.

threatening to those parents who seek to police the identity of their and other people's children, who want to reassert "family values" and existing social hierarchies through compulsory heterosexuality.

All Boys Aren't Blue asks its reader to identify with an anti-hero, a boy who doesn't fit into the mold of the hero monomyth and whose story doesn't conform to existing formulas. The memoir chronicles the author's struggles being a queer child, teen, and young man, an identity that put him at odds with his culture. "I had a longing to be perfect. To be right. To be in line with the societal norm. As much as I wanted to lead an openly gay life, I also didn't want to be a disappointment,"[89] he explains as he chronicles his experiences of coming out, of feeling pressured to conform to the storyline expected of him. "Notice my varying confidence and discouragement throughout this chapter. Notice my confusion in how strong I was in some moments and how weak I was in others, because that is what coming out truly is."[90] Johnson is emotionally aware throughout the memoir, even in his descriptions of his first awkward sexual encounters, which are also the scenes that draw the most ire from censors. He explains that he includes these frank discussions for the young queer people who are reading his book, who may not have been able to discuss their sexuality with others. "I often imagine what my first sexual experiences would have been like had I been given the ability to learn about what queer sex was when all my straight friends and classmates got to learn about what it looked like for them," he writes. "My queer sexuality was one big, risky crash course, much like the other aspects of my queer existence."[91] The reader he imagines is a young person like he was, who is not the "norm," who does not conform to hegemonic masculinity, and who does not see themselves or their perspective represented in mainstream narratives. Johnson explains that his memoir/manifesto is meant to serve as an example for younger people who are in situations similar to his: "I wanted to become the person that future Black queer folks could look to and know that their masculinity could be defined on their own terms."[92] Johnson constructs himself and his story as examples that challenge—through their "sassy" existence—the hegemonic masculinity that is central to neofascism. Significantly, he refers to his readers as future "Black queer folks," a choice of words that includes children, teens, young adults, and adults too. His writing is clear, his approach direct, like he's sharing vital information that queer young people need in order to survive, stories from which to learn.

The further one is from hegemonic white masculinity—and it's a spectrum, there is no either/or here, no "us" versus "them," not simply two kinds of masculine human—but, the further away one is from hegemonic masculinity, from access to the Phallus, the less likely they are to ever see their point of view represented: Pecola Breedlove, a trans child in some deep red state, a pregnant thirteen-year-old in a rural town in Texas, an unhoused queer kid living on the street in Chicago. These are the young people who will be crushed under the big black boot of neofascism, the Others, the queer, the untouchables, the undocumented, the underclass. The next chapter focuses on stories told from such neglected points of view, from the vantage point of "Others" who, as Elise McMullen-Ciotti put it, don't often "get the microphone."

4
From Margin to Center: An(Other) Point of View

> The dangers of fascist politics come from the particular way in which it dehumanizes segments of the population. By excluding these groups, it limits the capacity for empathy among other citizens, leading to the justification of inhumane treatment, from repression of freedom, mass imprisonment, and expulsion to, in extreme cases, mass extermination.
> —JASON STANLEY, *How Fascism Works: The Politics of Us and Them.*[1]

In the picture book, *The Monster at the End of this Book*, "loveable, furry old Grover" leads us on a metafictive journey of self-discovery. Grover, our narrator and fellow reader, reads the book's title and learns there is going to be a monster at the book's end, a terrifying prospect because Grover, one of the childlike Muppet monsters familiar to children who have watched *Sesame Street*, is terrified of monsters. He anxiously asks the child reader to stop reading: "Maybe you do not understand. You see, turning pages will bring us to the end of this book."[2] The playful and performative back-and-forth created by Grover's melodramatic antics—tying down pages, nailing pages together, desperately yelling "You turned another page!"—create subversive fun for the child reader who knows that silly Grover has no need to be afraid because Grover *is* the monster at both the beginning and the end of the book. This sense of dramatic irony, knowing more than the character/narrator, gives early readers a sense of power and control and makes turning the page into a daring and pleasurable act. Getting young readers excited about the act of reading is of course the point, but the book also comments on the relationship between the self and an Other, me and not me, human and monster. In other words, the idea that it is silly to be afraid of oneself can apply to humans as well: Would we be afraid to meet a human at the end of a book? What if we believed that human to be a monster?

In her analysis of *The Monster at the End of this Book*, children's literature scholar Megan L. Musgrave notes that, "From a posthuman perspective, a text like this one playfully invites readers to recognize that they are both Grover and not-Grover; they are the monster, the protagonist, and the antagonist all at once. Interacting with a text that simultaneously positions readers to align themselves with Grover and against him invites wonderfully rich deconstruction of the boundaries between self and other."[3] Posthumanist thinkers seek to deconstruct the boundaries that define "human" in terms of its opposition to Others who have been categorized as non-human, sub-human, monstrous, or animal. These Others, through their difference from it, are used to delineate the white, heterosexual, adult, able-bodied man, the human at the center of Western culture. Fascism, an extreme version of the white supremacist patriarchy, is grounded in such oppositional binaries—man/woman, self/other, white/black, insider/outsider, citizen/foreigner—that separate a population into an "us" and a "them," "we the people" against outsiders, illegals, and "enemies from within." As Stanley points out, fascist othering is pernicious because it can lead to the "justification of inhumane treatment, from repression of freedom, mass imprisonment, and expulsion to, in extreme cases, mass extermination."

Social scientists have found that authoritarian-minded people will often fear outsiders, immigrants, minorities, and other groups of people who are marked as Other, as cultural outsiders. Fascist leaders prey upon these fears by continuously constituting the borders that define a narrowly constructed homogenous social body, thus creating a unified "us" defined against and in opposition to "them." Amanda Taub writes that, "authoritarians are much more susceptible to messages that tell them to fear a specific 'other'—whether or not they have a preexisting animus against that group."[4] Fascist leaders gain power by amplifying fears of the Other, creating scapegoats, giving form to vague unease, and assigning blame for societal ills to groups already considered suspect. "Authoritarianism appeals, simply, to people who cannot tolerate complexity," writes Anne Applebaum. "It is anti-pluralist. It is suspicious of people with different ideas."[5] In Nazi Germany, the list of Others grew to include not only Jews but the Roma people and other ethnic groups, members of the LGBTQ+ community, Jehovah's Witnesses, and the disabled. In the contemporary United States, the Others currently being vilified by the Right include people of color, people with disabilities, Indigenous people, Muslims, Jews, members of the LGBTQ+ community, people who are unhoused, and immigrants.

Such constructions of Others create hierarchies when one group views itself as more deserving of human rights than the groups of Others it defines itself against. Alexa Wright notes that humans are constructed as being Other through hierarchies of race, sexuality, gender, or physical ability:

> Culturally and socially, the relationship between self and other is a hierarchical one, based on a need to justify and sustain existing power relations. Racial, sexual, or physically deformed "others" have so often been subordinated to the image of the straight, white, "rational," and able-bodied European male, which in Western culture has traditionally been the standard by which all "others" are judged.[6]

The most privileged positions in Western culture, like whiteness and heterosexuality, are the ones that often go unmarked because they are viewed as the norm against which others are compared. When these positions of power are threatened—women are elected to public office or minorities play leading roles in Hollywood films—Others are viewed as usurping power, and they become targets.

Othering is a complex concept because we all must distinguish between ourselves and Others, between what is "me" and what is "not me" in order to establish and maintain a sense of self. Children enter into the Symbolic Order through this recognition, and the acts of speaking, writing, and other forms of communication assume a split between self and Other. A distinction between authoritarian and non-authoritarian ways of thinking, then, comes not merely in the acknowledgement that there is a self and an Other; it lies in the characterization of one's relationship to Others. Are Others viewed as fellow humans, or are they viewed as wholly separate, as less-than-human, as abject or as monstrous? In his post-World War II essay attempting to understand and define antisemitism, Jean Paul Sartre explains that, "There is a disgust for the Jew, just as there is a disgust for the Chinese or the Negro among certain people,"[7] and that this feeling of disgust for Others is key to prejudice and discrimination. Similarly, in *Modernity and the Holocaust*, Zygmunt Bauman argues that antisemitism requires a "boundary which ought to be clearly drawn and kept intact and impregnable; and the intensity of antisemitism is most likely to remain proportional to the urgency and ferocity of the boundary-drawing and boundary defining drive."[8] Books aimed at younger readers can reveal and interrogate this process of "boundary-drawing," or they can participate in it.

One extreme example of a children's book that encouraged child readers to dehumanize Others and that instilled feelings of disgust, was *The Poisonous Mushroom*, published in Germany in 1938. It is a picture book that prompts young readers to view Jewish people as monstrous cultural outsiders. At the book's beginning, an Aryan mother asks her cherubic son, "Who are these bad men, these poisonous mushrooms of mankind?" to which he dutifully responds, "They are the Jews! Our teacher has often told us about them."[9] The picture book presents a series of vignettes meant to teach child readers that the Jew is fundamentally different from Christians: threatening and subhuman. For example, it shows children how they can identify a Jewish man because of his hooked nose, his "louse infested" beard, his bent legs, and his flat feet. The illustrations are caricatures and depict a Jewish tailor swindling people, a Jewish man tempting children with sweets, and a Jewish doctor with lascivious intents on his young, female patient. *The Poisonous Mushroom* demonstrates the way that some children's literature can reflect and encourage the most pernicious of authoritarian worldviews: that "we" are humans and those different from us are not.

Fascism insists on firmly drawn boundaries surrounding a uniform population, with clearly marked distinctions between who is outside and who is in. A firm border must be established between a homogenous citizenry and those who are seen as outside of these bounds because they are immigrant, transgender, Black, or queer. The "republic" imagined by American neofascists would be one that empowers a narrow group of citizens while disempowering others. In a nation becoming increasingly diverse, many white people are fearful of losing majority status, of being "replaced" by growing numbers of immigrants and people of color, which means that othering is also motivated by fear of a loss of one's status. Newer children's books depicting diverse cultures and perspectives pose a threat because they are "replacing" the canon and they are expanding the definition of "human." Parents who read *Catcher in the Rye* and *The Outsiders* as young people may view books like *The Hate U Give* or *All Boys Aren't Blue* as threats (and targets for censorship) because they challenge existing hierarchies by creating a space for Others to speak, which unsettles existing binaries.

Over the past few years, the Right's enmity toward children's and adolescent literature that challenges the status quo has become mainstream: This antagonism has emerged in challenges around the nation against books focused on combatting racism, homophobia, and transphobia. The Right also protests against the teaching of critical race theory in schools or drag queen story hours at libraries, which pose a double threat because they humanize the Others who are reading books to children. While such protests may seem to originate from concerned parents, these efforts are often deliberate and coordinated, coming from well-funded think tanks and organizations, and not merely from grassroots movements. For example, in 2021 the Heritage Foundation released a guide for parents titled "How to Identify Critical Race Theory," which alerts parents to look out for terms like "white privilege," "systemic racism," and "equity" that may seem benign but that all fall under the umbrella of dreaded critical race theory.[10] Well-funded and well-educated members of the Right, who know exactly what critical race theory actually is and is not, are redefining the phrase as a way to teach their followers to reject any kind of anti-racist teaching and anti-racist works of children's and young adult literature.

Some segments of the Right in the United States are so threatened by children's books that teach an acceptance of difference that they have created their own niche market of books meant to teach right-wing points of view. Michelle Ann Abate, in her book *Raising Your Kids Right: Children's Literature and American Political Conservatism,* chronicles the recent proliferation of conservative children's literature made possible by niche marketing on the internet and self-publishing technologies.[11] She found that, "While books for young readers have always been, to greater or lesser degrees, conservative in nature, some titles that began appearing during the latter half of the twentieth century greatly amplified those traits."[12] She also connects this successful cottage industry to a rise in literature written for the education of children increasingly being home-schooled or moved, through school choice, into charter or private schools that favor conservative ideas and avoid subjects like evolution, sex education, or climate change. More recently, Rebecca Klein examined several textbooks used in thousands of private schools around the country, and found that they "teach that President Barack Obama helped spur destructive Black Lives Matter protests, that the Democrats' choice of 2016 nominee Hillary Clinton reflected their focus on identity politics, and that President Donald Trump is the 'fighter' Republicans want."[13] These textbooks, she found, encourage fear with claims that the United States is in the midst of cultural decline that can only be remedied through right-leaning Christian nationalism.

A recent example of this publishing phenomenon is a series of picture books written by Eric Metaxas and illustrated by Tim Raglin: *Donald Builds the Wall, Donald and the Fake News,* and *Donald Drains the Swamp.*[14] It's not clear whether these are books written specifically for children or whether they are children's books for adults. In each book, a cartoon version of Donald Trump is depicted as a grinning caveman draped in an American flag and carrying a club inscribed with the words "We the people."[15] Donald's followers are "The Free People" and their enemies, Others whose status as outsiders the books work to reify, are people who don't love freedom: swamp creatures and caravans of immigrants. The swamp creatures are depicted as dinosaur-like monsters and their leader is George-o-saurus, a clear reference to billionaire George Soros, whom the Right often vilifies and who has been accused of multiple conspiracies. Soros has taken on the role of a shadowy bogeyman for many on the Right and has been accused of paying protestors to demonstrate, financing the Black Lives Matter movement, and funding caravans of refugees from South America. "Experts who study conspiracy theories say the new claims about Soros are a way to delegitimize the protests and the actual reasons behind them. Some see antisemitism, or a new spin on the age-old hoax that a shadowy cabal of rich men—whether it's the Illuminati, the Rothschilds, the Rockefellers, Bill Gates or Soros—is manipulating world events."[16] The visual depiction of George-o-saurus in this series of books is a caricature of a Jewish man: He has a large, hooked nose, big bushy eyebrows, and a big belly, a depiction that is strikingly similar to the illustrations of Jewish men in *The Poisonous Mushroom*. In one illustration he leers down at a dollar bill in his hands while saying, "But first we need other people's money!",[17] which reinforces another stereotype of Jewish people.[18]

George-o-saurus and his fellow swamp creatures, who have been exiled, are joined by refugees seeking to cross the southern border of the United States. "As they marched along, many other comrade cavemen joined them. The Swamp Creatures told them they would take care of them—once they got to the Land of the Free and took it over."[19] The word "comrade" implies that the immigrants are another kind of threatening Other, communists. Caveman Donald stands atop his completed wall and sees the caravan making its way toward the border while our narrator explains that "from so far away, it looked just like a snake."[20] Donald advises the Free People that they "must find out if the approaching crowd love[s] freedom or really [is] like a nasty snake."[21] Comparing humans to animals is one way authoritarians construct outsiders as non-human Others. The Nazis, for instance, produced propaganda that equated Jews with vermin that needed to be exterminated lest they infest the populace. Similarly, in the twenty-first-century United States, immigrants have been characterized as swarms and have been accused of bringing disease across our border. In late 2023, Donald Trump started to use the word "vermin" to further dehumanize his political enemies and he claimed that immigrants are "poisoning the blood" of the United States, language borrowed directly from Hitler.

Donald Builds the Wall offers a simple solution to the complex problems of immigration and the refugee crisis. Unlike its real counterpart, the fictional wall depicted in the book is impenetrable, which means refugees can only enter through a gate, where they are screened: "And if they were freedom-loving, they would be let in. And if they weren't, they wouldn't. It was that simple."[22] The "freedom-loving" immigrants depicted alongside this declaration are a white, heterosexual couple with a smiling baby boy, which sends a clear signal to readers about how outsiders and insiders are to be defined. In *Demagoguery and Democracy*, Patricia Roberts-Miller explains that, "Demagoguery is comfortable because it says that the world is very simple, and made up of good people (us) and bad people (them)."[23] *Donald Builds the Wall* reinforces a simple "us versus them" worldview where those constructed as Other—immigrants, Jews, liberals, and communists—must be expelled in order to preserve a homogenous social body. As Roberts-Miller explains,

> Once they have convinced their followers (or viewers) that it's kill or be killed, any policy short of complete purification makes no sense, and it's difficult to argue that normal politics is adequate. That is, *they* are no longer simply irritating, but incessantly and inevitably plotting the extermination of *us*. Therefore, we are justified in attacking, expelling, and even exterminating them—it's necessary self-defense."[24]

In *Donald Builds the Wall*, the immigrants and Swamp People trying to get across the wall are doing so in order to invade the United States: George-o-Saurus threatens, "If you cave people don't let us in, we'll come in by force! We are here to take back what is rightfully ours!"[25] The Others depicted in this book are an existential threat to a unified social body and the only solution offered is to expel them. It contributes to the construction of immigrants and Jews as scapegoats. Furthermore, the division between "us" and "them" is clear and simple: It just is, and it doesn't require interrogation.

As noted in Chapter 3, Klaus Theweleit noticed an obsession with boundaries and threats to bodily and social borders in his study of diaries and letters written by *Freikorpsmen* between the world wars. He argued that frequent mentions of communism, mires, swamps, floods, blood, dirt, and bodily secretions represented threats to the solid-seeming individual or social body constructed through fascism. Mires, swamps, and floods represent fluid, ill-defined landscapes that resist definition and control. Anything that can breach the body's border through orifices or that reminds us that our bodies are permeable is viewed with disgust and fear. Fascism, he argued, presents itself as a bulwark against ambiguous boundaries when it provides "erect, soldierly bodies"[26] that march in uniform order: "The threat of the 'flood' may be combatted with 'erections': towering cities, mountains, troops, stalwart men, weapons."[27] For example, Trump's promise to erect a wall at the United States's southern border both assuaged and reinforced existing fears of foreign others as it made tangible the idea of a firm, solid border between "us" and "them." Excessive fear of the Other, usually a set of Others, often takes the form of feelings of disgust: People in a homogenous social body view outsiders as barbarians, monsters, disease, filth, bad smells, vermin, or animals. Viewing other human beings as less than human, as targets of visceral hatred, creates conditions where humans are no longer seen as being worthy of human rights.

While *Donald Builds the Wall* depicts government workers as swamp creatures and immigrants as a "nasty snake," this sort of othering has also long occurred in children's books in ways that are less overt and therefore potentially more dangerous. In the *Little House on the Prairie* series of books, for example, Native Americans are repeatedly depicted as animals and savages.[28] In one scene, the narrator describes them as "thin, fierce-looking men. Their skin was brownish-red. Their heads seemed to go up to a peak, and the peak was a tuft of hair that stood straight up and ended in feathers. Their eyes were black and still and glittering, like snake's eyes."[29] Debbie Reese (Nambé Pueblo) writes of passages like these that, "[Laura Ingalls] Wilder depicts Native people as primitive, mostly naked, and more animal-like than human. And three times, a character says, 'The only good Indian is a dead Indian.'"[30] Depicting Native Americans as villainous, animal-like others makes the Wilders' squatting on Indian land seem justified, and that is the point of othering: It is used to rationalize atrocities, in this case the genocide of Indigenous Americans. In her book on children's historical fiction, Sara Schwebel writes:

> When my classmates and I listened to our teacher read the Little House books and then became Laura Ingalls on the playground, we absorbed a celebratory narrative of the nation-state and inserted ourselves into an American myth: the settlement of western lands was part of the nation's Manifest Destiny; pioneers were heroic, self-sufficient individuals who tamed the wilderness single-handedly; and this story of westward expansion, self-sufficiency, and rural democracy is the shared heritage of all Americans, regardless of their ancestry.[31]

The genocidal western expansion of white settlers is not only rationalized in this series of books, it is romanticized and celebrated, passing the American myth of Manifest Destiny on to younger generations.[32]

As is the case with other cultural constructs, othering is maintained and taught to younger generations through repetition and an accretion of detail. Small, everyday texts like commercials, news programs, films, internet memes, and books carry bits of ideology that accumulate over time and weave their way into individuals' worldviews. One way to challenge othering is to make its continuous construction visible. Cultural critics do this when they focus on the discourse used in various texts and the ways these create and reflect cultural attitudes about who is the norm or who is an outsider. We can learn to read against the grain of books like those in the *Little House* series by making the ideology of 'settler colonialism visible, by calling attention to Wilder's dehumanizing descriptions. There are, though, a number of books that reveal rather than reify existing social hierarchies, that actively work to humanize those considered to be Other, to expose the process of othering, and to demonstrate the harm caused when whole groups of people are dehumanized. In the next section, I discuss a few examples.

Invisible Others: The Subaltern

There are groups of humans who have been so dehumanized that they are viewed as invisible and disposable. Gayatri Spivak uses the term "subaltern" to describe people who live outside of the margins and, as such, are denied subject positions and a voice: "the illiterate peasantry, the tribals, the lowest strata of the urban subproletariat."[33] Subaltern people are refugees, the unhoused, Indigenous peoples, institutionalized and imprisoned people, the "untouchable," the "undocumented," all human beings who are denied a voice and subjectivity because they are viewed by dominant cultures as being less-than-human, as not belonging to any institution, nation, or dominant culture. These groups of people make up a significant portion of the nation's population but they are made invisible, except when they are viewed as a threat.

These most vulnerable members of a population are also the members most targeted by fascist policies. For example, right-wing media outlets and members of the alt-right focus on "swarms" of refugees threatening to "replace" the white population in Western nations, frightful depictions that have led to the dehumanization of migrants. Cristina Lash discusses the way recent US policies that have targeted refugees have directly harmed children. The US government, under the Trump administration, forcibly separated more than 5,500 children from their families with the purposeful intent of traumatizing them. They hoped that word of the trauma would deter refugees from seeking to cross the US's southern border. Lash reports that, during the Trump administration, "Children of immigrants showed awareness of Trump's policies and expressed fear that they would lose a parent as early as age three. Consequently, many young children displayed concerning new behaviors, including increased aggression, separation anxiety, and withdrawal from their social environments."[34]

The reality of Trump's border policies, depicted as so simple in *Donald Builds the Wall*, is that when human beings are constructed as less-than-human ("a nasty snake"), this creates an environment where humans are viewed as "disposable." The most horrible ends of fascism have involved "disposing" of humans that have been designated as less-than-human. Indeed, dehumanization is the first step toward genocide. Stories told from the point of view of marginalized characters can humanize by centering the perspectives and voices of those who have been othered. They can individualize stories so that groups of people are not depicted as "swarms." Most importantly, stories can also create mirrors so that children who are members of Othered groups can see their lives and the lives of their families and communities reflected, given representation. Many scholars studying diverse children's literature use Rudine Simms Bishop's conception of books as mirrors and windows to characterize works that act as mirrors for child readers from underrepresented cultures and as windows for people who are not part of the culture being represented. In her essay, "Mirrors, Windows, and Sliding Glass Doors," Bishop writes that accurate representation is vital for all children: "When children cannot find themselves reflected in the books they read, or when the images they see are distorted, negative or laughable, they learn a powerful lesson about how they are devalued in the society of which they are a part."[35]

In this chapter, I discuss several examples of books aimed at younger readers that work to humanize Others and to dismantle the boundaries that separate the United States into a population of "us" and "them." Representation, though, is never straightforward and well-meaning texts can sometimes backfire. For example, in *I See You*, a wordless picture book published by the American Psychological Association, the illustrator uses contrasts in color to highlight the wordless relationship between a boy and a woman experiencing homelessness. The woman is depicted in grey, but she is surrounded by colorful people who walk by her on the street, an artistic choice that shows how the woman is viewed as an outsider, as someone inherently different from those around her. While she is constructed as invisible or as abject by those who pass her on the street, the boy in the story sees her and worries about her. He also notices that passersby ignore her, turn their noses up at her as if she is a bad smell, glare at her, and sweep dirt at her. He witnesses as she searches through trash, as police shout at her, and as she sits shivering in the snow and cold at Christmas. In a too-tidy ending, the boy brings her a blanket as his parents look on smiling. Supplemental material at the end of the book provides information about homelessness, empathy, helping, giving, and getting involved that is largely geared toward adults: The author, Michael Genhart, explains that, "The idea is to foster greater awareness and empathic conversations about homeless people as people in order to help see them in more humanitarian ways."[36] The book is not without problems though—the main characters are all white, the woman is never given a voice, and she is left, at the end, sitting outside in the snow, gratefully smiling because she's been given a blanket. The book also does not depict unhoused children and does not tell the story from the point of view of people experiencing homelessness. The National Center on Family Homelessness reports that, "A staggering 2.5 million children are now homeless each year in America. This historic high represents one in every 30 children in the United States."[37]

A more child-centered book about homelessness is *Rich*, written by Nikki Grimes and illustrated by R. Gregory Christie, Book 2 in the Dyamonde Daniels early reader series. Dyamonde sees a girl in her class coming out of a shelter. The girl, Damaris Dancer, runs away when Dyamonde sees her because she is embarrassed. Damaris asks Dyamonde not to tell anyone where she lives, and she explains to Dyamonde that, "My mom was working two jobs and she lost one of 'em. She got late on the rent, so they threw our stuff on the sidewalk and said we had to go. . . . Now me and my two brothers and my mom have to stay in a shelter till we can save up enough to get a new apartment."[38] Dyamonde encourages Damaris to submit a poem to a contest about her experiences living in the shelter. Damaris is afraid the other children will laugh at her, but Dyamonde tells her that, "My mom says people laugh at other people 'cause they don't know better. . . . Maybe if they knew what it was like to live in a shelter, they wouldn't laugh. You could be the one to tell them."[39] In this way, Dyamonde encourages Damaris to speak on her own behalf, to no longer be invisible. Damaris's poem, which wins first prize in the contest and is published in the children's section of the local newspaper begins, "Home is a word / I forgot how to spell."[40] Unlike the silent woman in *I See You*, the child in *Rich* is given a name, a personality, and a voice.

Internment

Books told from the perspective of those who have been othered work to humanize those who have been dehumanized. One of the first things Trump did when he took office as US President was to institute a "Muslim Ban." According to the ACLU, he "signed an Executive Order that banned foreign nationals from seven predominantly Muslim countries from visiting the country for 90 days, suspended entry to the country of all Syrian refugees indefinitely, and prohibited any other refugees from coming into the country for 120 days."[41] He promised to reinstitute the ban if reelected in 2024. Trump had a history of expressing Islamophobic ideas long before his first run for the presidency: He falsely accused President Obama of being a Muslim and he accused Muslim Americans in New Jersey of celebrating the destruction of the World Trade Center on 9/11. When he was running for president in 2016, Trump floated the idea of closing mosques in the United States and creating a database of Muslims. As early as December 2015, he made targeting Muslims an official part of his campaign, releasing an announcement that read simply, "Donald J. Trump is calling for a total and complete shutdown of Muslims entering the United States."[42]

Trump and others on the Right accuse Muslims in America of wanting to institute Sharia law, an unfounded claim that incites further fear and division. For example, "Texas House Bill 45, the 'American Laws for Courts' bill signed into law by Texas governor Greg Abbott in June 2017, is intended to block Muslims from bringing Sharia law into the state,"[43] as if Sharia law is a genuine threat to the sovereignty of Texans. As is often the case with scapegoating, minorities are imagined as being far more powerful than they actually are. Their threat is exaggerated or, in this case, fully manufactured. Conspiracy theories such as the one behind this law provide justification for the fear and disgust authoritarians feel for Others and, worse, they incite violence against minority groups.

Samira Ahmed's 2019 dystopian novel *Internment* extends these trends to a conceivable dystopian near-future where Muslims in the United States are arrested and taken to an internment camp. Drawing on history of the internment of Japanese Americans during World War II, the detention of immigrants at the United States–Mexico border, and the Muslim travel ban enacted by the Trump administration, the novel feels all too plausible. The first-person narrator, seventeen-year-old Layla Amin, explains at the start of the novel that,

> I don't measure time by the old calendar anymore; I don't look at the date. There is only Then and Now. There is only what we once were and what we have become.
>
> Two and a half years since the election.
>
> Two years since the Nazis marched on DC.
>
> Eighteen months since the Muslim ban.
>
> One year since our answers on the census landed us on the registry.
>
> Nine months since the first book burning.
>
> Six months since the Exclusion Laws were enacted.

Five months since the attorney general argued that *Korematsu vs. United States* established precedent for relocation of citizens during times of war.

[. . .]

One month since the president of the United States gave a televised speech to Congress declaring that 'Muslims are a threat to America.'[44]

By listing the events—some real, others plausible—that lead up to Layla's internment, Ahmed makes a direct connection between the political and personal, and between public discourse and public policy, as she makes the fictional world she depicts believable. Dystopian fiction considers the question "What if certain trends continue into the future?" and the most frightening aspect of Ahmed's novel is how it doesn't need to veer very far from our own timeline. When Donald Trump was running for office, his Islamophobia was well known and strongly supported by his followers. Political Scientist Matthew MacWilliams found in a December 2015 study of authoritarianism in the GOP that, "A majority of Republican authoritarians in my poll also strongly supported Trump's proposals to deport 11 million illegal immigrants, prohibit Muslims from entering the United States, shutter mosques and establish a nationwide database that tracks Muslims."[45] For younger readers who may not have heard of the Trump administration's Muslim ban or the Right's rhetoric about Muslim Americans, Ahmed's novel draws out one possible trajectory of such rhetoric and policy: internment camps for Muslim Americans.

Layla and her parents are among the first to be rounded up and sent to a camp. While her parents try to make the best of their situation, she rebels: "People died in American internment camps during World War Two, and I'd rather die fighting back than going along with everything."[46] At multiple points in the novel, Layla reaches back into history to help her to make sense of their situation. For instance, when a Red Cross team visits the camp, Layla explains, "I learned about the Red Cross visit to the 'model' Nazi concentration camp Theresienstadt when I visited the Holocaust museum in DC on a trip with my parents . . . It was a sick hoax, and the Red Cross bought into the Nazi propaganda."[47] Such comparisons highlight the grave end results of othering, while also educating readers about past examples. An "author's note" at the end of the novel explains these connections in more detail by discussing family separations and the detention of migrants at the United States–Mexico border. Ahmed lists statistics about migrant detainment facilities and advises her readers to "pay attention to the racist demagoguery and scapegoating that aligns with that policy: immigrants and migrants are 'animals' who 'pour into and infest our country'."[48] In this way, she emphasizes how othering, portraying humans as animals, vermin or disease, goes hand-in-hand with instituting oppressive policies.

The Inquisitor's Tale: Or, Three Magical Children and Their Holy Dog

Adam Gidwitz's novel, *The Inquisitor's Tale: Or, Three Magical Children and Their Holy Dog*, illustrated by Hatem Aly, considers several kinds of otherness based in religion, race, and gender. It follows the adventures of three children living in medieval France: Jeanne is a peasant girl who has visions, William is an African boy with supernatural strength who is raised in a monastery, and Jacob is a Jewish boy with healing powers whose village has been burned to the ground by neighboring Christians. All three are Others as children in a medieval culture that places white, Christian men at its center. At the start, the three children even mistrust one another. William, for example, is trained to see the world in dichotomies. One of his teachers, Brother Bartholomew tells him, "The two kinds of people are these: those who are in league with the Devil, and those who stand on the side of God."[49] The same teacher tells William that, "All peasants are liars, loafers, or both!,"[50] to "[b]eware the sneaky, evil, diabolical Jew,"[51] and to mistrust girls and women, "the daughters of Eve, who tempted Adam to taste the forbidden fruit, and thus introduced evil into the world! The world was perfect before women came along and ruined it! Beware the daughters of Eve, for they indeed are in league with the Devil!"[52] Finally, Brother Bartholomew highlights William's status as Other by referring to Saracens, a term Christian Europeans used to use to refer to Muslims and people from African countries. "If peasants are the Devil's slaves and if Jews are his emissaries and if women are his spies, Saracens are his foot soldiers" says Brother Bartholomew, finishing by calling William's mother a "Saracen harlot."[53]

As the three children and their greyhound meet and then travel together to Saint-Denis, they learn about one another. They are fearful at first. Jeanne notes that "the last time she'd seen a giant monk, her friend Theresa had been taken away and burned at the stake";[54] after having his village burned, Jacob is nervous about being alone with two Christians; and William is wary about traveling with a peasant girl, a daughter of Eve, who brought evil into the world by biting into that apple. "So," the narrator explains, "the children sat in silent fear of one another."[55] Once they begin talking and traveling together, though, they address cultural misunderstandings through genuine dialogue and shared experiences, and their budding friendship influences those around them as well.

When they travel to Paris near the end of the novel they witness the king order the burning of Talmuds he has confiscated from throughout France: "We've collected thousands of Jewish books from all over the kingdom," explains the king's mother, adding that they plan to burn them "right on the old bridge, where the moneylenders are. Send the Jews quite a message."[56] The children are unable to prevent the book-burning but they do save a few Talmuds from the fire. In an afterword, Gidwitz explains that King Louis IX did indeed oversee the burning of 20,000 Talmuds. "We know that Louis hated Jews. He said so, more than once, and he complained of how many Jews lived in Paris."[57] Gidwitz based much of the novel on research and included real historical figures and events, as well as legends. In his afterword, he includes more details, especially about antisemitism in medieval Europe. "There were increasingly frequent reports of organized violence against Jewish communities as the Middle Ages went on," he writes. "Sometimes a group of Christians would descend on a Jewish neighborhood and beat them or set fire to their homes. And sometimes a king would force all the Jews to leave his kingdom."[58] Through his narrative of three children who become friends by building affinities across differences, Gidwitz encourages readers to think about the effects of othering as he personalizes a history of antisemitism.

Esperanza Rising

Members of the alt-right espouse the "great replacement" theory, a belief that immigrants, specifically non-white immigrants, are deliberately being encouraged to enter the United States and other Western nations in order to replace white populations, cultures, and votes. Ironically, this fear and hatred of immigrants crosses national borders as members of the alt-right in North America and in Europe share the same theories: It is their whiteness and their fear of nonwhites that unites them.[59] As is the case in *Donald Builds the Wall*, immigrants are often depicted as threatening swarms or animals, and they are accused of carrying disease. The great replacement theory is antisemitic as well, with some on the Right arguing that caravans of immigrants are being funded by a wealthy cabal of Jews. According to the National Immigration Forum, "Regardless of which version is referenced, proponents of the 'great replacement' theory almost always paint a life-or-death scenario concerning the fate of 'white America.' The theory contends that nonwhite immigration must be stopped, or else the country is on—as [Tucker] Carlson put it—a 'suicidal' path."[60] What was once a fringe theory among white supremacist groups has become mainstream as right-wing politicians and pundits have engaged in increasingly hyperbolic anti-immigration rhetoric.[61]

Children's books focused on immigration can help to counter anti-immigrant sentiments because they often tell stories of immigration from the point of view of an immigrant. In Pam Munoz Ryan's middle-grade novel about Mexican immigrants, *Esperanza Rising*, readers follow the year-long journey of a rancher's daughter who immigrates to the United States in 1930 and must work as a field hand in a California migrant camp. The novel is so effective at showing how Others are constructed because Esperanza begins her journey in a place of privilege oblivious to the plight of working class and indigenous Mexicans. We witness her journey from cultural insider to outsider. The novel is focalized through her so that, as she discovers her place within larger economic and social systems, young readers learn alongside her. At the start of the novel, Esperanza is a beloved and protected only daughter. As her family celebrates the start of the grape harvest, she ceremoniously cuts the first bunch of grapes of the season while wearing a silk dress and hair ribbon that mark her as being above menial labor: "Esperanza stood between Mama and Papa, with her arms linked to theirs, and admired the activity of the workers. 'Papi, this is my favorite time of year,' she said, watching the brightly colored shirts of the workers slowly moving among the arbors."[62] The workers, identified only by their clothing, are beneath her concern, as her status as a member of a wealthy family descended from Spanish ancestors places her in a class above them.

When her father dies and she and her mother must flee to the United States, we witness Esperanza horrified at having to travel in the third-class section of a train: "Trash littered the floor and it reeked of rotting fruit and urine. A man with a small goat on his lap grinned at Esperanza, revealing no teeth. Three barefoot children, two boys and a girl, crowded near their mother. Their legs were chalky with dust, their clothes were in tatters, and their hair was grimy."[63] This description—toothless, shoeless, chalky, grimy, smelling of urine—lets us know that Esperanza feels disgust for fellow humans she sees as being beneath her. Esperanza takes a porcelain doll out of her bag and a dusty and grimy little girl reaches up to touch the doll. As she approaches, "Esperanza quickly jerk[s] it away and put[s] it back on the valise, covering it with the old clothes."[64] This scene, in which the little girl cries, makes concrete the harm Esperanza's prejudice causes, and it also sets up a comparison for later in the novel when Esperanza will herself become dusty and grimy. Esperanza is both othered and othering, and through her transition from center to margin we come to understand the larger political, economic, and social systems at work in creating shifting and socially constructed borders and identities.

As the migrant workers around her become visible and individualized, readers follow along with Esperanza as she learns to see them as equals and herself as one of them. Cristina Rhodes highlights the ways in which Esperanza's body changes as she traverses the shifting border between rancher's daughter and field-worker, as well as the porous border between the United States and Mexico. Rhodes writes that, "When Esperanza finally understands that her body is not the ideal hegemonic body in the United States, as it had once been when she was a ranch owner's daughter in Mexico, she embraces her corporeal transformation."[65] The novel illustrates how bodily borders are socially constructed as part of an economic system. This emphasis on the body is also significant when considered in the context of authoritarian thinking, where the Other is often constructed in bodily, visceral ways as vermin or as diseased, as physically inferior, strange or even as monstrous. For example, the work camps depicted in the novel are segregated. The Okies, white workers from Oklahoma, get a camp that used to be an old army barracks, which means they have the luxury of inside toilets, running water, and even a swimming pool. The Mexican workers are allowed to swim in the pool only on "Friday afternoons, before they clean the pool on Saturday mornings." Upon learning this, Esperanza says, "Do they think we are dirtier than the others?"[66] As Rhodes notes, a character named "Marta recognizes that segregation is a way to discourage workers from organizing for better conditions, but it also pits the workers against one another."[67] *Esperanza Rising* highlights how racial identity intersects with socioeconomic class, how it is socially constructed, and how lower class and minority groups are pitted against one another so that they won't band together. In these ways, the novel moves beyond individual stories to make larger systems visible.

American Born Chinese

Gene Yang's graphic novel *American Born Chinese* also highlights larger systems in the way it depicts the harmful effects of stereotyping and microaggressions on the developing identity of its protagonist. *American Born Chinese* follows the story of Jin Wang, a child of Chinese immigrants who must confront cultural stereotypes in the media and in his relationships in school. On Jin's first day in a new school, his teacher mispronounces his name and a fellow student announces, "My momma says Chinese people eat dogs." Jin's teacher explains, "I'm sure Jin doesn't do that! In fact, Jin's family probably stopped that sort of thing as soon as they came to the United States!"[68] As is the case with Esperanza, the prejudice Jin encounters from both children and adults is most often fixated on his body—what he eats, how he wears his hair, how he smells, and whom he is allowed to associate with. Yang makes the stress on Jin tangible by intertwining his story with two others: the Chinese folk hero the Monkey King and a caricature named Chin-kee, who is an embodiment of multiple media stereotypes of Asians.

The graphic novel shows the effects of othering on Jin by depicting the prejudice he encounters in school and the onslaught of stereotypes he sees depicted in the media. The stereotypes are so ingrained that Jin becomes an Other to himself, identifying with white Americans rather than his Chinese heritage. He rejects his Asian identity, negatively represented by Chin-kee, who is a constant source of embarrassment to Danny, Jin's white alter-ego. Danny and Chin-kee are characters in a sitcom, which includes a laugh track that runs across the bottom of each panel. Whenever Chin-kee speaks in broken English, "ha ha ha ha" scrolls across the bottom of each frame: lines like "Ah-so! What big, bootiful Amellican school! Chin-kee rike! Chin-kee rike vely much. Heh heh!" are chillingly framed as humor.[69] Chin-kee is depicted with buck teeth and he wears a long braid and traditional Chinese dress. As the story progresses, he embodies increasingly exaggerated stereotypes of Asians seen in American film and television: He correctly answers every question posed by teachers, he knows martial arts, and he eats household pets—in other words, he is a physical incarnation of what Jin fears most, being othered. Danny/Jin defeats Chin-kee by knocking off his head. In its place, the head of the Monkey King appears, replacing stereotypes with authentic Chinese culture. By depicting Jin's battles with his own split identity, the graphic novel highlights the harmful psychological effects of othering on members of minority cultures and helps to foster empathy. Finally, rather than portraying a solid, singular identity, *American Born Chinese* depicts Jin as a fragmented, postmodern self, a strategy that can create affinities with the reader. In other words, readers who are able to see a character as psychologically complex can find the kinship they share.

Postmodern feminist theorists developed the term "affinities" to combat essentialist thinking (defining an individual by one trait or grouping individuals solely by identity categories). Affinities also are a way to embrace decentered, fragmented postmodern identity as an intersectional space where people can find commonalities with one another. If identity is multi-faceted, we can avoid stereotyping Others and can connect with one another across shared commonalities while still maintaining some borders. Finally, because identities are intersectional, in flux, performative, and shifting, the concept of affinities allows for temporary, evolving alliances. bell hooks wrote that, "Postmodern culture with its decentered subject can be the space where ties are severed or it can provide the occasion for new and varied forms of bonding."[70] Similarly, Donna

Haraway, in "A Cyborg Manifesto," advocates for building coalitions among groups through "affinity, not identity" as she breaks down solid-seeming Western categories and "constructs a kind of postmodernist identity out of otherness, difference, and specificity."[71]

Melissa (George) and 10,000 Dresses

As I discussed in the last chapter, authoritarianism, and especially fascism, has at its base the patriarchal family, which means that any variations from it are considered a threat. Feminists are accused of dismantling the family, as are movements to protect and gain rights for members of the LGBTQ+ community. In the United States, these fears of sexual minorities have recently taken the form of bathroom bills, bans against teaching about gender and sexuality in the classroom, and bans preventing transgender students from competing in athletics that align with their gender identity. Such laws are passed under the auspices of protecting women and children, the assumption being that transgender people are a threat because they are pedophiles or rapists. As Stanley writes, "Attacking trans women, and representing the feared other as a threat to the manhood of the nation, are ways of placing the very idea of manhood at the center of political attention."[72] He points out that trans women are an especial threat to hegemonic masculinity because "they *choose* femininity," which disrupts a hierarchy of gender identity that should make masculinity the better choice. The very existence of transgender individuals is a peril to them because it challenges the gender binary and reveals bodily borders as mutable.

A number of school systems around the United States have banned teachers from teaching about gender identity, and books about gender identity have been removed from classrooms and libraries. "[President] Biden and other Democrats argue that federal civil rights law protects trans students, and schools must respect students' gender identity. Republican legislators and governors in a growing number of states argue the exact opposite: Federal law doesn't protect trans students, and school policies—covering everything from bathrooms to sports teams and pronouns—should stick to students' sex assigned at birth."[73] The idea behind such policies is that children are too young to learn about gender identity even though many transgender people know from a young age that the gender they were assigned at birth does not reflect who they are.[74]

Alex Gino's middle-grade novel *Melissa* (published under the name *George* until April 2022) is the story of a ten-year-old trans girl, and it can be as instructive for adults as it is for child readers.[75] In an afterword to the novel, Gino explains that, "I can only imagine how my life would be if I had seen someone more like me in a book or three when I was younger. As many of us do, I wrote the book I wanted to read as a kid."[76] Melissa longs to play Charlotte in her school's production of *Charlotte's Web*, struggles to make her mother understand, and must endure violence from boys at school who bully her for not conforming. The story is focalized through Melissa, which means we get her perspective on the events of the novel. For example, we see Melissa's intense reaction when her mother says, "Whatever happens in your life, you can share it, and I will love you. You will always be my little boy, and that will never change. Even when you grow up to be an old man, I will still love you as my son."[77] In this way, the novel is also instructive for adult readers. It models ways that adult mentors can be encouraging or discouraging. Melissa's mother means well but her use of the words boy, man, and son signal that she has not yet accepted her child's gender identity. Similarly, other adults in the book also convey behaviors that discourage or encourage: Melissa's teacher won't allow her to play the part of Charlotte because it is not a part for boys, but her principal is far more understanding. When Melissa is called to the principal's office after a confrontation with a bully, she notices a sign with a rainbow flag, and "below the flag, the sign said SUPPORT SAFE SPACES FOR GAY, LESBIAN, BISEXUAL, AND TRANSGENDER YOUTH." Melissa draws hope from the sign and wonders "where she could find a safe space like that, and if there would be other girls like her there."[78] Principal Maldonado, who tells her mom that, "you can't control who your children are, but you can support them," is a role model for adult teachers and parents reading the novel.

The picture book *10,000 Dresses*, written by Marcus Ewert and illustrated by Rex Ray, is written for a younger audience but also contains a message for adults reading the book. In it, Bailey dreams each night about dresses, each with a different, fanciful design: "The first dress was made of crystals. When Bailey slipped the dress on, the crystals clinked against each other like millions of tiny bells. And when sunlight hit the dress just right, rainbows jumped out!"[79] When Bailey tells her family members about the dresses, she is rebuked. "Bailey, what are you talking about?" says his mother. "You're a boy. Boys don't wear dresses!" When Bailey tells her mother she doesn't feel like a boy, her mother says, "Well, you are one, Bailey, and that's that! Now go away . . . and don't mention dresses again!" Despite repeated discouragement, Bailey continues to dream of dresses until she meets a girl named Laurel who sews dresses, and the two work to design a new dress together. Bailey's persistence in the face of hostile reactions from her family—her brother even threatens to kick her—is a model for children who don't conform to normative gender expectations and a model for adults on how not to behave. Even though it presents a simple, unrealistic solution for Bailey's situation, it is one of a very small number of picture books that allow transgender children to see represented their identity and their struggles against oppressive systems.

El Deafo

Jason Stanley notes that, "Fascist governments have exhibited some of humanity's worst cruelty toward disabled populations."[80] This is because fascism promotes the idea of social Darwinism: People are seen as being valuable to society when they "rise above others in competitive struggle."[81] In Nazi Germany, people with disabilities were seen as a burden on the state. "On July 14, 1933, the German government instituted the 'Law for the Prevention of Progeny with Hereditary Diseases.' This law called for the sterilization of all persons who suffered from diseases considered hereditary, including mental illness, learning disabilities, physical deformity, epilepsy, blindness, deafness, and severe alcoholism."[82] People with disabilities were characterized as "useless eaters" and as "life unworthy of life," and many were eventually "euthanized" or sent to concentration camps.[83] People with disabilities were viewed as subhuman Others who were a threat to the ideal of a unified nation of like individuals, a threat to sameness.

Literature about disability told from the point of view of a main character living with a disability can be an effective way to learn about a particular disability without dehumanizing the character or making the disability a character's only defining attribute. Cece Bell's graphic novel *El Deafo* is an autobiographical story in which Cece, depicted as a rabbit, loses her hearing, is equipped with a hearing aid, and learns to lip-read. Bell makes clear in her afterword that hers is one experience, one story from the point of view of a person who is deaf, and that there are many other experiences of being deaf. She uses the affordances of the graphic novel form—specifically narration and speech bubbles—to portray Cece's difficulties communicating with those around her. Sara Kersten observes that, "The speech bubbles do not always clearly articulate what is being said as they are sometimes empty or filled with nonsense words, providing hints into how Cece is hearing or not hearing and understanding the world around her."[84] Through the use of speech and thought bubbles, the graphic novel shows readers how Cece hears sounds and how hearing peoples' well-meaning attempts to speak loudly or slowly only impede her lip-reading. In many panels, Cece takes on the role of narrator as she draws herself holding up placards that accompany illustrations or as she explains the Miracle Ear device that helps her to hear her teacher. While the graphic novel educates about deafness, it focuses largely on Cece's friendships and other elementary school events and relationships so that she is not defined only by her disability. Much in the way that

American Born Chinese depicts a multifaceted character, El Deafo depicts a complex main character who is humanized through the depiction of small, everyday experiences.

Allegories of the Other: *The Arrival* and *The Assassination of Brangwain Spurge*

Shaun Tan's wordless picture book *The Arrival* puts the reader in the uncomfortable position of being an Other. Readers follow the journey of a man who must leave behind his family to immigrate to a strange new land where everything—street signs, customs, foods, architecture, language, pets, home appliances, and transportation—is bewildering. The book begins with images from the man's home that feel familiar: a cracked teapot, a clock, a trunk with clothing, a child's drawing of a happy family.[85] But once the man travels away from home and arrives in a new land, both he and the reader are bombarded with enigmatic symbols and images that feel disorienting and require effort to interpret. We follow the man as he learns to use the mysterious appliances in his apartment, to read maps, to use public transportation, and to find a job. He meets other immigrants along the way, and they each help one another to adjust to new customs. *The Arrival* humanizes immigrants by depicting their stories of migration. The main character must leave his family behind in a dangerous situation until he can afford to send for them. Other immigrants share their stories of war, oppression, and violence through abstract images that convey the danger they fled. The reading experience is interactive and, at first, frustrating because the reader must work to make sense of an invented alphabet and system of symbols, much in the way immigrants must work to learn new languages and systems. By the end of the book, as the man adjusts to his new life in a new land, the strange becomes familiar.

The end pages of the book depict rows of photos, shaped in small squares like passport pictures, of a diverse array of individuals, some with head scarfs or hats, all of them staring straight ahead. None of them are smiling. Some look worried, tired, or anxious. They are the first images we see when opening the book and we return to them again at the close. The story of the book's protagonist also begins with squares arranged in rows on the page, creating a visual link to the end papers. These sixty images of individuals who seem "foreign" frame the text: At first they seem unfamiliar and enigmatic but by the end of the book, after we've seen stories of several immigrants and after we've been put into the readerly position of being an Other to the text, we can imagine a story for each individual pictured. Tan's book actively engages the reader through its wordless narrative because the reader must work to assemble the story. It's a book that invites multiple re-readings that each provide additional details and layers of meaning. One way to counter othering is to highlight complex individual stories so that the borders we construct around groups of people become porous, less fixed, and more difficult to differentiate.

M.T. Anderson's novel, *The Assassination of Brangwain Spurge*, illustrated by Eugene Yelchin, also demonstrates the process of othering and the ways that othering clouds our views of fellow humans. As the novel progresses, readers gradually learn, alongside the protagonist, that he has been duped by his own government into believing that the goblins in the neighboring kingdom are terrifying and monstrous. The book is an ambiguous text filled with enigmatic illustrations, mysteries, interruptions, and contradictions that force us to actively make meaning, to flip back and forth among its pages as we, alongside the protagonist, reconsider our initial impressions. Like a Brechtian play, the text works to continuously interrupt the flow of the narrative so as to continuously remind us that we are holding a book in our hands. The text shifts in focalization among three different characters as we follow the adventures of an elf named Brangwain Spurge, a historian who is catapulted in a barrel into the land of goblins from where he secretly transmits home images of his seemingly frightening and barbaric hosts.

The novel disrupts the reading experience by making Brangwain into an unreliable narrator whose perceptions are clouded by his prejudice. For example, the goblin archivist, Werfel, frets about how to show hospitality to his foreign guest, who arrives aloof and dismissive, showing scorn for Werfel's ways. "'And what are those?' [Brangwain] asked through a throat constricted with disgust. 'Oh!' Werfel laughed. 'My skins. My previous skins. When we shed every few years, we keep them . . . It's important to see who you're growing into and who you used to be'."[86] The goblins and elves are different, perhaps not as a species, as we discover later, but in their customs. For instance, Spurge witnesses Werfel mocking his neighbor and is shocked. He learns from Werfel that, "It is an old goblin custom: The closer you are with someone, the more you make fun of them. It is a sign of how friendly you are. [. . .] If you said them to a complete stranger, they would fight you in a duel to the death."[87] This cultural difference becomes a running joke throughout the book as Werfel insults his friends and neighbors and, as their relationship deepens, eventually Spurge.

The images, which are laid out in full two-page spreads interspersed between pages with text, work in tension with the narrative as we only gradually learn that they are inaccurate first impressions clouded by Spurge's fear and prejudice: As the Lord Spymaster explains to his superior, "It's not perfect. It's not exactly what he sees. It's whatever he pictures in his mind's eye."[88] Of course, the other elves have the same prejudices against the goblins Spurge does and they don't question the accuracy of the "mind's eye" transmissions. "Look in particular at the awful goblin women—brutish, roaring things," says the Spymaster. "We know that goblin women fight and rule alongside their men—hulking, ugly beasts, dreadfully unlike the beauties of our own elfin aristocracy, who are bred for their delicacy to be ornaments to society. This is yet another example of goblin savagery, their lack of nobility and chivalry."[89] As the book progresses, we only gradually come to understand that the visual transmissions are distorted. They only become realistic representations once Brangwain confronts his prejudice and develops a genuine friendship with his host. Because readers must work to assemble and reassemble meaning, the novel requires that readers reevaluate their initial impressions as well.

As we put together various illustrative and narrative puzzle pieces we gradually discover that poor Brangwain is a dispensable underling being used by government officials. We come to realize, alongside him, that the goblins initially described as "faceless swarms" pouring out of mountains to "burn our forests and our homes" are not swarms at all, but fellow humans, very much like elves, and that Brangwain's initial transmissions, which we see as illustrations, were colored by his ingrained prejudice. As his relationship with his host deepens, the images he transmits change to reflect his budding friendship with Werfel, the goblin Archivist. At the end, as they set out on a quest to learn and teach the forgotten histories of both their lands, the two scholars are depicted as equals, and what began as a fantasy quest narrative has become a significantly messier sort of text that challenges us consider how our views of Others are shaped by our understandings of history, nationhood, and cultural difference. Significantly, the novel also demonstrates how oppressive governments work to construct Others as a way to manipulate and divide their citizens.

Conclusion
The Ends of Story

Why, anyway, the commitment to literary ambiguity when writing for a young audience that is still using narrative to construct their world? Don't we want to participate in that construction? And even: What's wrong, in some cases, with a little propaganda? What's wrong with telling the lies that might come true if they are believed? These are difficult times, and worse times may come, and do we really want to abjure our power to argue fervently for what we believe in the forum of the young?

—M.T. ANDERSON, "Point of Departure."[1]

M.T. Anderson wrote that authors of children's literature dread being asked if their work provides lessons for younger readers: "If there is any accusation we fear as writers for children, it is that our books have been somehow instructive, that they have had a *message*."[2] Creative writers and literary scholars, he explains, are trained to value complexity and ambiguity, which means that a heavy-handed, transparent moral undermines the literary merit of a text. Anderson explains that,

> Most of us were brought up in a literary and critical tradition which suggested that literature is defined by ambiguity—the precise opposite (it would seem) of ideological clarity. Trained in high school and college English lit classrooms that assumed critical approaches vacillating between the modernist and the postmodern, we are eager to celebrate the sublimity of the artfully unclear and the polyvalent.[3]

In the literary tradition Anderson describes, a "great" work of literature is characterized by its universality, its ability to mean different things to different readers across different cultures and time periods. The "great works," we were taught, resonate with readers across time because they are malleable, able to carry multiple interpretations in varying contexts, which means they encourage readers to think in nuanced ways.

In his influential essay "Ideology and the Children's Book," Peter Hollindale cautioned scholars in our field against advocating for books that promote specific ideological stances, writing that, "A desire on the part of the child people for a particular set of social outcomes has led to pressure for a literature to fit them, and a simplistic view of the manner in which a book's ideology is carried."[4] Instead of insisting that texts promote a particular worldview, he argues that we should help young readers to read for ideology, to be critical of the ideological claims that a text makes. Hollindale also notes that readers, child or adult, don't uncritically, passively adopt the ideology of a given text, that it is simplistic to think that reading a book that promotes racism will lead readers to become racist or that reading a book that challenges the patriarchy will turn one into a feminist. On the other hand, though, stories do persuade. They affect us, sometimes profoundly. And they educate.

I have indeed been advocating for texts that promote specific ideological stances, ways of thinking about and perceiving the world, books that challenge authoritarian thinking and neofascist mythmaking, and that promote critical thought and ideals of social justice. I have discussed books that ask us to empathize with characters considered to be Other, to consider the world through another's point of view, ones that ask us to participate in the continuous reconstruction of history, that critique the patriarchy, and that highlight the rhetorical techniques fascists use to persuade. I am ending with a discussion of systemic narratives, stories that shift our attention from the depiction of individuals to the larger systems that govern our lives, that move the background to the foreground. In other words, just as there are texts that teach beginners how to read, there are also texts that may help beginners to read ideology, the sets of stories all around us that structure social relations.

Theory for Beginners

Throughout this book, I've done my best to convey theoretical ideas in ways that are accessible to non-experts. Theory helps us to make sense of our world and the ways it is constructed through narrative, but when this sense-making is limited only to those few who recognize arcane terms and concepts then it becomes inaccessible and, I would argue, ineffective. As Kenneth B. Kidd points out, everyone is a beginner at some point and everyone needs beginner books. In his book, *Theory For Beginners: Children's Literature as Critical Thought*, Kidd devotes a chapter to analyzing beginner books for adults, specifically graphic guides to the work of various theorists. He writes that "Theory often makes beginners out of experienced thinkers, even experienced readers of theory."[5] He focuses, for instance, on comics that help those studying in the humanities to grasp European critical theories. I still have my copies of *Brecht for Beginners*, *Foucault for Beginners*, and *Introducing Derrida* that I bought decades ago when I was a new graduate student struggling to understand what we used to call "high theory." Kidd argues that such guides, which many of us used to survive graduate school in the theory-saturated 1990s, "were launched with hope for political awareness and consciousness-raising and have morphed into something less ideologically revolutionary and more predictable, shoring up rather than challenging the middle-class professionalism of academia."[6] In other words, theory has been defanged and depoliticized by the institutions in which it is taught.

Cultural and literary theories provide lenses for understanding how the world works, but they are not ideologically neutral nor objective descriptions. Indeed, much of the theory I've applied to discussions in this book is overtly political: It seeks to understand the workings of fascism as an ideology so that it can be resisted. Theories about narrative and ideology, especially, can illustrate how stories shape our individual worldviews and our collective mythologies, which means they might also highlight areas of resistance, ways to recognize, read against the grain, and subvert fascist mythologies. While we wouldn't consider teaching Brecht, Derrida, or Foucault to children, there are books for younger readers that teach theory by distilling it. When theory is distilled it is, necessarily, simplified. It is explained using examples, characters, settings, or narrative structures that highlight the basic ideas undergirding a particular theory. While this risks oversimplification, I believe it is a way to return to the original intent of critical theory, much of which, unfortunately, is inaccessible to the average reader. Theory, much of which strives to understand the systems we inhabit and the way ideology works to shape institutions, can be made tangible in books for the young.

In response to threats of censorship and efforts to mandate school curricula, some educators and authors have claimed that critical race theory and gender theory are, of course, not things we teach to children. For the most part, they claim that these are ideas that are too theoretical and far too complex for a second grader or middle schooler to comprehend. That's only partially true though. As Kidd points out, books for children and young adults can indeed teach theory. He focuses specifically on queer theory, arguing that "the best children's literature challenges conventional perceptions and models philosophical thinking" and that "some children's literature functions like queer theory for kids."[7]

Most of the books I've discussed are ones that function like theory: They highlight political rhetoric, they analyze the construction of Others, they frame history, the patriarchy, and whiteness as social constructs, and they make visible the acts of genocide that are erased by authoritarian constructions of American history. For example, *Roll of Thunder, Hear My Cry* is a historical novel that teaches critical race theory in a distilled and accessible form. Even though the novel was written before the term critical race theory was coined, it is a text that highlights systemic racism and the way that the history of slavery is embedded in multiple US institutions. The novel helps readers to understand the complex systems involved in the creation and maintenance of the Jim Crow South and the way institutions like churches, schools, law enforcement, and land ownership worked together to keep Mississippi's Black population of the 1930s in an oppressed state. For example, the school for white children is named after the president of the Confederacy, and the land the sharecroppers work is owned by the same families who owned their enslaved ancestors. The Logan family has a deep understanding of their family history, the history of their community, and the larger systems they inhabit, and the adults in the family pass this understanding onto their children in multiple ways.

The Logans also work to educate others in their community about the social, legal, educational, and economic systems that make up the Jim Crow South. One such example occurs in Mary Logan's classroom when a group of white men, members of the school board, show up to observe her just as she is teaching the children of sharecroppers a history of slavery that is not included in their textbooks:

> But Mama did not flinch: she always started her history class the first thing in the morning when the students were most alert, and I knew that the hour was not yet up. To make matters worse, her lesson for the day was slavery. She spoke on the cruelty of it; of the rich economic cycle it generated as slaves produced the raw products for the factories of the North and Europe; how the country profited and grew from the free labor of a people still not free.[8]

Mrs. Logan is fired because the narrative she tells her students about history runs counter to the mythology that upholds Jim Crow apartheid. The segregated school system depicted in the novel is an institution designed to keep African American children in their place as sharecroppers. Her lessons are a threat to the system and to the white school board members, who maintain their power through a set of institutions that keep African Americans in debt, uneducated, and under a constant threat of violence from both the "night riders" and law enforcement. Through her child narrator and detailed examples that are accessible to young readers, Taylor makes visible the intersectional web of relations, histories, and institutions that worked to maintain structural racism and authoritarianism in the Jim Crow South.

Taylor depicts the ongoing construction of a white supremacist mythology, the ways that the monster of racism is created not only through institutions but also through ideology. One example involves Lillian Jean, a racist white girl, who is depicted as a product of her environment, which means that we are able to see the construction of racism. In one scene, Cassie Logan pretends to befriend Lillian Jean by behaving in a subservient way. Cassie knows enough about the system to know that this is what Lillian Jean expects of her. She tells her, "Then I seen how things was. I mean, I should've seen it all along. After all, I'm who I am and you're who you are."[9] As narrator, Cassie includes the reader in on her deception: "Lillian Jean looked at me with astonishment that I could see the matter so clearly. 'Well, I'm glad you finally learned the way of things.'" We, as readers, know, at this point in the novel, that the Logans have instilled in Cassie knowledge and pride, and that she is playing the trickster. She understands the web of relations that create the ideology of white supremacy even while Lillian Jean, as the child of dominators, is oblivious. Cassie says, "The way I see it—here, let me take them books for you, Miz Lillian Jean—the way I see it, we all gotta do what we gotta do." Lillian Jean is pleased with Cassie's apparent change of heart, with her willingness to take on the role that's been created for her under Jim Crow. She says, "Good for you, Cassie," "God'll bless you for it," and "God wants all his children to do what's right."[10] From this scene, we learn that Lillian Jean's white supremacy comes to her not only from her racist family and segregated school, but also from her church. Through tangible examples such as this one, the novel depicts a matrix of social relations and institutions that work together in order to create an ideology that makes white supremacy "common sense," or, as Lillian Jean puts it, just "the way of things."

As noted earlier, Hannah Arendt argued that narrative is especially central to fascist ideology, which creates "a society whose members act and react according to the rules of a fictitious world,"[11] The ideology of authoritarianism is so complete, so carefully crafted that it seems to be just "the way of things." Authoritarian leaders, she wrote, craft storied worlds, mythologies created through webs of story that their followers fully inhabit. "Before they seize power and establish a world according to their doctrines, totalitarian movements conjure up a lying world of consistency which is more adequate to the needs of the human mind than reality itself."[12] Reality is messy and contradictory, but fascists use story to create an illusion of order. Neofascists in the United States tell stories about a once great nation that has been corrupted by the Left and that is under siege by enemies—groups of scapegoated Others—from within and without. The stories they tell accumulate over time through addition and repetition to form a shared worldview, a dark vision of America in decline and under assault by groups of Others, of chaos in need of order.

Adolf Hitler understood the value of such stories in shaping a fascist ideology. He called the narratives he created "big lies" and explained in *Mein Kampf* that,

> in view of the primitive simplicity of their minds [the masses] more easily fall a victim to a big lie than to a little one, since they themselves lie in little things, but would be ashamed of lies that were too big. Such a falsehood will never enter their heads and they will not be able to believe in the possibility of such monstrous effrontery and infamous misrepresentation in others; yes, even when enlightened on the subject, they will long doubt and waver, and continue to accept at least one of these causes as true.[13]

Fascist leaders have contempt for their followers, their "primitive simplicity" and their willingness to believe in the lies they are told. In the United States, for example, various polls have demonstrated that millions believe Joe Biden won the presidency in 2020 through election fraud because this is a "big lie" Trump and his surrogates have repeated again and again for years, one they have woven into a web of stories that spreads out across our multimedia ecosystem. Even after it has been proven, again and again, that the 2020 election was fair and that Trump was defeated because Joe Biden simply got more votes, the belief in the "big lie" continues. Belief is more powerful than fact, especially when stories accumulate and reinforce one another to form a "lying world of consistency,"[14] a totalizing explanation for the way the world works. If fact-checking doesn't work to counter fascist ideology, perhaps we need to match stories with stories, especially ones that emphasize the role of story in shaping worldviews, ones that expose the totalizing narrative of fascism as fiction.

The Narrative Turn

Humans share stories for multiple reasons. We use narrative to give order and meaning to our days, to shape the passage of time, and to manage a complex and contradictory world. Fascists, though, use story for a particular purpose: they craft a narrative of "us" versus "them": It is "they" who stole the 2020 election from Trump, a figurehead standing in for "us," and "they" who are dangerous Others disrupting the order of things. Fascists don't always create new stories; oftentimes they borrow old stories that already exist in a culture to weave into their larger narrative. For example, Arendt explains that, "The most efficient fiction of Nazi propaganda was the story of a Jewish world conspiracy."[15] It was efficient because it was already believed. It could be woven together with other, newer stories under one totalizing mythology that made Jews into powerful, dangerous Others who needed to be controlled and, eventually, exterminated from the social body. The fiction of the solid, homogeneous social body is especially central to fascism, which relies on a "them" to define itself against, to delineate and reify its borders. Neofascists in the United States define their borders by telling frightful stories about disease-carrying, dangerous immigrants "swarming" across them; about "Democrat-run cities" that have been overtaken by Black Lives Matter protesters, drag queens, and the homeless; about schools "grooming" young people to adopt LGBTQ+ identities; and about works of children's literature that teach critical race theory to fragile white children. These stories accumulate, and weave together with other stories to create a master narrative of a wholesome social body with a shared history, national identity, and set of values under siege from all sides. The borders delineating this in-group are continuously reinforced through a collection of stories that create fear of the Other, which is feminized, brown, queer, and foreign, the "opposite" of the male, white, heterosexual citizen who is at the center of fascist fantasies of an authoritarian, white supremacist, patriarchal state.

In *Seduced by Story: The Use and Abuse of Narrative*, Peter Brooks argues that stories such as these can become "noxious" when they work together to construct a system of belief: "We do not need to look far back in history to see what happens when certain fictions gain the status of dominant and all-explaining myth."[16] Sets of stories become a mythology when they accumulate over time and reinforce one another to form an explanation, a set of patterns, a series of assumptions undergirding a system of belief, which make that system seem real and true, commonsense, or just the way things are. Authoritarians also work to suppress stories that run counter to the mythology they are building, stories that threaten to reveal the gaps that have been smoothed over in order to create big lies. They characterize the press as untrustworthy by referring to them as the lying media or fake news, they ban books that present diverse points of view, and they prohibit teaching that does not uphold their patriotic myths of America's founding. This is because the myth of American exceptionalism, a "great" past to which we need to return, is a story that is central to neofascist mythmaking. The present, for the authoritarian-minded, is characterized by decay, corruption, and decadence, while the past is pure and innocent. Authoritarian world-building involves constructing narratives of a pristine past, a degraded present, and a future that will return to something akin to the idyllic past once the corruption has been purged. A foundational, pristine mythology of nationhood and history is necessary to fascism, which means that stories that challenge these foundational myths, which reveal the ideology of the dominators as the ideology of the dominators, are especially threatening.

Cultural theorists, influenced by the work of thinkers like Roland Barthes and Antonio Gramsci, have long conceived of ideology as a mythology, a belief system constructed through speech acts, symbols, and stories that have taken on the function of myth. Our current media-saturated environment is ideal for mythmaking. Because the new authoritarianism is wired, whole mythologies can be constructed within the ideological bubbles made possible by our current media ecosystem. Anne Applebaum explains that, "Our new communications revolution has been far more rapid than anything we know from the fifteenth century, or even the twentieth"[17] and that this rapid revolution is fueling the new authoritarianism. In other words, the nature of narrative has changed significantly over the past few decades and in ways that have created increasingly polarized, insular, self-contained story-telling communities.

Brooks argues that this contemporary media environment is beset by an "overabundance of story," what he calls the "narrative turn."[18] This overabundance of story leads to totalizing myths "when their status as fictions, *ficciones*, is forgotten and they are taken as real explanations of the world, as something other than 'as if' constructions, as the object of belief. On the basis of such fictions become myths we erect theologies. Very much including political theologies."[19] Contemporary neofascist mythmaking works especially well because our current media environment is filled with convergence culture stories created through extensive, intertextual world-building that is participatory, embodied, and crosses various platforms.

Convergence culture storytellers build a world through a set of rules and a set of texts that adhere to those rules, and they continuously add stories that confirm the myth, that reinforce patterns through repetition. The storied world becomes "real" through an accretion of detail and through the creation of a web of interconnected, intertextual narratives. Unlike the novel or the stand-alone film, a convergence culture text spreads out. It is incomplete and unfinished. Stories organize our lives around the passage of time, but convergence culture narratives, especially non-fictional ones, assemble themselves in a continuous now so that the line separating real life and fiction evaporates. Wayne Booth wrote in *The Rhetoric of Fiction* that "if the gap between art and reality were ever fully closed, art would be destroyed."[20] Art, which is a rarified representation of reality, helps us to reflect and to make meaning of our world. The collapse between reality and fiction that characterizes our current media environment means there is no space for closure or reflection; there is just ever-expanding story. This "narrative turn," then, means that civic literacy must necessarily involve narrative literacy, an understanding of the stories that surround us, the way storied worlds are constructed, and how to tell the difference between fiction and reality.

Epistemic Narrative

Plot is a linear account of the passage of time but narrative can be ordered differently, it can tell events out of order or in flashbacks, it can speed things up or slow them down, it can move one story into the foreground and another into the background. Narrative creates order and, as it does so, it classifies, arranges, and distills reality. Most narratives, popular ones especially, follow familiar patterns and story structures but some challenge conventions, which can create delight or distress, depending upon the reader. Some readers, for example, are upset when a children's book does not end happily or when a romantic comedy does not end with marriage. This may be because dominant ideology is often reinforced through endings where order is restored to provide closure. For example, when dutiful, beautiful Cinderella is rewarded with a heterosexual marriage and wealth while her evil, ugly stepsisters are punished with birds pecking out their eyes, the order restored is that of the patriarchy. Patriarchal structures are also reified in the hero narrative when the hero comes into his own and takes his rightful place in the hierarchy.

Works of fiction can reproduce dominant ideology so well that readers (and perhaps authors too) might not see the ideology as constructed: It appears to be the natural way of things, obvious, or as Gramsci explained it, "common-sense." This is often the case with realistic fiction, a genre that can smooth over the gaps and contradictions that threaten to expose a book's underlying ideology as constructed. Catherine Belsey argued that realism, as a literary form, is especially adept at seeming "natural" and "true": "It is a set of omissions, gaps rather than lies, smoothing over contradictions, appearing to provide answers to questions which in reality it evades, and masquerading as coherence in the interests of social relations generated by and necessary to the reproduction of the existing modes of production."[21] She points to the way that texts are always influenced by the institutions that produce them and the larger systems within which they exist. In the case of children's literature, these institutions extend beyond the publishing industry and into the institutions of education and the family. Institutions reproduce ideas that uphold the institution, that reinforce dominant ideology, and these ideas are comfortable because they conform with our existing beliefs; they mesh with the other narratives we tell ourselves about ourselves as a nation and as a culture.

In a lecture titled "An Indigenous Critique of Whiteness in Children's Literature," children's literature scholar Debbie Reese (Nambé Pueblo) explains that when she shows adult white people the parts of *Little House on the Prairie* where Indigenous people are depicted as animal-like and as "savages," they are surprised because they don't remember them.[22] I read the *Little House* books in the early 1970s, when I was about eight years old, and I haven't re-read them since, except for those passages. I was also surprised the first time I heard about them because I didn't remember them. For eight-year-old me, the books had been about the relationships between family members and neighbors and I didn't focus my attention on the depiction of Native Americans in the books. I know now that Native children reading the books would have noticed them and would have been harmed by them because they are being constructed as Others both within the text and as readers. As a white child I didn't notice these details, these fragments of mythology, because they conformed with the dominant ideology of settler colonialism.

That's how dominant ideology works in a work of fiction. The text creates a believable world by maintaining verisimilitude through repetition, accretion of detail, referents to narratives outside of the book, and an adherence to the rules established as part of a universe of stories, the cultural context a book exists within. As a child, I believed in the world created in the *Little House* books because, even though the events of the books were set in the past, they depicted the world I knew at the time, a mythology of America maintained through stories of Manifest Destiny. In the 1970s, we learned about Columbus and the Mayflower, children played cowboys and Indians, and we watched Westerns on our television sets. The imperialist idea of Indian, the stereotype, was everywhere. That is the dominant ideology of settler colonialism at work. Dominant ideology makes itself invisible when something is depicted as normal, as just the way things are, even though it is something that has been socially constructed.

The most entrenched ideologies are the ones that make themselves appear to be "natural." The slave trade, for example, relied upon the reification of "race science," a set of ideas given credibility through discourses of rationalism. In other words, white people created the mythology of "race science" as a way to naturalize racism so that they could dehumanize and enslave Africans. It provided a rationale and, more importantly, it provided a set of ideas, a collection of stories that wove together to form a mythology in which slavery was viewed as just the way things are, the order of things, and in which people of

African descent were viewed as less than human. As I discussed in Chapter 2, this is the dominant ideology that is interrogated in Anderson's *Octavian Nothing* novels where we witness how the protagonist's identity is constructed by the institutions that bind him. The *Octavian Nothing* books make visible the ways in which the system of slavery is inexorably intertwined with our nation's founding, and they do so by using several narrative techniques that both make use of and disrupt the traditions of realism. Through Octavian's narration of the years leading up to 1776 the novel depicts the contradictions present at the founding of our democracy and the way these have been smoothed over in order to create a national mythology of freedom for all.

In earlier chapters I discussed the way that members of the Right are seeking to suppress stories that run counter to the foundational myth of American exceptionalism. Most of this suppression of stories is centered on America's schools, which the Right sees as institutions where a nationalist mythology should be cultivated. Schools, after all, are ideological state apparatuses, institutions that create, reflect, and reinforce dominant ideology, which is why they have been at the center of efforts to shape public opinion. In *The 1776 Report* released under the Trump administration the authors argue for reform of America's schools because "people must share a large measure of commonality in manners, customs, language, and dedication to the common good."[23] The authors of the report also argue that, "educators must convey a sense of enlightened patriotism that equips each generation with a knowledge of America's founding principles, a deep reverence for their liberties, and a profound love of their country."[24] Patriotic myths such as these should be questioned and are based on emotion rather than fact. Current efforts on the Right to expunge diversity, inclusion, and equity programs, critical race theory, books highlighting the experiences of under-represented groups, curricula focused on teaching complete, complex, and unflattering histories, and even critical thinking itself, are all efforts to "take control of the narrative," to (re)impose ideologies that are still dominant but are being challenged by changing cultural norms and more nuanced understandings of history.

Authoritarians fear change, difference of opinion, diversity, ambiguity, and complexity, all of which threaten the larger, cohesive fictions that bind their world together. Arendt argues that "[fascists] are able to create a believable fictive world because reality has the handicap that it is 'not logical, consistent, or organized'."[25] Fascist narratives impose order upon the imagination by glossing over nuance, but they are always under threat, which means they must be continuously maintained so that the seams of dominant ideology remain invisible, so that the myth being created feels real, true, consistent, and cohesive. Ruth Ben-Ghiat argues that authoritarian strongmen call upon narratives of utopia, nostalgia, and crisis: "the desire for a pristine and perfect community" and their "nostalgia for better times . . . involves the fantasy of returning to an age when male authority was secure and women, people of color, and workers knew their places."[26] In other words, they create a narrative about our nation's past, one that characterizes history, also a collection of stories, as stable, knowable, and unambiguous, as part of a cohesive mythology.

Eddie S. Glaude Jr. explains that this national mythology works to maintain a perception of coherence through collective acts of repression. White America represses what he calls "blasphemous facts" so that we can hold onto our nation's "innocence," a fantasy of a history where slavery and Jim Crow are somehow exceptions to our collective values instead of reflections of them. In the early 2020s multiple bills, all with the same boilerplate language, have been passed around the nation to restrict what is taught to young people in our nation's schools. They prohibit any instruction that asserts that the United States is "fundamentally racist" or that claims that individuals "should feel anguish, guilt or any other form of discomfort or stress" because of their race. It's a desperate, willful act of forgetting necessary to the maintenance of existing systems, institutions, values, and a coherent mythology of what it means to be an American: As Glaude explains, "Having secured our innocence, we feel no guilt in enjoying what we have earned by our own merit, in defending our right to educate our children in the best schools and in demanding that we be judged by our ability alone."[27] "Blasphemous facts" must be repressed so that they don't puncture this belief in the legitimacy of meritocracy and equality, bedrocks of neoliberal ideology.

Some stories can highlight "blasphemous facts" that challenge totalizing narratives, especially when they are focused on exposing the functioning of narrative, the way some stories are emphasized while others are repressed. Stories focused on revealing the maintenance of myth can also invite readers to read against the grain of fascist mythologies. Ideally, epistemic narratives teach reading and critical thinking skills that are transferable to other texts, especially those that make up the convergence culture narratives that dominate our current media ecosystem. In this way, books for younger readers can instruct us about the workings of ideology by teaching theory and modeling critical thought about the systems we inhabit, and in ways that are accessible to a broad range of readers.

Narrative Landscapes

M.T. Anderson's novel *Landscape with Invisible Hand* is another example of a book that makes larger systems visible, specifically laissez-faire capitalism, income inequality, and imperialism. In the novel, aliens called the vuvv have colonized Earth but instead of making humans into their slaves they impose their economic system, which further stratifies the human population according to class and further widens the income gap between the wealthy and the poor. The wealthy one percent of humans live in floating cities a mile above ground while everyone else lives on the neglected surface of the planet. In their negotiations with world leaders the aliens promised technology to cure diseases but "of course no one thought about the fact that all that tech would be behind a paywall."[28] The book is a satire that exaggerates existing social structures in order to highlight and critique them. It makes the inequality of late capitalism tangible by depicting a great physical distance between the wealthy and everyone else, by distilling and simplifying a complex system. Such allegories, R.T. Tally Jr. argues, serve a pedagogical purpose: "What almost certainly ought to be ridiculed as oversimplification may ultimately turn out to be one of the unforeseen political strengths of dystopian narrative,"[29] that it reveals the "invisible" social systems that structure our realities.

The narrator and protagonist, Adam, is an eighteen-year-old artist and each chapter is organized around the works he creates, landscapes in various mediums that depict his reality with titles like "The Looted Stop & Shop at First Light" and "My House, Underwater." Through Adam's narration we see the decisions he makes as he attempts to understand and depict his world. The book teaches an artist's point of view: seeing beauty amidst the everyday, making the normal seem strange. While the novel is focalized through its narrator, much of the meaning comes from the world-building, the way that Anderson crafts his written landscape: The floating cities block out the sun, the rendering sails the aliens use to extract Earth's resources glow at night so that people on the surface no longer experience dark, whole towns and neighborhoods are covered in black soot from alien factories, and the social infrastructure is crumbling because it is no longer funded or maintained. Adam gets a disease from untreated tap water because "as part of the vuvv's austerity measures, municipal water is no longer purified."[30] He is disabled by chronic illness, which threatens to kill him when he experiences sepsis. His family cannot afford treatment.

Through the use of satire and science fiction, Anderson conveys contemporary systems and the mythologies that maintain them in a way that makes them tangible. He uses what Brecht called distancing techniques in order to draw our attention to social structures that we normally wouldn't notice because they seem to be common sense or just the way things are. Brecht argued for what he called the "learning play" (also called "epic theatre"), one that would educate audiences about the workings of ideology and about larger systems of power. Brecht was an anti-fascist playwright who fled Germany in 1933, just after Hitler took power. Many of his plays and theoretical works were written during his twelve-year exile. He spent decades working to define political theatre that would help viewers to think about the larger systems—fascism, capitalism, imperialism—that are not apparent because they are all around us, they shape and are shaped by dominant ideology. He, like Belsey, argued that realism works to confirm dominant ideology by depicting it as common sense. Realistic texts, he argued, focus our attention on the lives of individuals rather than on social systems, much in the way that the Little House books foreground family relationships and place the context of settler colonialism in the background.[31]

Brecht wrote that, "When something seems 'the most obvious thing in the world' it means that any attempt to understand the world has been given up. What is 'natural' must have the force of what is startling."[32] Instead of saying, "It's only natural—it will never change—the sufferings of this man appall me, because they are inescapable," the epic theatre should leave the viewer saying, "That's extraordinary, hardly believable—it's got to stop—the sufferings of this man appall me, because they are unnecessary."[33] The protagonist in an epic text is not depicted as a "victim of an inevitable fate."[34] Their fate is shown as being alterable because man-made systems are alterable, not natural. Finally, the epic text shows how hegemony works because it depicts "the dominant viewpoint as the viewpoint of the dominators."[35] *Roll of Thunder* does this when Lillian Jean's oblivious opinion about "the way of things" is revealed to be part of a larger system of belief she has learned through her culture.

One way Brecht attempted to make larger systems visible was through a technique called distancing. He set plays in different times in history so that he could comment on the present from a distance and so that viewers would be emotionally distanced from the subject matter. *Landscape with Invisible Hand* uses similar techniques. The social and economic systems Anderson depicts are not so far removed from our own but he distances them through the plot device of an alien invasion. For instance, when Adam is explaining what happened when vuvv technology suddenly put a billion humans out of work, he says, "our leaders were making speeches about how America's middle class had to stop dreaming and start learning how to really work. By that point, I'm not sure there really even was a middle class anymore."[36] Adam notes several times that both the vuvv and the ruling classes focus on individual work ethic, on the neoliberal idea of pulling oneself up by one's bootstraps. They divert attention from their oppressive system by focusing on individual responsibility. Adam's optimistic mother echoes this ideology of laissez-faire capitalism saying, "Don't worry. The economy will get better. It always does. We just have to wait it out. The invisible hand of the market always moves to make things right."[37] The libertarian idea that the marketplace will correct itself is key to dominant ideology that benefits corporations that do not want to be regulated or taxed. The novel makes clear that this rhetoric is a way to justify and maintain an inhumane system, and that the stories those in power tell, and that the powerless repeat as if they are the natural way of things, help to hold that system in place.

Another system Anderson highlights is health care in the United States, where more than 10 percent of the population is uninsured. Adam's chronic illness is not a natural occurrence; it is brought on by the vuvv's austerity measures. It is also a disease that dehumanizes and demoralizes him, making him into a social outcast. Adam shits himself in public and narrates this experience of being an abject Other. "I clutch but can't hold" he says. "I feel it spilling down the backs of my legs. . . . She can tell what's happening. I can't stand her look of disgust."[38] He is another minority vilified by and left behind under the new authoritarianism of neoliberalism, the disposable human, the uninsured poor. His illness becomes progressively worse and threatens his life. When he passes out at a vuvv event, he is taken away on a gurney, treated, and unceremoniously dumped at a shuttle stop wearing a hospital gown. His cure is almost anti-climactic because it happens so quickly, so easily.

Adam and his family are victims of what Giroux characterizes as a "politics of disposability": "Discarded by the corporate state, dispossessed of social provisions, and deprived of the economic, political, and social conditions that enable viable and critical modes of agency, expanding populations of Americans now find themselves inhabiting zones of abandonment marked by deep inequalities in power, wealth, and income."[39] As I noted in the Chapter 4, the most vulnerable populations under American authoritarianism are groups considered to be disposable. "The practice of disposability expands to include more and more individuals and groups who have been considered redundant, consigned to zones of abandonment, surveillance, and mass incarceration. Disposability is no longer the exception but the norm."[40]

At the novel's end, Adam and his sister and mother abandon their underwater house and their debt so they can move someplace where his mother can get a job. "We need to leave this house, leave this town, leave this state and begin with nothing—because zero is more than negative something."[41] There is no deux ex machina or happy ending that reestablishes the social order. They simply survive. As Adam says, "We all have to find some way to live with the world as it is now."[42] Poverty does not ennoble or make characters in the novel behave well: Adam's father leaves the family he is unable to support and his mom takes in tenants who refuse to pay rent. There is no heart-warming story of neighborly love or charity. Unlike those "feel-good" stories we hear all the time on the news about some clever fund-raising idea to help a family with insufficient health insurance to pay medical bills, the novel emphasizes and places blame and responsibility on the system of unfettered capitalism rather than on individuals.

The Ends of Story

I teach children's and young adult books to adult university students. Over the past twenty years, I've gotten used to people suspiciously asking, "Why are college students reading children's books?" as if to say, "Aren't children's books too simple and easy for adults?" An easy answer that highlights the utility of the subject matter is to point out that our students go on to become teachers, librarians, professors, writers, editors, or parents, taking on a number of roles where a knowledge of literature for young people might come in handy. It's an incomplete and ingenuous answer though. The more complete answer is that books for children and young adults can teach important ideas to adults as well as children. Additionally, many of the adults in our courses are still in their late teens and early twenties, which makes them the target audience for many works of young adult literature.

In my "introduction to children's literature" course I sometimes begin the term by sharing the picture book *Hooray for Diffendoofer Day!*, which was written by Dr. Seuss and published posthumously. In the book, the students at Diffendoofer School are joyful as they learn about myriad delightful things from a staff of quirky teachers. But two-thirds of the way through the book, the state ordains a standardized test. Suddenly, everyone is sad and worried because, if they fail the test, they'll be sent to school in dreary Flobbertown. "'Not Flobbertown!' we shouted / And we shuddered at the name, / For everyone in Flobbertown / Does everything the same."[43] The next two-page black, white, and mostly grey spread depicts Flobbertown School atop a hill with search lights scanning the skies as if it's a prison. Frowning children, who all look and dress the same, walk single file through the rain.

> It's miserable in Flobbertown,
> They dress in just one style.
> They sing one song. They never dance.
> They march in single file.
> They do not have a playground.
> And they do not have a park.
> Their lunches have no taste at all.
> Their dogs are scared to bark.[44]

The children at Diffendoofer School avoid this terrible fate because they easily pass the test. As they're taking it, they realize that they're able to answer questions about unfamiliar material because their teachers have not taught them what to think, they've taught them *how* to think: "There were questions about other things / we'd never seen or heard / And yet we somehow answered them / enjoying every word." (I teach the book in the first few days of the semester because it sets up a major theme for the course, which is a focus on critical thinking: How can books for children and young adults teach readers *how* to think?)

The book is also a commentary on the standardized testing industry and on what happens at schools that teach to the test, that demand conformity, and that "drill and kill," sucking the joy and wonder out of learning in the process. Wonder, intellectual curiosity, and imagination are difficult, if not impossible, to measure but they are vital to anti-fascist and pro-democracy education. There's a reason America's neofascists are banning books and muzzling teachers: Critical thinking is anathema to authoritarianism. So are imagination and wonder. As I discuss in earlier chapters, authoritarians work to foment cynicism, disdain, and mass skepticism. Henry Giroux writes that, "authoritarianism does not just breed conformity and cynicism; it relies on the death of hope to reproduce its dominant ideologies and practices while depoliticizing young people and others who should care about the fate of democracy."[45] An education and literature that are anti-fascist and pro-democracy, then, should encourage intellectual curiosity, independent thinking, questioning, and imagination. Young people cannot strive toward a better, more democratic future without a rich imagination, the ability to envision possibilities for themselves beyond the present.

Giroux claims that under neofascism, children and adults are being educated by a "disimagination machine," which "depoliticizes, privatizes, and infantilizes Americans."[46] "The 'disimagination machine' is [. . .] a set of cultural apparatuses extending from schools and mainstream media to the next sites of screen culture, social media, and public pedagogy that function primarily to weaken the ability of individuals to think critically."[47] One way to counter the "disimagination machine," the "public pedagogy" of our media-saturated culture, is through books, films, shows, and games for children and young adults that equip them with the close reading skills they need in order to understand and critique the overabundance of narratives that surround us. I have focused here mostly on books, but there are multiple other texts in various mediums that can help to teach non-authoritarian ways of thinking, including narrative literacy, an awareness of how the stories all around us work to create meaning. In Chapter 1, I discuss the attention economy, the way our devices control, divert, and capture our attention. There is no better way to capture an audience's attention than with story, which is why young people, and older people too, need the kind of narrative literacy taught in departments of English, especially ones with a strong basis in cultural studies and rhetorical theory. In our media-saturated culture, we need the humanities to help us to understand how story works, how it manipulates our emotions, how narrative is a kind of rhetoric that persuades, and how lots of small and large stories work together to create a mythology, a belief system that supersedes facts and elides complexity, contradictions, and divergent perspectives.

Finally, an anti-fascist literature for younger readers assumes that we—adults and children—are fellow travelers, while also acknowledging that one group, adults, has far more rights, money, influence, voice, privilege, and power than the other group, children. I discuss in the Introduction how children's books, and the study of them, are often centered on power relationships, especially those between children and adults or children and institutions. Ours is a field that is self-aware of intersectional power relationships, and the way these manifest through narrative: Does an author address the child reader as an underling? Do they withhold important information, and why? Is the author an adult "authority" that cannot be questioned or challenged? Or, conversely, does the book invite young readers to co-construct meaning, to question, and to participate in larger, philosophical and political conversations? Works of anti-fascist literature for young readers acknowledge that young and old have much more in common than we do differences, that age is a continuum, that people of all ages share affinities and common goals, and that we all must work together to maintain and expand democracy.

Acknowledgments

I am grateful to my university and to my faculty union, the EMU-AAUP, for creating an environment where scholarship is valued and faculty research is supported. This project was only possible because I received four internal research grants from Eastern Michigan University: two faculty research fellowships, one sabbatical leave, and funding from the Josephine Nevins Keal Professional Development Fund.

Much thanks to my reviewers: Reviewer no. 1, whose enthusiasm for this project was encouraging and Reviewer no. 2, who challenged my arguments and pushed me to think differently. Thanks also to my editor Richard Morrison for having faith in this project.

The Children's Literature Association, my academic home for more than twenty years, provided a space where I could share ideas in progress and learn from others. I've tried to cite as many colleagues as possible in the manuscript to acknowledge this intellectual debt and the way so many clever people in our field have influenced my thinking and offered encouragement. What I can't cite is how Margaret Mackey helped to give form to an amorphous set of ideas; Michelle Ann Abate read an early, drafty introduction; Phil Nel generously shared ideas, resources, and encouragement; Gina Boldman and Jessica Kander shared titles of books I wouldn't have known about otherwise; and how Tamra Pica and Dawn Sardella-Ayres included me in their virtual writing group, which provided community during the Covid pandemic.

I am grateful for Elke and Martine Krantz Moheim for providing a valuable international perspective on events happening in the United States and for my dear friend Michelle Burdick, who got me out of my study to kayak all along the Huron River, writing breaks that put the world into perspective.

My parents, Bill and Irmgard Wannamaker, and my son, Will Krause, have been a constant source of support and love. Steven D. Krause, my partner for more than thirty years, is a fellow academic and writer. Because he does all the shopping and cooking, everyday acts of love, I'm able to write for hours on end in a room of my own. So many of the ideas in this book bounced around our living room as he helped me to work through rhetorical theory, suggested sources on new media technologies, and helped me to untangle the knots in my arguments. Quite simply, I would not have been able to complete this project without him.

Notes

Preface. Fascism, Resistance, and the Confounding Case of *Harry Potter*

1. Timothy Snyder, *On Tyranny: Twenty Lessons from the Twentieth Century* (New York: Tim Duggan Books, 2017), 13.
2. Snyder, 61.
3. Snyder, 62.
4. Snyder, 61.
5. I have chosen to put white into lower case and Black into upper case. White supremacists will often do the inverse to mark the superiority of whiteness, and I'd like to counter their efforts.
6. David Neiwert, "When white nationalists chant their weird slogans, what do they mean? Explaining 'You Will Not Replace Us,' 'Blood and Soil,' 'Russia is Our Friend,' and other catchphrases from torch-bearing marchers in Charlottesville," Southern Poverty Law Center. October 10, 2017, accessed April 2, 2022, Splcenter.org.
7. Ella Cerón, "Why 'Harry Potter' Means So Much to the Parkland Activists," *Teen Vogue*. March 26, 2018, accessed January 12, 2024, https://www.teenvogue.com/story/what-harry-potter-means-to-parkland-activists#:~:text=They%20have%20found%20a%20small,story%20is%20any%20less%20important.&text=If%20anything%2C%20Harry%20Potter%20suggests,the%20wrongs%20of%20our%20world.
8. Loris Vezzali, et al., "The greatest magic of Harry Potter: Reducing Prejudice," *Journal of Applied Social Psychology* 45, no. 2 (February 2015), 105–121.
9. Sarah Park Dahlen and Kallie Schell, "'Cho Chang Is Trending': What It Means to Be Asian in the Wizarding World" in *Harry Potter and the Other: Race, Justice, and Difference in the Wizarding World*, eds. Sarah Park Dahlen and Ebony Elizabeth Thomas (Jackson: University Press of Mississippi, 2022), 87.

10. Sarah Park Dahlen and Ebony Elizabeth Thomas, "Introduction" in *Harry Potter and the Other*, 6.

11. Our democratic republic is almost 250 years old but it didn't become a multiracial democracy until after the civil rights movements of the mid-twentieth century, which assured voting rights for racial minorities. These rights are currently being worn away by a conservative US Supreme Court and new voting restrictions being imposed by a number of state governing bodies.

12. In his essay "A Manifesto for Children's Literature; or, Reading Harold as a Teenager," Philip Nel makes a case for why adults should be reading works of literature written for younger readers. "Children's books are the most important books we read because they're potentially the most influential books we read," he argues, highlighting the impact of stories we learn at impressionable ages. Adults, he argues, should read or reread children's books: "Children's books have much to give those of us who are no longer children. There are levels of meaning we may have missed when we read the book as a child. Adults' experiences may grant us interpretations unavailable to less experienced readers, just as children may arrive at interpretations lost to adults who have forgotten their own childhoods. In children's books, there is art, wisdom, beauty, melancholy, hope, and insight for readers of *all* ages." Philip Nel, "A Manifesto for Children's Literature; or, Reading Harold as a Teenager," *The Iowa Review* 45, no. 2 (Fall 2015), https://iowareview.org/from-the-issue/volume-45-issue-2-%E2%80%94-fall-2015/manifesto-childrens-literature-or-reading-harold.

13. My approach to books and other texts is grounded in cultural studies, a field that taught me to think about the cultural context that stories are told within and the way narrative both reflects and affects our collective worldview. The relationship between a text and its readers is complex, and readers aren't empty receptacles: they have agency and critical faculties, they can read against the grain of a text that flows with dominant ideology, and they can repurpose or remake a text through their interactions with it. After all, ideology comes from the bottom up as well as from the top down as we all participate in its maintenance and reproduction. Dominant ideology is constructed through shared ideas that go largely unquestioned because they are so ingrained that they seem to be just the way of things or "common sense," something most everyone believes to be true. For example, it once was "common sense" in Western culture that the sun revolved around the earth. With hindsight, we can recognize when a paradigm shifts, when a Copernicus or Darwin comes along with an idea large enough to challenge the beliefs of a given culture and time. It's much harder though to study our current cultural context because we're in the midst of it. Cultural theories can help us to think about the workings of ideology by encouraging us to pose childish questions about things that seem obvious: Why do people believe what they believe? Where's the line that separates a "real" story from one that is "fiction"?

14. Adrienne Kertzer's 2002 book *My Mother's Voice: Children, Literature, and the Holocaust* is an excellent study of Holocaust literature for young people.

15. Philip Nel, *Was the Cat in the Hat Black? The Hidden Racism of Children's Literature and the Need for Diverse Books*. (New York: Oxford UP, 2017), 198.

16. bell hooks, *Teaching to Transgress: Education as the Practice of Freedom*. (New York: Routledge, 1994), 64.

17. The term "Third Culture Kid" was coined by researchers John and Ruth Useem in the 1950s to describe the children of military personnel or ambassadors who grow up living overseas. It's a small, spread-out subculture of global nomads who share a number of experiences and characteristics.

Introduction. American Neofascism, the Child, and Children's Literature

1. Umberto Eco, "Ur-Fascism," *The New York Review of Books* (June 22, 1995), accessed April 22, 2024, https://www.nybooks.com/articles/1995/06/22/ur-fascism/.

2. Robert O. Paxton, *The Anatomy of Fascism* (New York: Vintage Books, 2004), 202.

3. Paxton, 14.

4. Paxton, 218.

5. Robert O. Paxton. "The Five Stages of Fascism," *The Journal of Modern History* 70, no. 1 (March 1998), 10, accessed November 19, 2024, JSTOR.

6. Christian Fuchs. *Digital Demagogue : Authoritarian Capitalism in the Age of Trump and Twitter* (London: Pluto Press, 2018), 25.

7. In their book *The Black Antifascist Tradition: Fighting Back from Anti-Lynching to Abolition*, Jeanelle K. Hope and Bill V. Mullen argue that the "United States, not Europe" was the "epicenter of modern racial fascism," which started just after the Civil War ended when six former Confederate soldiers in Tennessee formed the KKK. Significantly, they argue that "unlike with European Fascism, there is no need for a singular Fascist regime or dictator to ensure its existence." Jeanelle K. Hope and Bill V. Mullen. *The Black Antifascist Tradition: Fighting Back from Anti-Lynching to Abolition* (Chicago: Haymarket Books, 2023) p. 9-10.

8. Adolf Hitler, *Mein Kampf*, translated into English by James Murphy, Chapter 10. PDF at https://www.livingston.org/cms/lib9/NJ01000562/Centricity/Domain/751/mein%20kampf.pdf.

9. Alt-right groups practice and perpetuate antisemitism in several ways: They deny the Holocaust ever happened and they accuse Jews of conspiring to commit all manner of crimes, some of which involve children. For example, the QAnon conspiracy theory that elites are kidnapping and torturing children has its roots in centuries-old accusations of blood libel, the widespread medieval European belief that Jews sacrificed Christian children in their religious rituals. Talia Lavin writes that, "For a millennium, the blood libel has flourished and, with it, accompanying tortures and murders of Jews in orgies of violence." The fiction of mutilated and murdered children creates grounds for attacking the alleged perpetrators. In this way, Jews were made to seem monstrous, not human, which justified their

oppression. "QAnon, Blood Libel, and the Satanic Panic," *The New Republic* (September 29, 2020), accessed February 20, 2024, https://newrepublic.com/article/159529/qanon-blood-libel-satanic-panic.

10. Michael Vavrus, *Teaching Anti-Fascism: A Critical Multicultural Pedagogy for Civic Engagement* (New York: Teachers College Press, 2022), 73.

11. Kevin D. Roberts, "Forward: A Promise to America," in *Mandate for Leadership: The Conservative Promise, Project 2025: Presidential Transition Project* (Heritage Foundation, 2023), 1. Hereafter referred to as Project 2025.

12. Roberts, 3.

13. *Project 2025*, 481.

14. *Project 2025*, 346.

15. The Child, when capitalized, refers to the concept of childhood rather than to actual children. A number of scholars in the field of children's literature studies have theorized the cultural construct of the Child, the ways it has evolved over time, how it differs in different cultures, and its role in shaping attitudes and policies that affect actual children. See, for example, Robin Bernstein's *Racial Innocence: Performing American Childhood from Slavery to Civil Rights* (New York University Press, 2011); Kate Capshaw and Anna Mae Duane's *Who Writes for Black Children?: African American Children's Literature Before 1900* (Minneapolis, University of Minnesota Press, 2017); Marah Gubar's *Artful Dodgers: Reconceiving the Golden Age of Children's Literature* (Oxford University Press, 2009); Caroline F. Levander and Carol J. Singley's *The American Child: A Cultural Studies Reader* (New Brunswick, NJ: Rutgers University Press, 2003); and Steven Mintz's *Huck's Raft: A History of American Childhood* (Cambridge, Harvard University Press, 2004).

16. Roberts, 4–5.

17. Roberts, 5.

18. As a result of these concerted efforts, the phrase "critical race theory" has become unmoored from its original meanings as the Right has co-opted it as shorthand for any teaching about systemic racism. "Among conservatives, the term has become a catch-all for any conversation about historical or present inequities. And it's been conflated with a host of other initiatives schools have taken up to improve outcomes for students of color, like culturally responsive teaching or restorative justice." Sarah Schwartz, "Who's Really Driving Critical Race Theory Legislation? An Investigation," *Education Week* (July 19, 2021), accessed January 22, 2023, https://www.edweek.org/policy-politics/whos-really-driving-critical-race-theory-legislation-an-investigation/2021/07.

19. Heritage Foundation, "How to Recognize Critical Race Theory" (2023), accessed May 30, 2023, https://www.heritage.org/civil-society/heritage-explains/how-identify-critical-race-theory.

20. Moms for Liberty, "Who we are," accessed February 29, 2024, https://www.momsforliberty.org.

21. Robin Bernstein, *Racial Innocence: Performing American Childhood from Slavery to Civil Rights* (New York University Press, 2011), 3.

22. Lee Edelman, *No Future: Queer Theory and the Death Drive* (Durham: Duke University Press, 2004), 21.

23. Ian Prior, *Parents of the World Unite! How to Save our Schools From the Left's Radical Agenda* (New York: Hachette Book Group, 2023), 6.

24. Benjamin Wallace-Wells, "What Do Conservatives Fear about Critical Race Theory?" *The New Yorker* (June 10, 2021), accessed February 29, 2024, https://www.newyorker.com/news/annals-of-inquiry/what-do-conservatives-fear-about-critical-race-theory.

25. Henry Jenkins, "Introduction: Childhood Innocence and Other Modern Myths" in *The Children's Culture Reader*, ed. Henry Jenkins (New York University Press, 1998), 5.

26. Kit Kelen and Björn Sundmark, "Introduction" in *The Nation in Children's Literature : Nations of Childhood*, eds. Kit Kelen and Björn Sundmark (Taylor & Francis Group, 2012).

27. Jason Stanley, *How Fascism Works: The Politics of Us and Them* (New York: Random House, 2018), 48.

28. Anna Mae Duane, *The Children's Table: Childhood Studies and the Humanities* (Athens: University of Georgia Press, 2013), 1.

29. Susan Campbell Bartoletti, *Hitler Youth: Growing Up in Hitler's Shadow* (New York: Scholastic, 2005), 38.

30. Bartolleti, 38.

31. Matthew C. MacWilliams, "The One Weird Trait That Predicts Whether You're a Trump Supporter," *Politico Magazine*, January 17, 2016, accessed June 6, 2023, https://www.politico.com/magazine/story/2016/01/donald-trump-2016-authoritarian-213533/.

32. Researchers look at both authoritarian leaders and their followers. Marc Hetherington and Jonathan Weiler explain that, "The scholarly literature tends to focus on followers rather than leaders, mostly painting an unflattering picture of authoritarians as angry people suffering from some cognitive defect, which causes them to blindly follow a Hussein, a Castro, or a Vader" (*Authoritarianism and Polarization in American Politics* [Cambridge University Press, 2009], 5). They go on to point out that "Authoritarianism is a not a set personality trait. People can and do change, and context matters too. Some researchers argue that people with some authoritarian traits can be activated in situations where they feel as though they are under threat: When those scoring lower in authoritarianism do perceive significant threat, we find that they are not heroic, small 'd,' democrats. In fact, under such conditions, their preferences on issues become indistinguishable from those who score high in authoritarianism" (7).

33. Hetherington and Weiler, 2.

34. The F-scale, a way to measure individual's tendencies toward an authoritarian mindset, was developed by Theodore Adorno and others in 1947. Although it has since been found to be problematic, it was highly influential among social scientists studying authoritarianism. The F-scale "fell into disrepute within a decade of its

introduction for any number of reasons, response acquiescence and poor reliability chief among them" (Hetherington and Weiler, 47). A modified version of the F-scale emerged in the late 1990s and early 2000s as researchers worked to understand an increase in authoritarian thinking in the United States. "In 1992, the NES introduced its four-item authoritarianism index. Specifically, it asked respondents to judge attractive attributes in children" (48). Some people value both choices, and that is measured as well. All choices are potentially positive and not necessarily in complete opposition to one another. "What is useful about this approach, we believe, is that it appropriately mirrors choices individuals are forced to make in politics" (48). This newer index, though, is also imperfect. For example, it doesn't account for cultural differences in parenting styles. "Recently, however, concerns have been raised about the cross-racial validity of the four childrearing questions. Early analysis of these questions found a higher percentage of authoritarians among African Americans than among whites. This finding by itself invited greater scrutiny of the questions themselves and how they are understood within different communities" (MacWilliams, 34).

35. Hetherington and Weiler, 49.

36. Nancy MacLean, *Democracy in Chains: The Deep History of the Radical Right's Stealth Plan for America* (New York: Viking, 2017), 105, 196.

37. The 1619 Project, *Education Materials Collection*, https://1619education.org/.

38. Nikole Hannah-Jones, "The 1619 Project," *The New York Times Magazine*, August 2019.

39. National Archives, "1776 Commission Takes Historic and Scholarly Step to Restore Understanding of the Greatness of the American Founding," Trump White House, January 18, 2021, accessed June 6, 2023, https://trumpwhitehouse.archives.gov/briefings-statements/1776-commission-takes-historic-scholarly-step-restore-understanding-greatness-american-founding/.

40. Civics Alliance, "American Birthright: The Civic Alliance's Model K-12 Social Studies Standards," July 2022, PDF accessed May 30, 2023, https://civicsalliance.org/american-birthright/.

41. Civics Alliance, 27.

42. Kenneth Kidd, *Theory for Beginners: Children's Literature as Critical Thought* (New York: Fordham University Press, 2020), 6.

43. Timothy Snyder, *On Tyranny: Twenty Lessons from the Twentieth Century* (New York: Tim Duggan Books, 2017).

44. Michelle Ann Abate, *No Kids Allowed: Children's Literature for Adults* (Baltimore: Johns Hopkins University Press, 2020), 3–4.

45. Kidd, *Theory for Beginners*, 8.

46. Terry Eagleton, quoted in bell hooks, *Teaching to Transgress: Education as the Practice of Freedom* (New York: Routledge, 1994), 59.

47. Kobabe uses e, em, eir pronouns.

48. Maia Kobabe, *Gender Queer* (Portland: Oni-Lion Forge Publishing Group, 2022), 211.

49. Perry Nodelman and Mavis Reimer, *The Pleasures of Children's Literature*, 3rd ed. (Pearson, 2003), 23.

50. Jacqueline Rose, *The Case of Peter Pan: The Impossibility of Children's Fiction* (Macmillan Press, 1984).

51. For example, in her work "Snanger Danger: SS/HG Fanfiction, Kinship, and an Affinity Space Model of Children's and Young Adult Literature" (in *Alt Kid Lit: What Children's Literature Might Be*, eds. Kenneth Kidd and Derritt Mason [Jackson University Press of Mississippi, 2024]), Amanda K. Allen analyzes online fan spaces as sites where readers/writers of varying ages share kinship. Vanessa Joosen explores the social construction of age categories in her entry titled "Age" (in *The Routledge Companion to Children's Literature and Culture*, eds. Claudia Nelson, Elisabeth Wesseling, and Andrea Mei-Ying Wu [New York: Routledge, 2023]). In his essay "Kidding Around: Children, Comedy and Social Media" in *The Routledge Comedy Studies Reader* (ed. Ian Wilkie [New York: Routledge, 2020]) Pete Kunze challenges constructs of the Child as passive reader in his analysis of young people's social media posts. Victoria Ford Smith examines the child as creator in her article, "Exhibiting Children: The Young Artist as Construct and Creator, *Journal of Juvenilia Studies* 1 (2018), 62–81, https://journalofjuveniliastudies.com/index.php/jjs/article/view/19/14.

52. In his article "Chaperoning Words: Meaning-Making in Comics and Picture Books" (*Children's Literature* 41 [2013], 57–90), Joe Sutliff Sanders uses the term "chaperoning" to characterize the experience of adults reading aloud to children. Adults chaperone meaning as they filter a text for the child, an act of selective interpretation that can emphasize certain aspects of a story or omit others.

53. Roberta Seelinger Trites, *Disturbing the Universe: Power and Repression in Adolescent Literature* (Iowa City: University of Iowa Press, 2000), 22.

54. Maria Nikolajeva, *Power, Voice and Subjectivity in Literature for Young Readers* (New York: Routledge, 2010).

55. Perry Nodelman, *The Hidden Adult: Defining Children's Literature* (Baltimore, MD: Johns Hopkins UP, 2008), 188.

56. Wayne Booth, *The Rhetoric of Fiction*, 2nd ed. (The University of Chicago Press, 1983).

57. Katharine Capshaw, "Singing a 'Sea Island Song': Alice Childress's Responsive Black Theater," *Alt Kid Lit: What Children's Literature Might Be*, eds. Kenneth B. Kidd and Derritt Mason (Jackson: University of Mississippi Press, 2024), 33.

58. Toni Morrison, *The Bluest Eye* (New York: Plume, 1970), 211.

59. Marah Gubar, *Artful Dodgers: Reconceiving the Golden Age of Children's Literature* (Oxford: Oxford University Press, 2009), 32-3.

60. Richard Flynn, "What Are We Talking about When We Talk about Agency?" *Jeunesse: Young People, Texts, Cultures* 8 no. 1 (2016), p. 254–265. Project MUSE, https://doi.org/10.1353/jeu.2016.0012. 256.

61. Kelly McDowell, "*Roll of Thunder, Hear My Cry*: A Culturally Specific, Subversive Concept of Child Agency." *Children's Literature in Education* 33, no. 3 (Sept. 2002), 215.

62. Kimberley Reynolds, *Radical Children's Literature: Future Visions and Aesthetic Transformations in Juvenile Fiction* (New York: Palgrave MacMillan, 2007), 2.

63. Michelle Ann Abate, *Raising Your Kids Right: Children's Literature and American Political Conservatism* (New Brunswick, NJ: Rutgers University Press, 2010), 37.

64. Jack Zipes, "Forward: The Twists and Turns of Radical Children's Literature," in *Tales for Little Rebels: A collection of radical children's literature*, eds. Julia L. Mickenberg and Philip Nel (New York: NYU Press, 2008), vii.

65. Reynolds, *Radical Children's Literature* 15.

66. Julia L. Mickenberg, *Learning from the Left: Children's Literature, the Cold War, and Radical Politics in the United States* (Oxford University Press, 2005), 13.

67. Peter Brooks, *Seduced by Story: The Use and Abuse of Narrative* (New York Review Books, 2022).

68. Brooks, 22-23.

69. Margaret Meek, *How Texts Teach What Readers Learn* (Stroud: The Thimble Press, 1988), 16–26.

70. Meek, 89.

71. John Stephens, *Language and Ideology in Children's Fiction* (New York: Longman, 1992), 16.

72. Adolf Hitler was a master of public pedagogy: He knew he had to teach the masses through repetition and simple language. In *Mein Kampf*, he wrote, "All propaganda must be presented in a popular form and must fix its intellectual level so as not to be above the heads of the least intellectual of those to whom it is directed;" "The receptive powers of the masses are very restricted, and their understanding is feeble. On the other hand, they quickly forget. Such being the case, all effective propaganda must be confined to a few bare essentials and those must be expressed as far as possible in stereotyped formulas;" and "Its chief function is to convince the masses, whose slowness of understanding needs to be given time in order that they may absorb information; and only constant repetition will finally succeed in imprinting an idea on the memory of the crowd" (chapter 6).

73. Kidd, *Theory for Beginners*, 3–4.

74. Kidd, *Theory for Beginners*, 12.

75. Snyder, *On Tyranny*, 55.

76. Books that directly and didactically present anti-authoritarian ideas may be less effective for two reasons. First, texts that prescribe a simple meaning (a heavy-handed "moral") are less likely to promote critical thinking, careful analysis, or an understanding of literary ambiguity. Second, nuance, ambiguity, and an ability to understand multiple perspectives are skills vital to anti-fascist ways of thinking.

77. In his book *On Bullshit*, Harry Frankfurt (Princeton University Press, 2005) defines bullshit as a particular type of rhetoric. A bullshitter differs from a liar

because a bullshitter does not care whether his statements are true or false: every rhetorical act is purely strategic. "His eye is not on the facts at all, as the eyes of the honest man and the liar are, except insofar as they may be pertinent to his interest in getting away with what he says. He does not care whether the things he says describe reality correctly. He just picks them out, or makes them suit his purpose" (56). Because a bullshitter doesn't care whether he is lying or telling the truth "bullshit is a greater enemy of the truth than lies are" (61). The proliferation of bullshit in our media-saturated environment can result in "various forms of skepticism which deny that we can have any reliable access to an objective reality, and which therefore reject the possibility of knowing how things truly are" (64).

78. Brooks, *Seduced by Story*, 26.
79. Hetherington and Weiler, *Authoritarianism and Polarization*, 112.
80. Amanda Taub, "The rise of American authoritarianism," *Vox* (March 1, 2016), accessed May 3, 2024, https://www.vox.com/2016/3/1/11127424/trump-authoritarianism.
81. Hetherington and Weiler, 43.

Chapter 1. Stories about Stories: Reading Fascistic Rhetoric

1. Adrienne Kertzer, *My Mother's Voice: Children, Literature, and the Holocaust* (Broadview Press, 2002), 49.
2. Kenneth Kidd, *Theory for Beginners: Children's Literature as Critical Thought* (New York: Fordham University Press, 2020), 134.
3. Karen Coats, *Looking Glasses and Neverlands: Lacan, Desire, and Subjectivity in Children's Literature* (Iowa City, Iowa: University of Iowa Press, 2004), 1.
4. Peter Brooks, *Seduced by Story: The Use and Abuse of Narrative* (New York Review Books, 2022), 22-23.
5. Stephen J. Hartnett, "'Lock Her Up!': Fascism as a Political Style from Mussolini to Trump," in *The Rhetoric of Fascism*, ed. Nathan Crick (Tuscaloosa, AL: The University of Alabama Press, 2022), 43.
6. Phillipe Lacoue-Labarthe, Jean-Luc Nancy, and Brian Holmes, "The Nazi Myth," *Critical Inquiry*, 16, no. 2 (Winter, 1990), 293.
7. Timothy Snyder, *On Tyranny: Twenty Lessons from the Twentieth Century* (New York: Tim Duggan Books, 2017), 66.
8. Snyder, 67.
9. Snyder, 69.
10. Steven Levitsky and Daniel Ziblatt, *How Democracies Die* (New York: Penguin Random House, 2018), 167–8.
11. "Convergence culture" is a term Henry Jenkins coined to describe the way contemporary stories are told across various platforms, which creates participatory, additive, spread-out storied worlds. Henry Jenkins, *Convergence Culture: Where Old and New Media Collide* (New York: NYU Press, 2006).
12. Social media is an attention economy. The goal is to keep users online and engaged as long as possible, and this often means manipulating their emotions.

Anger, outrage, and fear are especially engaging. According to Ally Mintzer, "Many firms understand the scarcity of our attention, and are adapting their business models to capitalize on it. For instance, music streaming services like Spotify have two revenue streams; you can either monetarily pay for ads to disappear, or pay with your attention and listen to ads. In the book *Hooked: How to Build Habit-Forming Products*, Nir Eyal attests that technology companies rely on Harvard psychologist B.F. Skinner's well-known study that found that rewards, especially at variable intervals, increase one's anticipation. As anticipation increases, such reward-seeking actions that technology companies have capitalized on to capture attention turn to instinct. Eyal argues 'When you're feeling uncertain, before you ask why you're uncertain, you Google. When you're lonely, before you're even conscious of feeling it, you go to Facebook. Before you know you're bored, you're on YouTube. Nothing tells you to do these things. The users trigger themselves.'" Ally Mintzer, "Paying Attention: The Attention Economy," *Berkley Economic Review*, March 31, 2020, accessed November 27, 2022, https://econreview.berkeley.edu/paying-attention-the-attention-economy/.

13. Ben Rhodes, *After the Fall: Being American in the World We've Made* (New York: Random House, 2021), 35.

14. Rhodes, 71.

15. Roland Barthes, *A Barthes Reader*, ed. Susan Sontag (New York: The Noonday Press, 1988), 99.

16. Eddie S. Glaude Jr., *Begin Again: James Baldwin's America and Its Urgent Lessons for Our Own* (New York: Crown, 2020).

17. Hannah Arendt, *The Origins of Totalitarianism* (New York: Harcourt, 1985), 364.

18. Arendt, 353.

19. Jason Stanley. *How Fascism Works: The Politics of Us and Them* (New York: Random House, 2018), xxx.

20. Stanley, xxx–xxxi.

21. Shoshana Zuboff, *The Age of Surveillance Capitalism: The Fight for a Human Future at the New Frontier of Power* (New York: Public Affairs, 2019), 191.

22. Johann Hari, *Stolen Focus: Why You Can't Pay Attention—and How to Think Deeply Again* (New York: Crown, 2022) 125.

23. Hari, 136.

24. Zac Gershberg and Sean Illing, "The Spectacle of Fascism," in *The Rhetoric of Fascism*, ed. Nathan Crick (Tuscaloosa, AL: The University of Alabama Press, 2022), 58.

25. Marc Hetherington and Jonathan Weiler, *Authoritarianism and Polarization in American Politics* (Cambridge University Press, 2009).

26. Hetherington and Weiler, 11.

27. Hetherington and Weiler, 34.

28. Hetherington and Weiler, 37.

29. Hetherington and Weiler, 45.

30. Arendt, 353.

31. Brooks, *Seduced by Story*, 23.

32. Michael Vavrus, *Teaching Anti-Fascism: A Critical Multicultural Pedagogy for Civic Engagement* (New York: Teachers College Press, 2022), 10.

33. Bruce McComiskey, *Post-Truth Rhetoric and Composition* (Denver, CO: Utah State University Press, 2017), 5.

34. McComiskey, 6.

35. Slavoj Žižek, *The Sublime Object of Ideology* (Brooklyn, NY: Verso, 1989), 33.

36. When journalist Jeff Sharlet interviewed people whose homes were adorned with Trump, Confederate, and other right-wing flags, he found that they often repeated ideas from right-wing media verbatim: "Not a word Jerry said was fully his own. I'd been listening to Fox, to right-wing radio, as I drove and I'd already heard variations of every syllable he uttered. Jerry followed the news. He was a follower. He had not been a good student as a boy, he said. But now he had learned his lesson. The lesson was fear, the lesson was bitter, the lesson was that other people were getting more than their fair share." Jeff Sharlet, "'Fuck Biden,' 'Don't Tread on Me,' and a Wisconsin Death Trip for Our Times." *Vanity Fair*. (November 30, 2022), accessed June 5, 2023, https://www.vanityfair.com/news/2022/11/america-new-civil-war.

37. Sharon Crowley and Debra Hawhee, *Ancient Rhetorics for Contemporary Students*. Fourth Edition (New York: Allyn and Bacon, 2009), 7.

38. Brooks, 26.

39. Brian Milner, *The World Made Meme: Public Conversations and Participatory Media* (Cambridge, MA: MIT Press, 2016), 15.

40. Stephanie Pappas, "Fighting fake news in the classroom," *Monitor on Psychology* 53, no. 1 (January 1, 2022), accessed May 30, 2023, https://www.apa.org/monitor/2022/01/career-fake-news.

41. Cambridge Social Decision-Making Lab, "Bad News," 2018, accessed May 30, 2023, https://www.getbadnews.com/books/english/.

42. Pappas.

43. Cambridge.

44. Zara Abrams, "Controlling the spread of misinformation," *Monitor on Psychology* 52 , no. 2 (March 1, 2021).

45. Hari, 115.

46. Hari, 81.

47. Hari, 81.

48. Hari, 85.

49. Shaun Tan, *Tales from Outer Suburbia* (New York: Scholastic, 2008), 74.

50. Tan, 74.

51. Tan, 75.

52. Tan, 74.

53. Tan, 75.

54. Laurie A. Finke and Martin B. Shichtman, "'Men shal nat maken ernest of game': The Knights of the Alt-Right," *Arthuriana* 32, no. 4 (2022), 61–78, 65.

55. Harry G. Frankfurt, *On Bullshit* (Princeton, NJ: Princeton University Press, 2005), 56.

56. Frankfurt, 61.

57. Frankfurt, 64.

58. McComiskey, *Post-Truth Rhetoric*,12.

59. Jeff Smith, *Bone: The Complete Cartoon Epic in One Volume* (Columbus, Ohio: Cartoon Books, 2020), 419.

60. Smith, 497.

61. Smith, 556.

62. Smith, 555.

63. Smith, 605.

64. Mark Keierleber, "How White Extremists Teach Kids to Hate," The 74, accessed June 20, 2024, https://www.the74million.org.

65. M.T. Anderson, *Feed* (MA: Candlewick Press, 2012).

66. Henry A. Giroux, *Dangerous Thinking in the Age of the New Authoritarianism* (New York: Routledge, 2016), 89.

67. Bertolt Brecht, *Brecht on Theatre*, trans. John Willett (New York: Hill and Wang, 1964).

68. Elizabeth Bullen and Elizabeth Parsons, "Dystopian Visions of Global Capitalism: Philip Reeve's Mortal Engines and M.T. Anderson's *Feed*," *Children's Literature in Education* 38, 127–139 (2007), 136.

69. Anderson, 85.

70. Anne Applebaum, *Twilight of Democracy: The Seductive Lure of Authoritarianism* (New York: Anchor Books. 2020), 111.

71. Zuboff, *Surveillance Capitalism*, 255.

72. Applebaum, 113–4.

73. Anderson, *Feed*, 48.

74. Anderson, 48–9.

75. Zuboff, 139.

76. Zuboff, 78.

77. Arendt, 382.

78. Anderson, 296.

79. Coats, 1.

80. Henry Jenkins, et al., *By Any Means Necessary: The New Youth Activism* (New York University Press, 2016), 47.

81. Jenkins, et al., 47.

82. Marah Gubar, *Artful Dodgers: Reconceiving the Golden Age of Children's Literature* (Oxford University Press, 2009), 42.

83. Angie Thomas, *The Hate U Give* (New York: HarperCollins. 2017), 26.

84. Thomas, 113.

85. Thomas, 205.

86. Thomas, 205.

87. Audre Lorde, "The Master's Tools Will Never Dismantle the Master's House," in *Sister Outsider: Essays and Speeches* (Berkeley, CA: Crossing Press, 2007), 110–114.

Chapter 2. The Order of Story

1. Chimamanda Ngozi Adichie, "The Danger of a Single Story," TED Talk, July 2009, https://www.youtube.com/watch?v=D9Ihs241zeg.

2. In August 2019, *The New York Times Magazine* launched "The 1619 Project" with an article of the same name by Nikole Hannah-Jones, followed by a series of articles, books, videos, and teaching materials that reframe US history by centering the Black experience. The project provides resources to educators working to teach about the legacy of slavery and how it is woven throughout our history and culture. As a curriculum guide for K-12 teachers frames it, "The project calls us to do the work of truth-telling as a baseline for collective healing, understanding, and growth" (1). The project aims to augment and to fill in gaps in traditional histories taught in schools, which often gloss over the atrocities of slavery and ignore the accomplishments of Black Americans.

3. Nikole Hannah-Jones and Renée Watson, illustrated by Nikkolas Smith, *Born on the Water* (New York: Penguin Random House, 2021).

4. Mike Gonzalez, "'1619' Pulitzer Will Boost Socialist Teaching in Schools," The Heritage Foundation, May 11, 2020, accessed June 6, 2023, https://www.heritage.org/education/commentary/1619-pulitzer-will-boost-socialist-teaching-schools.

5. Nikole Hannah-Jones, "The 1619 Project," *The New York Times Magazine*, August 14, 2019, 12.

6. Hannah-Jones, 5.

7. Cornel West, *Democracy Matters: Winning the Fight Against Imperialism* (New York: Penguin, 2004), 41.

8. Trump White House, "1776 Commission Takes Historic and Scholarly Step to Restore Understanding of the Greatness of the American Founding," January 18, 2021, accessed May 30, 2023, https://trumpwhitehouse.archives.gov/briefings-statements/1776-commission-takes-historic-scholarly-step-restore-understanding-greatness-american-founding/.

9. President's Advisory 1776 Commission, *The 1776 Report*, January 2021.

The *1776 Report* uses the word democracy only one time, relying instead on the words "republicanism," "republic," and "republican people" to describe US citizens and government. While the United States is indeed a democratic republic, the point here seems to be to avoid any positive connotations with variations of the word "democratic." It is not only partisan, it reflects growing sentiment on the Right that the United States doesn't need to be a democracy.

10. Stanley, 15.

11. "Executive Order on Establishing the President's Advisory 1776 Commission," November 2, 2020, accessed May 30, 2023, https://trumpwhitehouse.archives.gov/presidential-actions/executive-order-establishing-presidents-advisory-1776-commission/.

12. "Executive Order."

13. Sarah Schwartz, "Map: Where Critical Race Theory Is Under Attack," *Education Week*, January 17, 2023, accessed January 22, 2023, https://www.edweek.org/policy-politics/map-where-critical-race-theory-is-under-attack/2021/06.

14. Sarah Schwartz, "Who's Really Driving Critical Race Theory Legislation? An Investigation," *Education Week*, July 19, 2021, accessed January 22, 2023, https://www.edweek.org/policy-politics/whos-really-driving-critical-race-theory-legislation-an-investigation/2021/07.

15. Heritage Foundation, "Protecting K-12 Students from Discrimination," accessed June 6, 2023, https://www.heritage.org/protecting-k-12-students-discrimination.

16. Heritage Foundation, "Protecting."

17. Brooks, 26.

18. Heidi Perez-Moreno, "Texas' 1836 Project aims to promote 'patriotic education,' but critics worry it will gloss over state's history of racism," *The Texas Tribune*, June 9, 2021, accessed February 13, 2023, https://www.texastribune.org/2021/06/09/texas-1836-project/.

19. Anne Applebaum. *Twilight of Democracy: The Seductive Lure of Authoritarianism* (New York: Anchor Books. 2020), 75.

20. Applebaum, 74–75.

21. Applebaum, 106.

22. A concise description of the origins, meaning, and purpose of "critical race theory" is included in the 2017 essay, "Race to the Bottom: How the post-racial revolution became a whitewash," written by one of the theory's early founders, legal scholar Kimberlé Williams Crenshaw, https://thebaffler.com/salvos/race-to-bottom-crenshaw.

23. Angela Glover Blackwell, "How We Achieve a Multiracial Democracy." *Stanford Social Innovation Review.* Spring, 2023, accessed June 6, 2023, https://ssir.org/articles/entry/how_we_achieve_a_multiracial_democracy#.

24. Henry Giroux and Ourania Filippakou, "Critical Pedagogy in the Age of Authoritarianism: Challenges and Possibilities," *Revista Izquierdas* 49, March 2020, 2087.

25. Giroux and Filippakou, 2087.

26. Bill V. Mullen. *We Charge Genocide! American Fascism and the Rule of Law* (Fordham University Press, New York: 2024), 7.

27. Vavrus, 30.

28. Vavrus, 73.

29. Vavrus, 5.

30. Vavrus, 11.

31. Adichie.

32. Charles C. Mann, *Before Columbus: The Americas of 1491* (New York: Atheneum. 2009), ix.

33. Mann, xi..

34. Mann, 108.

35. Elizabeth Gargano, "Oral Narrative and Ojibwa Story Cycles in Louise Erdrich's *The Birchbark House* and *The Game of Silence*." *Children's Literature Association Quarterly* 31, no. 1, 2006, 27–39, at 29, Project MUSE, doi:10.1353/chq.2006.0027.

36. Louise Erdrich, *The Birchbark House* (New York: Hyperion Children's Books, 1999), 233.

37. Roxanne Dunbar-Ortiz, *An Indigenous Peoples' History of the United States* (New York: Beacon Press, 2014), 212.

38. Dunbar-Ortiz, 212–213,

39. Jenny Kay Dupuis and Kathy Kacer, illustrated by Gillian Newland. *I Am Not a Number* (Toronto: Second Story Press, 2016).

40. Ian Mosby and Erin Millions, "Canada's Residential Schools Were a Horror," *Scientific American*, August 1, 2021, accessed November 17, 2022, https://www.scientificamerican.com/article/canadas-residential-schools-were-a-horror/.

41. Mosby and Millions.

42. One area of study that provides some guidance for how to think about difficult historical subject matter for younger readers is the study of Holocaust literature for children. Scholars of Holocaust literature ask, how do authors balance the desire to protect children, especially younger children, from reading about trauma with the duty to preserve and create memory? If we believe that we must educate future generations about history so that it will not repeat itself, how do we do so in productive ways that encourage a sense of responsibility and stewardship? As Adrienne Kertzer asks in *My Mother's Voice: Children, Literature, and the Holocaust*, "How do we tell children about the Holocaust without terrifying them, and what kind of knowledge do we convey when we are determined not to frighten? If to write poetry after Auschwitz is barbaric, what can we say about telling children stories about genocide?" (Kertzer 12). In many ways, children's literature about genocide is a contradiction because many see the purpose of children's literature to be to protect children from horrors and from knowledge they are not yet ready for. If horror must be shared, most agree, it must be done in a way that provides hope, much in the way that *Born on the Water* focuses on drawing strength and inspiration from past generations' struggles.

43. Dupuis.

44. Dupuis.

45. Dunbar-Ortiz, 214.

46. Dunbar-Ortiz, 174.

47. Dunbar-Ortiz, 174.

48. Charlene Willing McManis, with Traci Sorell, *Indian No More* (New York: Tu Books, 2019), 1.

49. McManis, 2.
50. McManis, 20.
51. McManis, 119.
52. McManis, 122.
53. McManis, 116.
54. McManis, 123.
55. McManis, 28.
56. McManis, 29.
57. McManis, 30.
58. McManis, 168.
59. McManis, 195.
60. McManis, 198–199.
61. Ashleigh, "INDIAN NO MORE, by Charlene Willing McManis with Traci Sorell: A Review by Ashleigh, 13." Indigo's Bookshelf. https://indigosbookshelf.blogspot.com/search?q=Indian+no+more.
62. Joe Sutliff Sanders, *A Literature of Questions: Nonfiction for the Critical Child* (Minneapolis: University of Minnesota Press, 2018) 49, JSTOR, accessed June 24, 2024, https://doi.org/10.5749/j.ctt1pwt67w.
63. Anderson quoted in Heather Snell and Lorna Hutchison, eds., *Children and Cultural Memory in Texts of Childhood* (Routledge, 2014).
64. M.T. Anderson, *Octavian Nothing: Traitor to the Nation, Volume 1: The Pox Party*. (Somerville, MA: Candlewick Press, 2006), 323.
65. M.T. Anderson, *Octavian Nothing: Traitor to the Nation, Volume 2: The Kingdom on the Waves*. (Somerville, MA: Candlewick Press, 2008), 568–569.
66. Anderson, Volume 2, 264.
67. Anderson, Volume 2, 559.
68. *1776 Report*, 5.
69. Anderson, Volume 2, 450.
70. West, 41.
71. Mildred Taylor, *Roll of Thunder, Hear My Cry* (New York: Puffin, 1976), 13.
72. Taylor, 24.
73. Taylor, 13
74. Taylor, 48.
75. Taylor, 49.
76. Taylor, 30.
77. Taylor, ii.
78. John Lewis and Andrew Aydin, illustrated by Nate Powell, *March: Book Two* (New York: Top Shelf Productions, 2015), 125.
79. Lewis and Aydin, 124.
80. Lewis and Aydin, 170.
81. Lewis and Aydin, 80–81.
82. Lewis and Aydin, 82.

83. John Lewis and Andrew Aydin, illustrated by Nate Powell, *March: Book Three* (New York: Top Shelf Productions, 2016), 38.
84. West, 23.
85. West, 23.

Chapter 3. Fascism Is the Patriarchy

1. Susan Campbell Bartoletti, *Hitler Youth: Growing Up in Hitler's Shadow* (New York: Scholastic, 2005), 7.
2. Barbara Ehrenreich, "Forword" in Klaus Theweleit, *Male Fantasies*, trans. Erica Carter and Chris Turner (Minneapolis: University of Minnesota Press, 1987), xv.
3. Guus Kuijer, *The Book of Everything*, trans. John Nieuwenhuizen (New York: Arthur Levine Books, 2006), v.
4. Kuijer, 9.
5. Kuijer, 62–63.
6. Kuijer, 81.
7. Kuijer, 84.
8. Kuijer, 98–99.
9. After World War II, when European scholars were trying to figure out what had happened in Germany and Italy and how to prevent it from happening again, Theodor Adorno and his colleagues developed the F-Scale, a way to assess how authoritarian an individual is. While the F-Scale was later found to be flawed, it was an early attempt at trying to understand the mindset of people who would follow someone like Hitler or Mussolini. Adorno and others theorized that an authoritarian mindset is the result of a rigidly structured household, that authoritarian parents, especially fathers, produce authoritarian children. Contemporary scholars no longer use the F-Scale, but they still connect the structure of the patriarchal family to the structure of a fascistic government, where the male leader, a "strongman," is patriarch to the nation.
10. William Reich, *The Mass Psychology of Fascism* (New York: Farrar, Straus and Giroux, 1970), 53.
11. Reich, 35.
12. Theo Horesh, *The Fascism This Time: And the Global Future of Democracy* (Boulder, CO: Cosmopolis Press, 2020), 33.
13. Ruth Ben-Ghiat, *Strongmen: Mussolini to the Present* (New York: W.W. Norton and Company, 2020), 67.
14. Kristin Kobes Du Mez, *Jesus and John Wayne: How White Evangelicals Corrupted a Faith and Fractured a Nation* (New York: Liveright Publishing Corporation, 2020), 3.
15. Kobes Du Mez, xvii.
16. Kobes Du Mez, 268.
17. Kobes Du Mez, 85.

18. Horesh, 43.
19. Stanley, 127–128.
20. Stanley, 12.
21. Stanley, 129.
22. Stanley, 133.
23. David Frum, "Trump Promises a 'Bloody Story'," *The Atlantic*, September 8, 2024, https://www.theatlantic.com/politics/archive/2024/09/donald-trump-bloody-story/679751/.
24. Southern Poverty Law Center, "Proud Boys," accessed May 30, 2023, https://www.splcenter.org/fighting-hate/extremist-files/group/proud-boys.
25. SPLC.
26. Alexandra Hall, "Controversial Proud Boys embrace 'Western values,' reject feminism and political correctness," *Green Bay Press Gazette*, November 27, 2017, accessed June 7, 2023, https://www.greenbaypressgazette.com/story/news/2017/11/27/controversial-proud-boys-embrace-western-values-reject-feminism-and-political-correctness/888519001/.
27. Susan Faludi, *Stiffed: The Betrayal of the American Man* (New York: Harper Perennial, 1999), 9.
28. Samantha Kutner, "Swiping Right: The Allure of Hyper Masculinity and Cryptofascism for Men Who Join the Proud Boys," International Center for Counter-Terrorism. May 2020, 6, accessed June 7, 2023, https://doi:10.19165/2020.1.03.
29. Kutner, 7.
30. Kutner, 9.
31. Michael Kimmel, *Angry White Men: American Masculinity at the End of an Era.* (New York: Bold Type Books, 2013), 9.
32. Kimmel, 63.
33. Kimmel, 245.
34. Vavrus, 65.
35. Vavrus, 63.
36. Vavrus, 41.
37. Jared Yates Sexton, "The Fascist Cult of Masculinity," Dispatches from a Collapsing State, accessed June 10, 2023, https://jaredyatessexton.substack.com/p/the-fascist-cult-of-masculinity?s=w.
38. Klaus Theweleit, *Male Fantasies*, trans. Erica Carter and Chris Turner (Minneapolis: University of Minnesota Press, 1987), 402.
39. Theweleit, 155.
40. Vavrus, 41.
41. The Southern Poverty Law Center explains that domestic violence is a term that does not fully encompass the systems that support violence against women. They cite a definition developed by several Black feminist groups that reads, "Patriarchal Violence (PV) is an interconnected system of institutions, practices, policies, beliefs, and behaviors that harm, undervalue, and terrorize girls, women, femme, intersex, gender non-conforming, LGBTQ, and other gender-oppressed people in our communities. PV is a widespread, [normalized] epidemic based on the

domination, control, and colonizing of bodies, genders, and sexualities, happening in every community globally. PV is a global power structure and manifests on the systemic, institutional, interpersonal, and internalized level. It is rooted in interlocking systems of oppression."

42. Jennifer Mathieu, *Moxie*, (New York: Roaring Book Press, 2017), 39.
43. Mathieu, 28.
44. Mathieu, 29.
45. Mathieu, 46.
46. Mathieu, 48.
47. Mathieu, 96.
48. Mathieu, 97.
49. Mathieu, 112.
50. Mathieu, 277.
51. Mathieu, 302–303.
52. Laurie Halse Anderson, *Speak* (New York: Penguin, 1999), 185–186.
53. Anderson, 159.
54. "As his beliefs have seeped into homes and classrooms, children as young as 11 think Andrew Tate is their 'god.'" Lindsay Dodgson and Bethany Dawson, *Business Insider*, January 29, 2023, accessed June 6, 2023, https://www.businessinsider.com/teachers-and-parents-talk-about-andrew-tates-influence-on-kids-2023-1.
55. Dodgson and Dawson.
56. Madeline Will, "Misogynist Influencer Andrew Tate Has Captured Boys' Attention. What Teachers Need to Know," *Education Week*, February 2, 2023, accessed June 6, 2023, https://www.edweek.org/leadership/misogynist-influencer-andrew-tate-has-captured-boys-attention-what-teachers-need-to-know/2023/02.
57. Kimmel, 59.
58. Margery Hourihan, *Deconstructing the Hero: Literary Theory and Children's Literature* (New York: Routledge, 1997), 72.
59. Dan Spinelli, "The Fight Over Captain America's Legacy Isn't Just Happening on TV," *Mother Jones*, April 29, 2021, accessed July 28, 2022, https://www.motherjones.com/media/2021/04/captain-america-punisher-symbols-nazis-donald-trump/
60. "Crossover" texts appeal to an audience of children, teens and adults and are created with this multigenerational audience in mind. Sandra Beckett analyzed such texts in her book *Crossover Fiction*, and Rachel Falconer wrote about them in her book, *The Crossover Novel*.
61. Dom Nero, "*Star Wars* Fans Fundamentally Misunderstand *Star Wars*," *Esquire*, June 7, 2018, accessed July 19, 2022, https://www.esquire.com/entertainment/movies/a21205523/star-wars-kelly-marie-tran-harassment-controversy/.
62. Ian Sherr and Erin Carson, "GamerGate to Trump: How video game culture blew everything up," CNET, Nov. 27, 2017, accessed July 19, 2022, https://www.cnet.com/culture/gamergate-donald-trump-american-nazis-how-video-game-culture-blew-everything-up/.
63. Hourihan, 9.

64. Bethany Lacina, "The smash success of 'Captain Marvel' shows us that conservatives are ignoring the alt-right," *The Washington Post*, March 15, 2019.

65 Lacina.

Additionally, in "Weaponizing the haters: The Last Jedi and the strategic politicization of pop culture through social media manipulation," (*First Monday* 23, vol. 11 [2018], https://doi.org/10.5210/fm.v23i11.9388) Bay Morton writes that his "study finds evidence of deliberate, organized political influence measures disguised as fan arguments. The likely objective of these measures is increasing media coverage of the fandom conflict, thereby adding to and further propagating a narrative of widespread discord and dysfunction in American society" (2).

66. Corinne Engber, "Neo-Nazis, The Punisher, and Cognitive Dissonance," *Jewish Boston*, January 12, 2021, accessed July 26, 2022, https://www.jewishboston.com/read/neo-nazis-the-punisher-and-cognitive-dissonance/.

67. Jon Jackson, "Marvel's Punisher Problem," *Newsweek*, March 10, 2021, accessed July 26, 2022, https://www.newsweek.com/marvels-punisher-problem-1574579.

68. Engber.

69. Spinelli.

70. "[Captain America's] early appearances valorized the US war effort and depicted Japanese soldiers as demented caricatures, complete with fangs and yellow skin" (Spinelli), a contradiction Yang works through in his afterword.

71. Aja Romano, "Can Captain America serve two dramatically different versions of America?" *Vox*, January 14, 2021, accessed July 28, 2022, https://www.vox.com/22219034/captain-america-stacey-abrams-trump-supporters-marvel-chris-evans.

72. Hourihan, 9.

73. Gene Luen Yang, illustrated by Gurihiru, *Superman Smashes the Klan* (New York: DC Comic, 2020), 7–8.

74. Yang, 44.

75. Yang, 33.

76. Yang, 180.

77. Yang, 45–47.

78. Yang, 35.

79. Yang, 220.

80. Yang, 221.

81. Yang, 229.

82. Yang, 237.

83. Yang, 237.

84. George M. Johnson, *All Boys Aren't Blue: A Memoir Manifesto* (New York: Farrar Straus Giroux, 2020), 54.

85. Johnson, 59.

86. Johnson, 60.

87. Johnson, 61.

88. According to PEN America, in 2022 "the top 3 banned titles all are centered on LGBTQ+ individuals or touch on the topic of same-sex relationships: *Gender*

Queer: A Memoir by Maia Kobabe, banned in 30 districts, *All Boys Aren't Blue* by George M. Johnson, banned in 21 districts, and *Lawn Boy* by Jonathan Evison, banned in 16 districts. *Out of Darkness* by Ashley Hope Pérez, a love story between a Black teenage boy and a Mexican-American girl set in 1930s Texas, was also banned in 16 districts. *The Bluest Eye* by the late Nobel Prize laureate Toni Morrison is the fifth most banned book, in 12 districts" (PEN America, "Report: 1,586 School Book Bans and Restrictions in 86 School Districts Across 26 States," *PEN.org*, April 7, 2022, accessed October 15, 2022).

Jonathan Friedman, Director of PEN America's Free Expression and Education program, said:

Book challenges in American schools are nothing new, but this type of data has never been tallied and quite frankly the results are shocking. Challenges to books, specifically books by non-white male authors are happening at the highest rates we've ever seen. What is happening in this country in terms of banning books in schools is unparalleled in its frequency, intensity, and success. Because of the tactics of censors and the politicization of books we are seeing the same books removed across state lines: books about race, gender, LGBTQ+ identities and sex most often. This is an orchestrated attack on books whose subjects only recently gained a foothold on school library shelves and in classrooms. We are witnessing the erasure of topics that only recently represented progress toward inclusion (PEN America).

89. Johnson, 236–7.
90. Johnson, 237.
91. Johnson, 273.
92. Johnson, 261.

Chapter 4. From Margin to Center: An (Other) Point of View

1. Jason Stanley, *How Fascism Works: The Politics of Us and Them*, (Random House, 2018), xxix.
2. Jon Stone, illustrated by Michael Smollin, *The Monster at the End of This Book* (Boston: Western Publishing Company and Children's Television Workshop, 1971).
3. Megan L. Musgrave, "The Monster at the End of This Book: Posthumanism and New Materialism in the Scholarship of Children's Literature," in *The Routledge Companion to Children's Literature and Culture*, eds. Claudia Nelson, Elisabeth Wesseling and Andrea Mei-Ying Wu (New York: Routledge, 2024), 60.
4. Amanda Taub, "The rise of American authoritarianism," *Vox*, March 1, 2016, accessed May 30, 2023, https://www.vox.com/2016/3/1/11127424/trump-authoritarianism. Dead link
5. Anne Applebaum, *Twilight of Democracy: The Seductive Lure of Authoritarianism* (New York: Anchor Books, 2020), 16.
6. Alexa Wright, "Monstrous Strangers at the Edge of the World: The Monstrous Races," *The Monster Theory Reader*, ed. Jeffrey Andrew Weinstock (Minneapolis: University of Minnesota Press, 2020).

7. Jean-Paul Sartre, *Anti-Semite and Jew: An Exploration of the Etiology of Hate*, trans. George J. Becker (New York: Schocken Books, 1944), PDF (1995).

8. Zygmunt Bauman, *Modernity and the Holocaust* (Ithaca, NY: Cornell University Press, 1989), 34.

9. Ernst Hiemer, *The Poisonous Mushroom* (Clemens and Blair, 1938).

10. Heritage Foundation, "How to Recognize Critical Race Theory," 2023, accessed May 30, 2023, https://www.heritage.org/civil-society/heritage-explains/how-identify-critical-race-theory.

11. Abate's book *The Big Smallness* closely examines a number of children's books written for niche markets (Routledge, 2019). These books are self-published or published by small presses, but are financially viable because they can reach a broad, international audience via sites like Amazon.com. As Abate writes, "niche markets and the World Wide Web were made for each other" (13). Both have increased access for authors and readers, both have helped to build and maintain a multitude of subcultures and interest groups, and, in both cases, the effects of these recent trends have been double-edged. While scholars in the twentieth century lamented the bland, commercial products and texts created by the culture industry through mass-production, these twenty-first century texts, "emerging from a powerful combination of the ease of affordability of desktop publishing software [and] the promotional, marketing, and distribution possibilities made possible by the internet" (2), raise a whole new series of possibilities, challenges, and questions. While the volume of texts sold by big, multinational media conglomerates able to use horizontal and vertical integration to create convergence across media platforms is vast and represents, by far, the greatest number of books sold to American children, post-Fordist means of production, marketing, and distribution are proliferating, creating and catering to a multitude of audiences segmented into sub-subcultures. Much in the way that Americans have created news bubbles for ourselves that echo and reinforce our already held beliefs, so too can parents create similar bubbles for their children.

12. Abate, *Raising Your Kids Right: Children's Literature and American Political Conservatism*, Rutgers Series in Childhood Studies (Rutgers University Press, 2011), 9.

13. Rebecca Klein, "The rightwing US textbooks that teach slavery as 'black immigration,'" *The Guardian*, August 12, 2021, accessed June 6, 2023, https://www.theguardian.com/education/2021/aug/12/right-wing-textbooks-teach-slavery-black-immigration.

14. Metaxas is well-known in right-wing Christian circles and is quite a colorful character. He gained brief notoriety after punching a protestor at the Republican National Convention (Kobes, xvi). He initially didn't support Trump's candidacy but rallied behind him after Trump received the GOP nomination writing, "With all his foibles, peccadilloes, and metaphorical warts, he is nonetheless the last best hope of keeping America from sliding into oblivion, the tank, the abyss, the dustbin of history, if you will" (Kobes, 262). As is the case with many evangelicals, Metaxas excused Trump's un-Christian behaviors because Trump "was the perfect embodiment of a different set of masculine 'virtues' that evangelical men had been touting for nearly half a century" (262).

15. Eric Metaxas, illustrated by Tim Raglin, *Donald Builds the Wall* (Metaxas Media, 2019), 3.

16. David Klepper and Lori Hinnant, "George Soros conspiracy theories surge as protests sweep US," *Associated Press*, June 21, 2020, accessed June 6, 2023, https://apnews.com/article/ap-top-news-racial-injustice-mn-state-wire-united-states-us-news-f01f3c405985f4e3477e4e4ac27986e5.

17. Metaxas, 23.

18. The visual similarity between George-o-saurus and the Jewish men in *The Poisonous Mushroom* is so striking that I thought of presenting both images side-by-side. I decided against including these though because I cannot bring myself to pay permissions fees to the author and illustrator of such damaging books.

19. Metaxas, 42–43.

20. Metaxas, 45.

21. Metaxas, 4.

22. Metaxas, 58.

23. Patricia Roberts-Miller, *Demagoguery and Democracy* (New York: The Experiment, 2017), 24.

24. Roberts-Miller, 88.

25. Metaxas, 49.

26. Theweleit, 409.

27. Theweleit, 402.

28. Brigitte Fielder and Katrina Phillips write that, "Children's and youth literature are rife with both implicit and explicit depictions of racism and cultural appropriation. Laura Ingalls Wilder's *Little House on the Prairie* series—books that have permeated the American imagination since the first book was published in 1935—has come under fire in recent years, particularly for Wilder's depictions of Native peoples. The books are 'brimming with casual racism,' writes Laura June Topolsky, and the Osage Indians the family encounters are shown not as human, but as 'a brooding pack of inconvenience' (Topolsky). Wilder's father, Charles Ingalls, moved his family from Wisconsin to Kansas in 1869, choosing to build a cabin within the borders of the Osage Diminished Reserve—land that was not open to white settlement" (Fielder and Phillips, "Editors' Introduction," *Research on Diversity in Youth Literature* 3, no. 1 [April 2021], 6).

29. Laura Ingalls Wilder, *Little House on the Prairie*, excerpted in *Crosscurrents of Children's Literature: An Anthology of Texts and Criticism*, eds. J. D. Stahl, Tina L. Hanlon, and Elizabeth Lennox Keyser (New York: Oxford University Press, 2007), 957.

30. Debbie Reese, "Lecture: An Indigenous Critique of Whiteness in Children's Literature," Association of Library Service to Children (2019), 8, PDF accessed Feb. 7, 2023, https://journals.ala.org/index.php/cal/article/view/7101/9662.

31. Sara Schwebel, *Child-Sized History: Fictions of the Past in U.S. Classrooms* (Nashville, TN: Vanderbilt University Press, 2011), 4.

32. Another famous children's author who advocated for genocidal Western expansion was L. Frank Baum, the author of the *Wizard of Oz* series. Roxanne

Dunbar-Ortiz writes in *An Indigenous People's History of the United States* that he callously wrote in 1891, that "[t]he Pioneer [sic] has before declared that our only safety depends upon the total extermination of the Indians. Having wronged them for centuries we had better, in order to protect our civilization, follow it up by one more wrong and wipe these untamed and untamable creatures from the face of the earth" ([Beacon Press, 2015], 156). His use of the word "creatures" illustrates the extreme act of othering required to call for the extermination of an entire people.

33. Gayatri Chakravorty Spivak, "Can the Subaltern Speak?" in *Colonial Discourse and Post-Colonial Theory: A Reader*, eds. Patrick Williams and Laura Chrisman (New York: Columbia University Press, 1994), 78.

34. Cristina L. Lash, "Multicultural citizenship education as resistance: Student political development in an anti-immigrant national climate," *Teaching and Teacher Education* 105 (2021), accessed July 9, 2024, https://www.sciencedirect.com/science/article/abs/pii/S0742051X21001293.

35. Rudine Sims Bishop, "Windows and Mirrors: Children's Books and Parallel Cultures," Proceedings of the 14th Annual Reading Conference (California State University, San Bernardino), 15, PDF at https://files.eric.ed.gov/fulltext/ED337744.pdf#page=11.

36. Michael Genhart, illustrated by Joanne Lew-Vriethoff, *I See You* (Washington, DC: Magination Press, 2017).

37. Ellen L. Bassuk, et al., *America's Youngest Outcasts: A Report Card on Child Homelessness* (America Institutes for Research), 6, PDF at https://www.air.org/resource/report/americas-youngest-outcasts-report-card-child-homelessness.

38. Nikki Grimes, illustrated by R. Gregory Christie, *Rich* (New York: Puffin Books, 2009), 58–60.

39. Grimes, 57.

40. Grimes, 91.

41. American Civil Liberties Union, "Timeline of the Muslim Ban," accessed August 19, 2024, https://www.aclu-wa.org/pages/timeline-muslim-ban.

42. Jenna Johnson and Abigail Hauslohner, "'I think Islam hates us': A Timeline of Trump's comments about Islam and Muslims," *The Washington Post*, May 20, 2017.

43. Stanley, *How Fascism Works*, 65.

44. Samira Ahmed, *Internment* (New York: Little, Brown and Company, 2019), 2.

45. Matthew C. MacWilliams, "The One Weird Trait That Predicts Whether You're a Trump Support," *Politico Magazine*, January 17, 2016, accessed June 6, 2023, https://www.politico.com/magazine/story/2016/01/donald-trump-2016-authoritarian-213533/.

46. Ahmed, 178–9.

47. Ahmed, 232–3.

48. Ahmed, 378.

49. Adam Gidwitz, illustrated by Hatem Aly, *The Inquisitor's Tale: Or, The Three Magical Children and Their Holy Dog* (New York: Dutton Children's Books, 2016), 34.

50. Gidwitz, 35.

51. Gidwitz, 36.

52. Gidwitz, 36.

53. Gidwitz, 39.
54. Gidwitz, 85.
55. Gidwitz, 86.
56. Gidwitz. 249.
57. Gidwitz, 348.
58. Gidwitz, 347.
59. "Ironically, nationalism has sorted people into borderless tribes. On the one hand, the mass of people who have responded to globalization in Hungary by turning to Viktor Orban have a lot more in common with the Americans who turned to the Tea Party and Trump. . . " (Rhodes, 53).
60. National Immigration Forum, "The Great Replacement Theory Explained," accessed June 6, 2023, https://immigrationforum.org/wp-content/uploads/2021/12/Replacement-Theory-Explainer-1122.pdf, 6.
61. In 2006, Marc Hetherington and Jonathan Weiler conducted a survey linking attitudes about immigration to respondents' affinities for authoritarianism. They found that those scoring high in authoritarianism were overwhelmingly anti-immigration. For example, while only 38 percent of non-authoritarians agreed with the statement "Illegal immigrants are lawbreakers, plain and simple," 82 percent of those who scored high in authoritarianism agreed (*Authoritarianism and Polarization in American Politics* [Cambridge University Press, 2009], 169).
62. Pam Muñoz Ryan, *Esperanza Rising* (New York: Scholastic, 2000), 6.
63. Ryan, 66.
64. Ryan, 69.
65. Cristina Rhodes, "Corporeal, Phenomenological, and Activist Transformations in Pam Muñoz Ryan's *Esperanza Rising*," *Children's Literature Association Quarterly* 46, no. 1 (Spring 2021), 41–56.
66. Ryan, 218.
67. Rhodes, 51.
68. Gene Luen Yang, *American Born Chinese* (New York: Square Fish, 2008), 31.
69. Yang, 110.
70. bell hooks, *Yearning: Race, Gender, and Cultural Politics* (Boston: South End Press, 1990), 31.
71. Donna Haraway, "A Cyborg Manifesto," in *Simians, Cyborgs, and Women: The Reinvention of Nature* (New York: Routledge, 1991), 155.
72. Stanley, *How Fascism Works*, 137.
73. Patrick Wall, "Biden vs. GOP states: Where will the battle over transgender rights leave students?" *Chalkbeat*, August 10, 2022, accessed June 6, 2023, https://www.chalkbeat.org/2022/8/10/23298986/transgender-children-kids-students-rights-biden-lgbtq-title-ix.
74. Children are constructed in ways that are contradictory: They are viewed as asexual and also as innately heterosexual and cisgendered. That's why any discussion of gender and/or sexuality is considered a threat and is often conflated with pedophilia.

75. Based on the number of times *Melissa* has been challenged or banned since its publication, there are clearly a lot of adults who resist its message of inclusion. According to *The New York Times*, "A few parents, weighing in on the Oregon Battle of the Books Facebook group, objected to the book because it features a transgender child. More parents, however, singled out the older brother character, Scott, who, they say, behaves inappropriately in a book aimed at a younger audience. Scott appears on page 6, banging on the door of a locked bathroom and demanding that George get out. Scott surmises that George is taking so long because she's 'looking at dirty magazines.' Later Scott is more explicit, talking about copies of *Girls' Life* that George keeps hidden in a bag. 'Dude, I thought you had porn or something in there,' he says." Author Alex Gino told the *Times* that "arguments about Scott were 'a decoy' for discomfort with a book about a transgender child: 'One would have to search through the whole book to find a few vague references. And if you are really looking, there are a few vague references. But the reason you were looking is because you were afraid about the trans issue.'" (Sarah Lorge Butler, "Parents Are Divided Over a Book in a Popular Student Reading Program in Oregon," *The New York Times* (May 8, 2018).

76. Alex Gino, *Melissa/George* (New York: Scholastic, 2015), 199.

77. Gino, 47.

78. Gino, 125.

79. Marcus Ewert, illustrated by Rex Ray, *10,000 Dresses* (New York: Seven Stories Press, 2008).

80. Stanley, 177.

81. Stanley, 178.

82. United States Holocaust Memorial Museum, "Nazi Prosecution of the Disabled: Murder of the 'Unfit,'" accessed September 11, 2022, https://www.ushmm.org/information/exhibitions/online-exhibitions/special-focus/nazi-persecution-of-the-disabled.

83. United States Holocaust Memorial Museum.

84. Sara Kersten, "'We are Just as Confused and Lost as She is': The Primacy of the Graphic Novel Form in Exploring Conversations Around Deafness," *Children's Literature in Education* 49 (2018) 282–301, 284.

85. Shaun Tan, *The Arrival* (New York: Scholastic, 2006).

86. M.T. Anderson, *The Assassination of Brangwain Spurge* (Somerville, Mass: Candlewick Press, 2018), 112–113.

87. Anderson, 117.

88. Anderson, 159–160.

89. Anderson, 160–161.

Conclusion. The Ends of Story

1. M.T. Anderson, "Point of Departure" in *Handbook of Research on Children's and Young Adult Literature*, eds. Shelby A. Wolf, Karen Coats, Patricia Enciso, and Christine A. Jenkins (New York: Routledge, 2011), 373.

2. Anderson, 372.
3. Anderson, 372.
4. Peter Hollindale, "Ideology and the Children's Book," *Signal* 55 (January 1988), 7.
5. Kenneth B. Kidd, *Theory For Beginners: Children's Literature as Critical Thought* (Fordham University Press, 2020), 62.
6. Kidd, 75.
7. Kidd, 93.
8. Mildred D. Taylor, *Roll of Thunder, Hear My Cry* (Dial Press, 1976), 183.
9. Taylor, 172.
10. Taylor, 172.
11. Hannah Arendt, *The Origins of Totalitarianism* (New York: Harcourt, 1985), 364.
12. Arendt, 353.
13. Adolf Hitler, *Mein Kampf*, translated into English by James Murphy, Chapter 10, PDF at https://www.livingston.org/cms/lib9/NJ01000562/Centricity/Domain/751/mein%20kampf.pdf.
14. Arendt, 353.
15. Arendt, 354.
16. Peter Brooks, *Seduced by Story: The Use and Abuse of Narrative* (New York Review Books, 2020), 120.
17. Anne Applebaum. *Twilight of Democracy: The Seductive Lure of Authoritarianism* (New York: Anchor Books. 2020), 112.
18. Brooks, 26.
19. Brooks, 22–23.
20. Wayne Booth, *The Rhetoric of Fiction*, 2nd ed. (Chicago: The University of Chicago Press, 1983), 121–122.
21. Catherine Belsey, *Critical Practice*, 2nd ed. (New York: Routledge, 2002), 57–58.
22. Debbie Reese, "Lecture: An Indigenous Critique of Whiteness in Children's Literature," Association of Library Service to Children (2019), PDF accessed February 7, 2023, https://journals.ala.org/index.php/cal/article/view/7101/9662.
23. President's Advisory 1776 Commission, *The 1776 Report* (January 2021), 4, PDF at https://trumpwhitehouse.archives.gov/wp-content/uploads/2021/01/The-Presidents-Advisory-1776-Commission-Final-Report.pdf.
24. *1776 Report*, 17.
25. Arendt, 362.
26. Ruth Ben-Ghiat, *Strongmen: Mussolini to the Present* (New York: W.W. Norton and Company, 2020), 67.
27. Eddie S. Glaude Jr., *Begin Again: James Baldwin's America and Its Urgent Lessons for Our Own* (New York: Crown, 2020), 174.
28. M.T. Anderson. *Landscape with an Invisible Hand.* (Somerville, Mass: Candlewick Press, 2017), 14.
29. R.T. Tally Jr., "The End-of-the-World as World System," *Other Globes: Past and Peripheral Imaginations of Globalization*, eds. Simon Ferdinand, Irene Villaescusa, and Illán Esther Peeren (Palgrave Macmillan, 2019), 272.
30. Anderson, 41.

31. Brecht and his contemporaries, worked to highlight the relationship between art and ideology, to illuminate the way that aesthetics are not ideologically neutral and can work with the grain of dominant ideology or against it. Among the questions Brecht asked are: Is emotional identification with a character at odds with conveying larger social structures and systems of power? Are some forms and narrative structures more or less adept at encouraging activism than others? Can different textual forms and aesthetics encourage or discourage different readerly stances?

32. Bertolt Brecht, *Brecht on Theatre*, trans. John Willett (Hill and Wang, 1964), 71.

33. Brecht, 71.

34. Brecht, 78.

35. Brecht, 109.

36. Anderson, 16.

37. Anderson, 113.

38. Anderson, 69.

39. Henry A. Giroux, *Dangerous Thinking in the Age of the New Authoritarianism* (New York: Routledge, 2016), 98.

40. Giroux, 76.

41. Anderson, 143.

42. Anderson, 74.

43. Dr. Seuss, Jack Prelutsky, and Lane Smith, *Hooray for Diffendoofer Day!* (New York: Knopf Books for Young Readers, 1998).

44. Seuss.

45. Giroux, 81.

46. Giroux, 74.

47. Giroux, 74

Index

Abate, Michelle Ann, 13, 22, 115, 176n11
Abrams, Zara, 50
Adichie, Chimamanda Ngozi, 65–66, 72
Adorno, Theodore 159–60, 171
Aesop, 1
Ahmed, Samira, 122–23
All Boys Aren't Blue (Johnson), 108–10, 114
allegory, 34–35, 132–34
Allen, Amanda, 161n51
alt-Right, x, 4, 10, 55, 62, 88, 93–95, 101–4, 119, 125, 157–58n9
American Born Chinese (Yang), 127–29, 132
"The Amnesia Machine" (Tan), 51–55, 57, 58, 59, 61
Andersen, Hans Christian, 56
Anderson, Laurie Halse, 98
Anderson, M. T., 57, 79–80, 133, 135–6, 145–49
anti-fascism, 4, 12, 20, 22–23, 25–27, 37, 47, 64, 71–72, 101, 104–5, 107, 151–52
Applebaum, Anne, 59–60, 70, 112, 142
Arendt, Hannah, 40, 46, 61, 139–41, 145
The Arrival (Tan), 51, 132–33
The Assassination of Brangwain Spurge (Anderson), 132–34
Aydin, Andrew, 83

"Bad News," 49–51, 57
Barthes, Roland, 39–40, 142
Bartoletti, Susan Campbell, 9, 86
Baum, Frank L., 177–78n32
Bauman, Zygmunt, 113
Beckett, Sandra, 173n60
Before Columbus (Mann), 72–73

Bell, Cece, 131–32
Belsey, Catherine, 143, 148
Ben-Ghiat, Ruth, 90–91, 145–46
Bennett, William, 22
Bernstein, Robin, 6, 158n15
Biden, Joe, 68, 129, 140
The Birchbark House (Erdrich), 73
Bishop, Rudine Simms, 120
Blackwell, Angela Glover, 71
The Bluest Eye (Morrison), 19–20
book bans, 5–7, 11, 108, 129, 174–75n88, 180n75
The Book of Everything (Kuijer), 88–90
The Book of Virtues (Bennett), 22
Bone (Smith), 56–57
Booth, Wayne, 18, 142
Born on the Water (Jones and Watson), 65–66, 85
"The Boy Who Cried Wolf," 1
Bradbury, Ray, ix
Brecht, Bertolt, 58, 133, 147–48, 182n31
Brooks, Peter, 23, 27, 35, 47–48, 70, 141–42
Bullen, Elizabeth, 59
bullshit, 26, 55–57, 162–63n77

Capshaw, Katharine, 18–19, 21, 158n15
Captain America, 101, 104, 105
Carson, Erin, 102
Catcher in the Rye, 114
censorship, 14, 20, 23, 108–10, 114, 137, 174–75n88
Cerón, Ella, x
Charlotte's Web, 130
the Child, 5–11, 14, 17–19, 69, 158n15

183

child rearing, 9–10, 21, 63, 74, 93, 159–60n34
Christians, 2, 90, 124–25, 176n14; Christian family, 27, 88–89; Christian nationalism, 37–38, 87, 115
"Cinderella," 143
civil rights movements, 7, 21, 81–85, 87, 129, 156n11
Clinton, Hillary, 91
Coats, Karen, 33, 62
convergence culture narratives, 23, 37–40, 44–50, 101–2, 104, 142–43, 146, 163n11
Crenshaw, Kimberlé Williams, 168n22
Critical Race Theory, 5, 6, 23, 67, 69, 71, 114–15, 138, 141, 145, 158n18, 168n22
Crowley, Sharon, 48

Dahlen, Sarah Park, xi
Dodgson, Lindsay, 99
Donald Builds the Wall (Metaxas), 115–19, 125
Duane, Anna Mae, 8, 158n15
Dupuis, Jenny Kay, 74
Dunbar-Ortiz, Roxanne, 74, 76, 177–78n32

Eagleton, Terry, 13
Eco, Umberto, 1
Edelman, Lee, 6–7
Ehrenreich, Barbara, 86
1836 Project, 70
El Deafo (Bell), 131–32
"The Emperor's New Clothes" (Andersen), 56
Engber, Corinne, 103
Erdrich, Louise, 73
Esperanza Rising (Ryan), 125–27
Ewert, Marcus, 130
Eyal, Nir, 164n12

F-scale, 159–60n34, 171n9
Falconer, Rachel, 173n60
Faludi, Susan, 93
Fielder, Brigitte, 177n28
fascism, 1–4; Arendt on, 40, 140–41, 145; Bartoletti on, 9; Brecht on, 148; Eco on, 1; Fuchs on, 3; Gershberg and Illing on, 43; Giroux on, 151; Giroux and Filippakou on, 71; Horesh on, 90; Mullen on, 71–72, Lacoue-Labarthe, Nancy, and Holmes on, 36; Paxton on, 2–3; Reich on, 89–90; Rhodes on, 37–38; Sexton on, 71, 95; Snyder on, 1, 36; Stanley on, 8, 41, 68, 91–92, 111; Theweleit on, 86–87, 95; Vavrus on, 4, 72, 94–95
fascist myth-making, xv, 3, 8–11, 12, 23, 28–29, 36–37, 39–41, 43, 46–47, 67–68, 71, 141–42, 145–46

Feed (Anderson), 57–62
feminism, 5, 87, 92–96, 100, 102, 128–29
Filippakou, Ourania, 71
Finke, Laurie A., 55
Flynn, Richard, 20
Ford Smith, Victoria, 161n51
Frankfurt, Harry G., 55, 162–63n77
Franklin, Aretha, 84
Friedman, Jonathan, 175n88
Fuchs, Christian, 3

Gamber-Thompson, Liana, 62
Gargano, Elizabeth, 73
Garner, Eric, 63
Gender Queer (Kobabe), 14–16
Genhart, Michael, 120
Gershberg, Zac, 43
Gidwitz, Adam, 124–25
Gino, Alex, 129–130, 180n75
Giroux, Henry A., 58, 71, 149, 151
The Giver (Lowry), 35
Gladiator, 104
Glaude, Eddie S., Jr., 40, 146
*Go the F**k to Sleep*, 13
Goodnight Bush, 13
Gonzalez, Mike, 66
Grimes, Nikki, 121
Gubar, Marah, 20, 63, 158n15

Hannah-Jones, Nikole, 66–67, 167n2
Haraway, Donna, 129
Hari, Johann, 42, 51
Harris, Kamala, 91
Harry Potter (Rowling), ix–xii, 19, 34–35, 44–46, 96, 100, 102
The Hate U Give (Thomas), 63–64, 114
Hawhee, Debra, 48
Heritage Foundation, 4, 6, 66, 69, 71, 115
hero narrative, xi, 96, 100–5, 108–9, 143
Hetherington, Marc J., 10, 43–44, 159n32, 159–60n34, 179n61
Hitler, Adolf, 2, 3, 4, 9, 38, 86, 92, 104, 116, 148; *Mein Kampf*, 3–4, 9, 140, 162n72
Hitler Youth: Growing Up in Hitler's Shadow (Bartoletti), 9, 86
Hollindale, Peter, 136
Holmes, Brian, 36
Holocaust, 74–75, 123; denial, 157n9; education, 34–35; literature, xiii–xiv, 31, 34, 169n42
hooks, bell, xiv, 128
Hooray for Diffendoofer Day (Seuss), 150–51
Hope, Jeanelle, 157n7
Horesh, Theo, 90–91
Hourihan, Margery, 100–4

I Am Not a Number (Dupuis and Kacer), 74–76
I See You, 120–21
Illing, Sean 43
immigrants, 3, 28, 40, 45, 46, 66, 91, 92, 112, 114, 179n61; in literature, 105–7, 115–19, 125–29, 132–33
Indian No More (McManis and Sorell), 76–79, 107
The Inquisitor's Tale (Gidwitz), 124–25
Internment (Ahmed), 121–24

Jenkins, Henry, 7, 38, 62, 163n11
Jews, x, 41, 92, 104, 112–14, 116–17, 124–25, 141, 157n9, 177n18
Jim Crow laws, 3, 7, 8, 21, 81–82, 138–39, 146
Johnson, George M., 108–110, 175n88
Joosen, Vanessa, 161n51

Kacer, Kathy, 74–75
Kelen, Kit, 8
Kersten, Sara, 131
Kertzer, Adrienne, 31, 156n14, 169n42
Kidd, Kenneth, xiv, 12, 13–14, 25, 33, 136–38
Kimmel, Michael, 94, 100
King, Dr. Martin Luther, Jr., 84
Klein, Rebecca, 115
Kliger-Vilechik, Neta, 62
Kobabe, Maia, 14, 174–75n88
Kobes Du Mez, Kristin, 90–91, 176n14
Ku Klux Klan, 4, 92, 105–7, 157n7
Kuijer, Guus, 88
Kunze, Pete, 161n51
Kutner, Samantha, 93

Lacina, Bethany, 103
Lacoue-Labarthe, Philippe, 36
Landscape with Invisible Hand (Anderson), 146–50
LGBTQ+, xii, 27, 87, 90, 91, 108, 112–13, 129, 141, 172–73n41; in literature, 5, 7, 12, 108–10, 129–31, 174–75n88
Lash, Cristina L., 119
Lavin, Talia, 157–58n9
Levander, Caroline, 158n15
Lewis, John, 83–85
Levitsky, Steven, 36
Little House on the Prairie (Wilder), 20–21, 118–19, 144
The Little Mermaid, Disney's, 38–39
The Lord of the Rings (Tolkien), 44, 46
Lorde, Audre, 64
Lowry, Lois, 34–35

MacLean, Nancy, 11
MacWilliams, Matthew C., 9–10, 159–60n34
Mad Max, 104
MAGA, 2, 4, 39, 62, 103
Mangen, Anne, 51
Mann, Charles C. 72–73
March (Lewis and Aydin), 83–85
masculinity, 86–88, 94–95; alternative, 91, 96, 98, 108–110, 129; hypermasculinity, 86–88, 90–93, 95, 97–100, 101, 104, 106
Mathieu, Jennifer, 97
McComiskey, Bruce, 47–48, 56
McDowell, Kelly, 20–21
McInnes, Gavin, 92–93
McManis, Charlene Willing, 76, 78
McMullen-Ciotti, Elise, 78, 110
Meek, Margaret, 23–24
Mein Kampf, see Hitler
Melissa (Gino), 129–30, 180n75
memes, 48–49, 50, 55, 101, 118
Metaxas, Eric, 115, 176n14
Mickenberg, Julia L., 22
Milner, Brian, 49
Mintz, Steven, 158
Mintzer, Ally, 164
Moms for Liberty, 6, 108
The Monster at the End of This Book (Stone), 111–12
Morrison, Toni, 19–20, 175n88
Morton, Bay, 174n65
Moxie (Mathieu), 96–99
Mullen, Bill V., 71–72, 157n7
Musgrave, Megan, 112
Mussolini, Benito, 2, 3, 4, 171n9

Nancy, Jean-Luc, 36
narrative literacy, 23–24, 37, 44, 45, 47–49, 143–44, 151, 152
Nazis 86–88. 105; Nazi Germany, 9, 88, 112, 131; iconography, ix, 67, 103; neo-Nazis x, 67, 103; propaganda, 116, 123, 141
Neiwert, David, x
Nel, Philip, xiv, 156n12
Nero, Dom, 102
Nikolajeva, Maria, 17–18
Night (Wiesel), 34
1984 (Orwell), ix, 58
Nodelman, Perry, 15, 18
Number the Stars (Lowry), 34

Obama, Barack, 83–84, 115, 122
Octavian Nothing (Anderson), 79–81, 145
Orwell, George, ix, 2, 58
The Outsiders, 114

parental rights, 5, 6
Parsons, Elizabeth, 59
patriarchy, 5, 19, 27, 47, 86–91, 97, 98, 108, 141, 143, 171n9; patriarchal family, 5, 21, 88–91, 94–95, 129, 171n9; patriarchal violence, 172–73n41
Pappas, Stephanie, 50
Paxton, Robert O., 2–3
pedagogy, xiii; critical, 4, 47, 71–72; public, 151, 162n72
PEN America, 174–75n88
Peter Pan, 18
Phillips, Katrina, 177n28
The Poisonous Mushroom (Hiemer), 114–116, 177n18
Prior, Ian, 7
Project 2025, 4–5
Proud Boys, 87, 92–94
The Punisher, 103–4

Ray, Rex, 130
"Red Riding Hood," 33
Reimer, Mavis, 15
Reese, Debbie, 118, 144
Reich, Wilhelm, 89–90
replacement theory, 40, 66, 125
residential schools, 8, 74–77
Reynolds, Kimberley, 21–22
Rhodes, Ben, 37–38
Rhodes, Cristina, 127
Rich (Grimes), 121
Roberts, Kevin D., 4–5
Roberts-Miller, Patricia, 117
Roll of Thunder, Hear My Cry (Taylor), 21, 81–82, 138–39, 148
Romano, Aja, 104
Rose, Jacqueline, 17
Rowling, J.K., x, xiii
Runescape, 45–46
Ryan, Pam Muñoz, 126

Sanders, Joe Sutliff, 78–79, 161n52
Sartre, Jean-Paul, 113
Schell, Kallie, xi
schools, 6, 8, 9, 11–12, 20–21, 66, 68–71, 74–77, 81–82, 145–46, 151, 158n18, 167n2, 174–75n88. See also residential schools
Schwartz, Sarah, 69
Schwebel, Sara, 118
Sesame Street, 111
Seuss, Dr., 150

The 1776 Report, 11, 67–69, 80, 145
Sexton, Jared Yates, 95
Sharlot, Jeff, 165n36
Sherr, Ian, 102
Shichtman, Martin, 55
Shresthova, Sangita, 62
Sims Bishop, Rudine, 120
Singley, Carol, 158n15
"The 1619 Project," 11, 65–67, 70
Smith, Jeff, 56
Snyder, Timothy, ix, 12–13, 25, 36
Sorell, Traci, 76, 78
Southern Poverty Law Center, x, 155n6, 172n41
Speak (Anderson), 98–99
Spiegler, Jinnie, 57
Spinelli, Dan, 101, 174n70
Spivak, Gayatri Chakravorty, 119
Stanley, Jason, 8, 41, 68, 91–92, 111–12, 129, 131
Star Wars, 13, 46, 88, 100, 102–4
Stephens, John, 24
Sundmark, Björn, 8
Superman Smashes the Klan (Yang), 105–7

Tales from Outer Suburbia (Tan), 51
Tally, R. T., Jr., 147
Tan, Shaun, 51–55, 132
Tate, Andrew, 99–100
Taub, Amanda, 28, 112
Taylor, Mildred, 21, 81
10,000 Dresses (Ewert), 130–31
Theweleit, Klaus, 86–87, 95, 117
Thomas, Angie, 63
Thomas, Ebony Elizabeth, xi
transphobia, xii, 4, 26, 28, 114
Trites, Roberta Seelinger, 17
Trump, Donald, 4, 9–10, 28, 36, 40, 68, 90–92, 115–17, 119, 121–23, 140–41, 176n14, 179n59; administration, 11, 67–69, 119, 122, 145

Useem, John and Ruth, 157n17

Vance, J.D., 87
Vavrus, Michael, 4, 47, 72, 94–95

Wallace-Wells, Benjamin, 7
Weiler, Jonathan, 10, 43–44, 159n32, 159–60n34, 179n61
West, Cornel, 67, 80, 84–85
Western civilization, 8, 11, 12, 19, 36, 66, 76, 112–13

white supremacy, xi–xii, 11, 18–20, 41, 71–72, 81, 92, 107, 112, 139, 141; white supremacist groups, x, 46, 55, 66–67, 105–6, 125–126, 155n5. *See also* Ku Klux Klan
Wilder, Laura Ingalls, 118–19, 177n28
Wright, Alexa, 113

Yang, Gene Luen, 105, 107, 127–28, 174n70

Zipes, Jack, 22
Ziblatt, Daniel, 36
Zimmerman, Arely M., 62
Žižek, Slavoj, 48
Zuboff, Shoshana, 42, 60–61

Annette Wannamaker is Professor of Children's Literature in the Department of English at Eastern Michigan University. She has served as North American Editor-in-Chief of *Children's Literature in Education* and as President of the Children's Literature Association. She is the author of *Boys in Children's Literature and Popular Culture: Masculinity, Abjection, and the Fictional Child.*

www.ingramcontent.com/pod-product-compliance
Lightning Source LLC
Chambersburg PA
CBHW031150020426
42333CB00013B/597